MAX
VERSTAPPEN

James Gray is a sports journalist for *The i*, specialising in Formula One, boxing, football and tennis.

MAX VERSTAPPEN

BORN TO RACE:
A BIOGRAPHY

JAMES GRAY

ICON

First published in the UK in 2021
by Icon Books Ltd, Omnibus Business Centre,
39–41 North Road, London N7 9DP
email: info@iconbooks.com
www.iconbooks.com

This edition published in the UK in 2022 by Icon Books Ltd

Sold in the UK, Europe and Asia
by Faber & Faber Ltd, Bloomsbury House,
74–77 Great Russell Street,
London WC1B 3DA or their agents

Distributed in the UK, Europe and Asia
by Grantham Book Services, Trent Road,
Grantham NG31 7XQ

Distributed in Australia and New Zealand
by Allen & Unwin Pty Ltd, PO Box 8500,
83 Alexander Street, Crows Nest, NSW 2065

Distributed in India by Penguin Books India,
7th Floor, Infinity Tower – C, DLF Cyber City,
Gurgaon 122002, Haryana

Distributed in South Africa
by Jonathan Ball, Office B4, The District,
41 Sir Lowry Road, Woodstock 7925

ISBN: 978-1-78578-919-9

Text copyright © 2021, 2022 James Gray

Typeset by Cecile Berbesi Rault

Printed and bound in Great Britain by Clays Ltd, Elcograf S.p.A.

CONTENTS

PROLOGUE

'We need a miracle.'

Red Bull boss Christian Horner meant it. Max Verstappen was trying to chase down Lewis Hamilton in the final stages of the most dramatic title race of the modern era, the two drivers perfectly level on points before the race but the British driver now ahead on the track. In the stands, thousands of orange-clad Dutch fans with nails bitten down to the quick clasped their hands together in prayer to whatever deity they thought could bring the intervention that Max needed to close the gap.

On that day, Mercedes had the faster car. Abu Dhabi had often been a place they had dominated the racing, but Red Bull had been close enough for Verstappen to pinch pole position on Saturday. Hamilton, though, produced the perfect start off the line and surged into the lead, despite running on the harder medium tyre. Max's soft tyre should have given him an early advantage, but Hamilton had cancelled it out. Formula One is a sport of compromise: reduce downforce for speed on the straights and you will have less grip in the corners; spend more money on a driver and you will have less to develop the car; pit for fresh tyres and be faster or stay out and maintain track position but with slower rubber.

Tyre strategy is crucial: softer tyres are faster but don't last as long, so Max knew he had to make the first part of the race count. Running behind Hamilton was not part of the plan and would end in defeat. He lunged down the inside of the hairpin. For weeks, the chatter in the paddock had been about how aggressive Max would be in the final race of a season that will be remembered by many for a series of crashes between him and Hamilton. Just six corners in, Verstappen showed that once again, no quarter would be given.

Hamilton, knowing a crash that ended both their races would hand Verstappen the title, veered away from the corner. In Monaco he would have hit the wall. In Silverstone he'd have beached in a gravel trap. But in Abu Dhabi there is endless space. He circumvented turns six and seven, effectively going straight on. Max drove the track as it was intended and emerged from the corners more than a second behind Hamilton. His left thumb slammed down on the radio button.

'He has to give that back,' Max pleaded on the radio, a message less for his team and more for race director Michael Masi, the much-maligned referee of such incidents. The Australian disagreed and Hamilton continued in the lead. Red Bull's lawyers scribbled furiously. Mercedes' probably did too. No one was under any illusions about whether there would be a protest after the race. There would almost inevitably be a protest. It was simply a matter of who would be protesting what. Both hoped it would be the other.

And for the majority of the race, even as Sergio Perez played an invaluable pawn role in holding up Hamilton to bring Max back within a few seconds of the lead, it looked as though Mercedes would be celebrating and Red Bull would be litigating late into the Middle Eastern night and beyond.

Then, the miracle. Nicholas Latifi, who finished 17th in the World Drivers' Championship, may never again have such a seismic impact on a world title race. The Williams driver hit the barriers with five laps to go, blocking the track and bringing out the safety car. It eradicated Hamilton's lead and allowed Max to dive into the pits for fresh tyres.

But Red Bull needed a little more of the miracle dust. There were still a number of back-markers who, by coincidence, had been caught between Hamilton and Verstappen in the safety car queue. They formed a protective barrier for Hamilton, who was probably starting to plan the acceptance speech that would see him crowned a record-breaking eight-time world champion.

Fate though had one final twist for him. Race director Masi ordered the lap cars to unlap themselves, but only those who were at risk of interfering in the race for victory. Had he ordered all of those behind Verstappen to follow as well, the race would have ended behind the safety car. There simply was not time to complete all the protocols. Hamilton would win the title ahead of Verstappen at 70 miles an hour. There would be more drama at the roundabout outside the circuit. Masi would not have it. He made a call. The safety car pulled in with a lap to go and the two mighty drivers were given a minute and a half to sort out the small matter of who would take the world title. It was a sudden death situation, the like of which Formula One has never seen and may never see again. The ultimate test of nerve.

On the pit wall, nerves, fingernails and race plans were long since lost. Mercedes boss Toto Wolff, an increasingly animated figure as the year wore on, was straight on the radio to Masi.

'Michael, this isn't right,' Wolff said. He knew that Hamilton had old tyres and Verstappen new ones. It would take yet another miracle for the Mercedes driver to hold him off.

Things were no less tense next door in the Red Bull garage. While Wolff tends to sit at a monitor in the garage, Horner prefers to be up on the pit wall with Adrian Newey, whose technical brilliance has been at the heart of so much success at Red Bull, sitting on his left. Horner's eyes were on stalks, as wide as if he himself were driving the car, scanning the countless screens with every possible piece of data for any signs of trouble or opportunities for advantage. The truth was that there was nothing he could do. It was up to Max.

The driver himself was virtually silent. He had a few moments earlier voiced his frustrations at the 'typical' decision not to let the cars unlap themselves and give him a shot at Hamilton. As they moved out of the way, there was a mutual understanding on the airwaves of what this meant. His engineer Gianpiero Lambiase calmly talked him through the engine modes required for the final lap. After giving his technical instructions, he simply said: 'This is it.' 90 seconds later, he was screaming:

'OH MY LORD, MAX.'

Max's response was an unintelligible cry of pure emotion, the kind that had not been building for just a few seconds, minutes or hours, but for a lifetime. From practically the minute he was born, Max's life had been leading to this point.

This is the story of how he got there.

1

BORN TO RACE

In a sport governed by the stopwatch, having a good sense of timing is important. Max Verstappen has never lacked that. Even his birth was conveniently timed.

With a due date at the beginning of October, it was likely that his mother Sophie Kumpen would have to rely on friends and family for support in the days after giving birth to her first child, rather than husband Jos. This was not because he didn't want to be there, but because it was a busy time of year for a full-time F1 driver that would include the longest trip of the season to Japan.

Instead, Jos happened to be racing at the Nürburgring on 28 September 1997 while his wife crossed her legs at home in Belgium. He had been looking to challenge for a rare top ten finish for Tyrrell before he retired from eleventh place, seventeen laps from the end of the race. Some joked that he was hoping to get an early start on the 124-mile trip back to Belgium so as not to miss the birth of his son – he had already driven further than that on the track before being forced to leave his car parked at the side of the road. Fortunately for both parents, Max was born on 30 September 1997, two days after the Luxembourg Grand Prix. Even if he had been forced to drive his ailing Tyrrell home, Jos would have made sure that he made it back in time.

Max Emilian Verstappen seemed to be a healthy enough baby. Jos' personal website, which remarkably existed way back in the late 1990s, records the birth in oddly forensic detail: his son's weight was seven pounds, two ounces, his length 48.5 centimetres long and the delivery lasted just 40 minutes. Max, to quote, 'had chosen the right moment to come out'. It goes on to predict that 'if Max has inherited the racing talents of both his parents, a new F1 driver for the year 2020 has been born'. The prescience of that comment, which turned out not to be optimistic enough when you consider that Max made his F1 debut four years earlier than that, was not merely the exuberance of a new father. The racing pedigree of Verstappen Junior was impressive. That said, Jos was not overly enamoured with the trials of early fatherhood.

'I have to say, the first year I wasn't really into babies,' Jos said in a 2021 documentary. 'They don't do very much.' He added with a smile: 'I was no expert when it came to changing nappies.' His expertise lay on the track, he felt.

Jos had two nicknames in his career: 'Jos the Boss' and 'Vercrashen'. Between them, they rather succinctly sum up how he was viewed by the racing community, as a strong, dominant character with a boot full of talent but an unfortunate habit of ending races in the wall.

Jos grew up a few miles from Hasselt, where he raised Max, across the border in the Dutch town of Montfort. He had come up through karting from the age of eight with no shortage of speed, and in 1984 and 1986 he won the Dutch Championship. In the modern era he might have been fast-tracked into a driver academy or one of the larger teams with seats in various series.

Perhaps due to a lack of funding or political influence though, or just because he was such a talented karter and thoroughly enjoyed the success at that level, he was content to remain on the karting track until much later. Whatever the reason, Jos did not make the transition into car racing until he was nearly twenty. In those teenage years he went from winning national championships in the Netherlands and in Belgium to Continental ones; by the end of 1991, his victories could not be ignored any longer.

Triumphs in the 1993 Marlboro Masters (a Formula Three race day held at the famous Zandvoort Circuit) and the German Formula Three Championship in the same year earned him the chance to test an F1 car for a team then known as Footwork, although Arrows is how most race fans will remember them. They put him in their car at Estoril the day after the Portuguese Grand Prix, his first ever drive in the monstrous V10 engines that were prevalent at the top of motor sport at the time. It was a tremendous step up in pace for Jos, having only driven in F3 before jumping into the Footwork in 1993. He was going from 175 brake horsepower to 750, more than four times as much power under his right foot, as well as having to deal with a semi-automatic gearbox, traction control and carbon brakes. The extra speed through corners alone would make most drivers' necks ache with G-force. Nevertheless, Jos the Boss took to it like a duck to water.

In his very first fifteen-minute run, he was on pace with the backmarkers of Sunday's Grand Prix. After another five minutes on track he had matched Aguri Suzuki, the man usually behind the wheel of the car he had been given.

'I must say I thought it would be quite difficult, the jump from F3 to F1,' Jos told reporters at the time. 'But really, it was not so difficult. On the first lap I thought, 'Shit!' I never thought it would be so fast. But by the third lap I was really enjoying it; it was fantastic. After ten to fifteen laps it feels normal and you find yourself wanting more. Still, it's very fast.'

By the end of the day, in which he logged 65 laps and was left with a sore neck and shoulders, he produced a lap time that would have qualified him tenth on the grid if he had done it a few days earlier. He was only 0.07 seconds slower than Derek Warwick, Footwork's lead driver with twelve years of F1 experience.

Even in that very first experience of F1 though, the watching media were treated to a reminder of the two-faced nature of speed. Verstappen returned on Thursday, still sore from his efforts two days before, and while he immediately started punching in lap times, he then lost it through the high-speed final sector and spun into the barriers. It signalled a premature end to the day – but it did not appear to do much to dampen the excitement around the name Verstappen. The phone started to ring off the hook.

'We had contact with ... most teams,' Jos said in a revealing 2019 Beyond the Grid podcast appearance. 'We did a day of testing with McLaren at Silverstone, we had contact with Eddie Jordan, Flavio [Briatore, boss of Benetton].'

Eventually, Jos chose what he felt was the secure option above all else, signing for Benetton because they offered him a two-year contract rather just a one-year deal. Initially, he was supposed to be a test driver in 1994 but when JJ Lehto broke his neck in a pre-season crash, Verstappen made his debut at the Brazilian Grand Prix alongside one Michael Schumacher. His meteoric rise, having spent barely two years in professional racing driving, was eerily similar to what his son would achieve two decades later.

Jos' debut was no fairy tale. He had plenty to prove after Schumacher had out-qualified him by nearly two seconds to start second on the grid with Verstappen seven places behind him. Caught up in a frantic midfield battle for eighth place, he pulled out to overtake Eddie Irvine 36 laps into the race, only for the Jordan to move over to lap a backmarker, unaware he was being challenged, and collide with him. In a terrifying scene, Verstappen was powerless to stop his spinning car which then hit the braking McLaren of Martin Brundle and was thrown into the air, completing a full barrel roll before hitting the tarmac again and skidding off into the barriers. Remarkably, no one was seriously hurt, despite Brundle's helmet splitting, so great were the forces involved.

'I was never scared and it didn't hurt my confidence at all. I never had a problem with that,' Jos said with typical bravado.

He spun out of his second race too – 'every time I was trying to match Michael's pace, [the crashes] never stopped me trying' – before Lehto came back from injury.

If Jos had learned anything from his first taste of F1 it was that physically he was not up to the game, but he had also quickly twigged that politically Benetton was Schumacher's team first and foremost. That was not to say they did not rate Verstappen – after all, they had offered him a longer contract than any other team and when Lehto failed to produce his best form on returning from injury, Verstappen was reinstalled. By that point though, Schumacher had won five of the first six races and if they were predisposed towards him before, they were now entirely on Michael's side. Jos insists that he understood but the frustration of feeling abandoned in his first ever season in F1, with less than three years of racing experience behind him, is clear.

'All the testing went into the [mid-season] rule changes, not into helping me get confident in the car to make me faster. It wasn't like it is today where they really help the other driver who is struggling but at that time they didn't care.'

When his son found himself in a similar position as the youngest driver on the grid and teammate to the vastly more experienced Daniel Ricciardo, Max did not lie down and accept any suggestion of a role as second fiddle. Perhaps his father, a close adviser throughout his life, had learned a valuable lesson from his rocky Benetton ride.

Despite the difficulties, Jos' accession to the fastest circus in motor sport was a cause for celebration in Montfort and the town became, according to Jos' father Frans, 'a place of pilgrimage'. For years, Frans ran a pub called the Cafe De Rotonde, named after the large roundabout in the middle of town where it sits, and when his son was racing, he did big business. 'Especially in the early years it was a madhouse,' Frans said in 2015. 'Back then, the entire street was closed off and there was a large tent running across the length of it. I had eighteen TV sets and the crowd numbered 2,000 or 3,000. This was the case during the races in Hungary and Belgium, where Jos finished third. After that, it was complete mayhem – the whole *rotonde* was jam-packed.' Even now, only 3,000 people live in the whole of Montfort.

This is no exaggeration though. Blurry VHS footage from the day of the 1994 Hungarian Grand Prix, in which Jos drove from twelfth on the grid to finish third while his Benetton teammate Michael Schumacher took the win, shows Frans being held aloft on the shoulders of some pub patrons who, from their pained expressions, look as though they might have underestimated his hefty frame. Outside, the pavement is packed with parasols and beer barrels being used as tables. A group of men are dressed in traditional Flemish costume, which for the uninitiated might not look out of place in a German beer hall a few miles away, and they chant 'Jos, Jos, Jos', as well as some very lyric-heavy songs they have written about his exploits and heroism. One of them has a signed picture of Jos tucked into his hatband.

'Jos brought that about and it is my belief that Max will stir up even more,' Frans said. No pressure, kiddo.

By the time his grandson had made it into F1, Frans had given up the pub and moved to the other side of the roundabout to run an ice cream parlour, but that did not stop the partying, albeit with a bit less alcohol involved. When Max made his debut in F1 in Australia, the race was too early in the morning back in the Netherlands to run any sort of event but his second event in Malaysia would start at 9am, a reasonable hour for Frans to get a licence to start dishing out ice cream breakfasts.

He put up a marquee next to the shop and kitted it out with a speaker system and large TVs before filling it to the rafters with *Montfortenaars*. In his Toro Rosso, Max finished seventh, beating his teammate Carlos Sainz and both drivers for the more senior Red Bull team. There were jubilant scenes in Montfort. A lot of ice cream was sold. Frans said: 'I am the most proud grandpa in Holland, rather yet ... the world. I have never hidden that.'

The tradition continued with the party moving from a temporary marquee into Zaal Housmans, a cafe a couple of hundred yards down the road from the roundabout owned by Frans' friend Harald Hendrikx. On race day, the street would practically be blockaded by fans trying to get parking close to the bar, Dutch flags with Max or Jos' name painted on them hanging out of their windows, and Red Bull Racing caps and shirts everywhere.

The races would be shown on an enormous projector at the end of the room with memorabilia and sometimes a giant portrait of Max's face sitting on the stage, more often host to a local band or an open mic night, next to the screen. The whole venue was bedecked in supportive flags and banners.

Contrary to what you might think, Frans wasn't in it for the money. The proudest 'Opa' in the world convinced Harald to keep the beer prices reasonable and encouraged entire families to come and spend the afternoon watching the racing. He wasn't profiteering, he merely wanted everyone to share in his joy (although if they wanted to buy any merchandise, he would also happily sell it to them). 'Every Grand Prix live here at Opa Verstappens, free entry, everyone welcome,' proclaims the sign outside Housmans, underneath which sits a replica of Max's Red Bull Racing F1 car.

When Max won for the first time in Spain, Frans stood on the stage as his grandson sprayed champagne behind him, waving an enormous flag in celebration. Confetti dropped from the ceiling. Beers were downed. Frans had been at parties like this before, but never with a Verstappen on the top step of the podium. Finally, they had a Grand Prix win.

Frans passed away in 2019 at the age of 72, after a long battle with cancer, just a few days after Max had won his eighth Grand Prix. The hearse processed from the roundabout where he had poured beer for Jos' fans in the nineties up to the hall where Max's face adorns every surface. He left his bar for the last time with townsfolk holding red flares in the air. Despite their presence on the walls, Jos and Max were conspicuous by their absence. The grandson had only just won the race in Brazil and had not yet finished his racing season. Jos meanwhile did attend the funeral along with Max's sister Victoria, but not the memorial in Housmans. It hinted that while Frans had always made out that his family were close-knit, it was not always the case.

In 2016, police were called after a heated argument between Jos and Frans. It's not clear what had caused the flashpoint. Max had just finished fifth at the Hungarian Grand Prix, meaning the party had been going for several hours which could explain it, but the police report records that Jos had pushed his father off his chair and he had fallen against the wall. Understandably, the incident made the national media in Holland. Having initially tried to deny anything ever happened, three days later Frans withdrew the complaint, calling it 'a private matter between me and Jos', before adding that 'we've seen before that Jos has loose hands but this was the limit'.

What his father was referring to was the famous temper of 'Jos the Boss'. He had a reputation as a driver of being someone not to be crossed but once he had retired, he found himself outside the F1 paddock where the deadly nature of the sport seemed to legitimise the odd outburst or confrontation; he was in the 'real world', where his actions had real consequences.

Frans was hardly a shrinking violet either. In May 1998, an argument broke out at a karting track in the Belgian town of Lanaken between Jos, who was there with his father, his group of friends and another group who wanted to use the facility. It quickly turned into a fight, in which a 45-year-old man was left with a fractured skull with Jos identified as the culprit in court. Under Belgian law, a financial settlement with the victim can reduce a defendant's sentence, and sure enough the Verstappens, both of whom were found guilty of assault, got the chequebook out and were handed five-year suspended sentences each.

At the time of the incident, Jos was without a drive. He was dropped by Tyrrell for the simple reason that he was not fast enough and having tested back at Benetton, he was not given a contract because he could not raise the sponsorship. He was desperate to get back into an F1 car as soon as possible, with his reputation for raw speed ensuring his name was never far from the newspapers and magazines when someone was struggling.

It is easy therefore to see how he might have been eager to throw his weight around, with an ego still inflated enough to believe he had been wronged and to ensure he would take umbrage at being asked to share or even vacate a parochial karting track. Fortunately for him, the case took two years to go through the courts and the controversy did not stop Stewart giving him a drive just a month after the widely reported fracas, replacing the poor-performing Jan Magnussen (whose son Kevin would go on to race against Max in F1).

Jos' temper did not seem to fade despite the close shave with time in prison. He appeared before the courts again in 2008, with assault on the docket once again, and Max's mother Sophie the alleged victim. The pair had separated by then and she had a restraining order against him, but he was accused of an assault and a series of threatening text messages. He was found not guilty of the more serious violent charge but was guilty of breaching the restraining order and, not for the first time, was handed a suspended prison sentence.

The Dutch public opened their newspapers in January 2012 to discover that Verstappen Sr had once again been arrested, this time on suspicion of attempted murder. Jos had been detained in the Dutch city of Roermond after an incident involving his ex-girlfriend Kelly van der Waal. Some suggested he had driven his car at her, explaining the gravity of the charge. The case was dropped two weeks later and in 2014 the pair reconciled and got married. The ceremony was small and happened largely in secret. He and Kelly, along with a few guests, jetted off to the Dutch Caribbean island of Curaçao in January to get married by the beach. Jos wore a three-piece beige suit with bright white shoes while his bride wore a strapless bridal gown in a mermaid cut and a slightly sweetheart neckline. It was a setting and occasion from which the memories should have lasted for years to come – but the marriage lasted just three years.

The pair did have a child together; Kelly gave birth to a daughter, Blue Jaye, a half-sister to Max seventeen years his junior, whom he happily welcomed into the family just as he had his little sister Victoria when she came along a good few years before. Jos had a fourth child with partner Sijtsma on 4 May 2019, a boy named Jason Jaxx, and the four children regularly spend time together as a family.

Max is a caring and kind older brother. He had just turned two when his mother came home from the hospital with a little sister for him, but he was gentle and sympathetic, a skilled peacekeeper.

'Victoria was the boss,' his mother Sophie recalled years later. 'Max would always give her the sticker or colouring book to keep the peace. It sums up his character, really: open and sweet. Max is an emotional person and will always want to solve things by talking first.' She adds, a slight against her ex-husband: 'He got that fierce racing instinct from Jos. The gentleness he got from me.'

Family life was not a struggle in the Verstappen household in the early years; Jos was making good money in F1, although he could have done without losing his drive after a contract holdout with Jordan that left him out in the cold once again. He was stripped of the chance to lead Honda back into F1 when the project crumbled due to the sudden death of his friend and former Tyrrell boss Harvey Postlethwaite. Nevertheless, his progress was perhaps stifled due to the fact that his manager,

Huub Rothengatter, still believed he could extract hefty retainers for Jos' services from teams despite the nickname 'Vercrashen' still following him round the paddock. 'No one parks a car better than Jos Verstappen,' the joke used to go, so often would he find himself stationary by the side of the track.

Little Max was blissfully unaware of the highly political nature of the F1 paddock. To him, his father was a travelling, conquering hero whom he hated to see leave. He would cry when Jos would leave home for a race weekend, not just because his father was going away but also because he knew he was going racing and he wanted to go with him. He would hang on to Jos and sob. He wanted to be at the racetrack, where everything smelled of petrol and speed.

Even before he could walk or talk, Max would play with toy cars or bikes, obsessed with anything with wheels. His parents tried to keep up with his hobby, insisting that they never pushed him into it but just let him do what he wanted to do. When he was two, Jos bought him a quad bike for Christmas. It was the Verstappens' first Christmas as a four-person family with Victoria born in the October, so perhaps Jos was just trying to keep the peace, but more likely he was beginning his son's training. More than a decade later, after a spectacular save in the wet during the Brazilian Grand Prix, Max cited his time riding a quad bike in the snow when explaining how he went about trying to stop an F1 car skidding. As he got older, and the quad and motocross bikes grew bigger and more powerful, he would ride around with his friends, racing them and messing around in the snow or the mud. He himself is not sure whether he was trying to hone his skills by competing or just enjoying himself; the upshot was the same – the development of an innate understanding of grip, especially in tricky conditions.

His mother Sophie said: 'With his first balance bike, a kind of car that he had received from Mercedes, I can still see him skidding and making turns. The speed was there early on.'

Max did have other interests as a child. The house was something of a menagerie, with five cats, four dogs and a cockatoo. Max remembers that every now and again his father would come home with a new pet, and Sophie would be expected to look after them while Jos went around the world with work. An eighth-floor flat in Monaco is a little less pet-friendly, but that did not stop Max from getting two cats in 2021, Jimmy and Sassy, and enjoying their company while also getting frustrated at their habit of curling up underneath the pedals of his simulator on the rare occasion he would forget to shut them out of the room.

Young Max played football, not very well it should be said, but he was left-footed and tried hard, two qualities often high on the agenda for youth football coaches, and his father noticed that he always had good balance while running during the game, probably from spending so much time on bikes of one sort or another. He rarely enjoyed school, finding it hard to sit still and look at the board. He felt trapped. Sometimes he would ask to go to the toilet and never come back. On Wednesdays, lessons finished at 12pm and he would head straight to the track. Once he turned eleven and started secondary education, Jos picked the school he would go to on the basis that the principal had agreed to be flexible, because Max's karting would require him to travel abroad. As long as Max kept his grades above a certain level, he would get the days off he needed to make the trips to bigger and better competitions. At 3.15pm on a Friday he would sprint through the school gates and jump in the van with his dad, off to some karting track in Italy or Holland or Germany. Sometimes all he would have in his rucksack was a spare set of underwear. Everything else he needed was in the workshop.

He did like geography though, probably the only subject he did like. His bedroom walls were not covered with posters of his favourite racing drivers like Ayrton Senna or Michael Schumacher, or stars of his favourite football team PSV Eindhoven, or even the great Johan Cruyff whose approach he said would later shape his approach to racing; instead, he had pictures of different countries and a world map. He wanted to know where everything was and to be able to point to the city his father was away in that week.

The first time he got to go with his father, his first real experience of F1 cars as far as either Jos or Max can remember, was when Verstappen Sr was testing for Arrows in 2000.

'When we went testing I took him with me – just him and me – and someone from the team was looking after him when I was driving,' Jos says. The team effectively ran a crèche for Max but the cars on the track were enough to fascinate him. Keeping him off the circuit itself was perhaps a greater struggle than keeping him entertained.

It got to a point where taking Max along with him was less of a battle than leaving him at home in Belgium, and Max's face became a regular sight, running around the paddock and in and out of garages. It started in 2001 in Malaysia, when Max was just three and a half years old and Jos was into his second year at Arrows, the only time in his career that he completed two full consecutive seasons with the same team.

It cannot have been entirely pleasant for Max, with temperatures on the Friday afternoon reaching 37.6 degrees Celsius and humidity at 50 per cent, although his own memories were that the whole place looked like a giant playground.

'Finishing is the most important thing,' said a pessimistic Jos after qualifying eighteenth on Saturday. The team had been forced to replace the engine during practice on Saturday and the car was still understeering badly and needing a front suspension upgrade that would not arrive in time for the race. On the most physically taxing circuit of them all, he did not sound like he was looking forward to the race or expecting to produce anything for his son's first appearance at a Grand Prix weekend. What followed was a race that his son's modern-day fans would have recognised.

After an aborted start, Verstappen went from seventeenth to sixth on the very first lap after a late adjustment to the clutch that just seemed to work and sliced through several seemingly impossibly narrow gaps. 'How on earth did that get there,' commentator Murray Walker remarked upon telling viewers it was indeed the Arrows of Verstappen running in the points before noting that 'this is Jos the Boss's opportunity, and he knows it'.

The rain started to fall just a few laps into the race, catching both Michael Schumacher and Rubens Barrichello, the leading Ferraris, out on the same corner. Fortunately for them, the extensive run-off areas at Sepang allowed them to keep the cars running and get on to the right tyre but it allowed the likes of Verstappen to move up the field even further. At one point, he was running second behind David Coulthard when his mirrors were filled with his former teammate Schumacher coming up behind. The German was on intermediate tyres, faster but less able to withstand large amounts of water on the track, while Jos was on the full wets. One-time teammates at Benetton, Verstappen was determined to make life as difficult as possible for Schumacher. He succeeded. Afterwards, Jos took it as a compliment when the reigning world champion mentioned it was 'miserable' trying to overtake him, although he did still manage to get past and went on to win the race.

Jos finished just outside the points in an agonising seventh place, the last car to remain on the lead lap: Schumacher had lapped everybody else. The Dutchman was torn between the emotions of a result far better than anyone could have predicted and missing out on an invaluable championship point by such a narrow margin. The rain had even taken the edge off the gruelling conditions. By the time he got to see Max again though, he was still understandably exhausted.

A friend snapped the two of them sitting in the hospitality area at the back of the Arrows garage at Sepang. Jos has his racing overalls peeled down and tied around his waist. Max, hair much blonder than it is in adulthood, has dressed up for the occasion, in a short-sleeved checked shirt with a button-down collar. He gestures to his father with two fingers while Jos looks quizzically at him. One hand on his father's arm, Max looks as though he is giving him a stern debrief. 'You were second, Papa, you could have finished second,' he seems to say. Few would have predicted that the same boy would celebrate his twentieth birthday with a victory on that very track sixteen years later.

2

A DUTCH FLAG ON A BELGIAN RACER

The Netherlands is not traditionally known as a powerhouse of motor racing. It is a sport that in general comes as a by-product of other industries: America's obsession with NASCAR came as a direct result of bootleggers building custom cars to outrun the police; in Finland, driving skills in all conditions are an essential part of survival which explains their love of rallying; Italian and German regimes set car production at the centre of their economic plan and their cars dominated, and still do dominate, the top end of motor racing; the British Empire similarly put England at the forefront of car technology in the first half of the 20th century.

For the Dutch though, the path to petrol-fuelled passion is not so clear. Traditionally a great seafaring nation, their flat, fertile land did little to inject racing into their veins and there were no multinational motoring giants based in the Netherlands to power their teams. While Max Verstappen is very much the present and future of Dutch motor racing, it is not altogether clear where the past originated.

Race cars were first seen in the Netherlands, it seems, back in 1898. At the time, there were estimated to be just twelve cars in the whole country, so when the Paris–Amsterdam–Paris race blew through the country in July, it was not without some intrigue. The race was organised by the Automobile Club de France and inspired the inauguration of a similar Dutch body – the Nederlandsche Automobiel Club, which later became the Koninklijke Nederlandsche Automobiel Club (KNAC) thanks to royal recognition – to 'promote the automobile industry in the Netherlands'. They would run club trips and conferences, lobby governments and even built hotels to improve the lives of motorists as the car began to take over Europe. They earned their 'royal' title in 1913 by helping the armed forces keep up with automotive progress elsewhere as war on the Continent approached. They fought hard for civilian rights on the road too, petitioning the government not to introduce speed limits or tolls. The three things they wished to promote among members were: road safety, driving skills and speed competitions.

A few races best described as 'primitive' were held in Scheveningen, another seaside resort close to The Hague, before World War I, but racing in earnest did not take place in the Netherlands for a few more decades. Sports cars were popularised, or at least entered the public consciousness, in the 1930s when Prince Bernhard, a KNAC member for more than 60 years, brought his two-seater Ford V8 to the Netherlands, and was also often seen in an Italian Alfa Romeo 8C 2900, of which only 40 were built. He was a popular if often controversial figure with a love for fast cars, boats and aeroplanes, but his work in World War II enamoured him to the Dutch public. For his wedding to Princess Juliana in 1937, Queen Wilhelmina ordered a Maybach Zeppelin, a particularly opulent German car with a twelve-cylinder engine, and had a custom four-seater convertible based on it built. Just a year later, in one of his other sports cars, the prince broke his neck and ribs in a 100 mph crash.

The appetite for fast cars was seized upon by the mayor of Zandvoort, Henri van Alphen. The town was a popular seaside resort, in striking distance of Amsterdam and The Hague, and is mentioned as a summer haunt of the family in Anne Frank's diaries. Hoping to use the event as a billboard for the seaside resort, Van Alphen set up a street circuit through the town and managed to attract a number of global motor racing superstars to perform exhibition races on it. The highlight of the 1939 event was the presence of Manfred von Brauchitsch, one of the best drivers in the world who had won the 1937 Monaco Grand Prix and was employed as a works driver for the then-dominant Mercedes-Benz team. He drove his Mercedes W154 around the street circuit, which met itself in the middle, separating the two sides of the track with just a few straw bales, to the delight of the locals.

Just a few months later though, war broke out. It could have stopped Van Alphen's grand plans to make Zandvoort the capital of motor racing in the Netherlands in their tracks, but like all great visionaries, he was not to be deterred.

After the German invasion of Holland and subsequent occupation, Van Alphen managed to convince the Nazi forces to continue his plans for the town's racing infrastructure – although he dressed it up as something quite different. He presented them with a plan for a new park in the north of the town with a hiking trail winding its way around it that coincidentally looked a little like a rather handy racetrack. He included in the plans a long straight road that he said would make a fine street for a grand victory parade once the war was over. His plan was feasible, but the idea that it would make an idyllic hiking spot was rather far-fetched; the area he had chosen had been largely demolished by the Nazis, including hundreds of houses and hotels, to build the Atlantic Wall, a defensive structure that was designed to keep the Allies at bay should they attempt to land on the Dutch beaches.

Nevertheless, the Germans bought into Van Alphen's plan and gave him the manpower to execute it, making it a happy unintended consequence (or not?) that many of the working-age men who would otherwise have been sent to Germany to help with the war effort remained in Zandvoort to work on the project. And even though Van Alphen was removed as mayor to be replaced by a candidate from the National Socialist Movement, a fascist political party sympathetic to the Nazi cause, the construction continued until Van Alphen was reinstated when the country was liberated in 1945 and the NSB outlawed. He did retire of his own will in 1948, and Zandvoort's circuit was opened later that year, but his successor Hector van Fenema did not forget Van Alphen's mighty input: the complex was officially named 'Burgemeester Van Alphenweg', literally 'The Road of Mayor Van Alphen'.

Once the circuit had been built, the town of Zandvoort then took on their next challenge: actually putting on a race, something they had no real idea how to do. Over the sea in Britain though, they were a little more experienced and so they recruited Desmond Scannell – then secretary of the British Racing Drivers' Club and who had a great part in the early days of making Silverstone the fixture it is today – to help organise the first Zandvoort Grand Prix.

'Prijs van Zandvoort, internationale autoraces' the 70 cent programme proudly proclaimed with a large Firestone advert on the bottom half of it. It notes the date as 7 August 1948, arguably the birth of motor sport in the Netherlands. In a country with not much motor-sport history to speak of, it had an improvised feel. There were no real garages at the circuit so most cars competing came over by boat several days in advance and parked up in the middle of Harlem, the nearest large town. One gentleman claiming to be the King of Siam, whose nephew was racing, arrived to watch with his entourage and was initially turned away by the ticket inspectors. Not wishing to risk a public embarrassment, one of his superiors ushered the group through without asking them to purchase a ticket. It is not clear whether he really was the monarch.

In the end, all 50,000 who attended the historic day were not disappointed. Sammy Davis, a British racer who won Le Mans in 1927, had been the chief adviser on design; he used what was available to him, namely the road that had been built by the occupying Germans, Van Alphen's hiking trail and the natural undulations of the sand dunes. Corners wound their way around mounds and dunes at improbable angles, sometimes banked for speed, other times off-camber to persuade cars away from the racing line. In that sense, it has a feel not unlike a links golf course, of which the town boasts a number for anyone wishing to combine the speed of the racetrack with something a little more sedate.

Early on, with sand being regularly blown on to the driving surface by the rough winds off the North Sea to distress the tyres of any car willing to take the track on, Zandvoort was seen as a challenge of driving skill. The high-speed first corner, at the end of a long straight, slightly banked and called Tarzan, is still one without a common consensus on the fastest way around it, making it a popular overtaking spot in the early races.

The grid for that first event in 1948 was predominantly British, Scannell convincing a number of his members to make the trip over, many of whom would form part of the first Formula One World Championship two years later. After two 24-lap heats, the deciding 40-lap race was a thriller: a battle between Prince Bira of Siam, a member of the Thai royal family who had been sent to England to attend Eton and had subsequently settled down in London, and Tony Rolt, an army officer who had been captured shortly before the Dunkirk evacuation and spent nearly two years as a prisoner of war in Colditz. He was best known as the man who had helped build a giant glider in an escape attempt from the East German castle, but was liberated before needing to use it. As such, both men were minor celebrities and having them battle it out for the win – which Bira eventually claimed – was something of a success for the track that had initially been built as an attempt to attract more tourists to the seaside resort.

The drivers enjoyed it too and within two years of the inauguration of the Formula One World Championship, the Dutch Grand Prix at Zandvoort had become a favourite on the calendar. It began to add famous names such as Alberto Ascari and Juan Manuel Fangio to its roll of honour. What had started off as essentially a marketing stunt had turned into a serious sporting event.

However, this was still a Europe picking itself up after World War II and a Netherlands reeling from the sustained occupation of the Nazis. In short, money was tight and nothing was immune. The 1954 race was not held due to the expense of putting it on while the Suez Crisis of 1956 and 1957 meant that oil tankers delivering to the Netherlands were affected and the price of fuel was so high that for two years the race was not held. When it returned in 1958, another famous name etched his name on to the history of the track as Stirling Moss took victory.

More realities of motor sport started to strike too though. Just eleven laps into the 1960 race, Dan Gurney had arrived at the famous Tarzan corner at full speed in his BRM, only for the brakes to fail at the crucial moment. He sped up the banked corner and flew over the fences at more than 100 miles an hour, landing on the grassy mound behind, hitting and killing a spectator, an eighteen-year-old named Piet Alders from Harlem. Gurney, who broke his arm in the accident, became a far more cautious driver because of it; for the rest of his career, he would sometimes gently tap the brake before a heavy braking zone, just to check it was still there, and generally looked after his brakes better than his rivals.

Gurney though appeared to be the only one in the sport who was seriously affected by the accident. The early days of F1 had little concern for matters of safety, whether of drivers or spectators, and deaths were a tragic but occupational hazard. The death of Alders was, the town's local newspaper *De Zandvoortse Courant* reported, quickly forgotten by the massed crowd. 'It seemed to have happened far away, on another planet,' the race report recorded. Europe had perhaps become all too used to the idea of the sudden loss of life after years of war. That or the racing was too enthralling to be ignored, with Jack Brabham dominating the field, two greats in Jim Clark and Graham Hill in a race-long duel in the midfield and Stirling Moss producing a brilliant comeback drive after a flat tyre that seemed to capture the crowd's imagination.

For all the race's popularity, the Dutch Grand Prix has still never had a Dutch winner. In the 1952 race, two Dutchman had raced – Jan Flinterman and Dries van der Lof – but neither ever raced in F1 again. The first regular Dutch driver of an F1 car was Carel Godin de Beaufort, or to give him his full title, Count Karel Pieter Antoni Jan Hubertus Godin de Beaufort, a free-spirited aristocrat who lived on the familial Maarsbergen estate just outside Utrecht who once tied a bratwurst stand to the back of his car at the Nürburgring before setting off, which ended up as a heap of splintered wood, bent metal and ruined sausage. (As a child, he had once played a similar trick on some dignitaries visiting the house and his father ran into the house to fetch his hunting rifle. Fortunately, his son had scarpered.) Despite De Beaufort's eccentric sense of humour, he was known as a true gentleman of the paddock and referred to by the Germans, who admired him greatly, as 'Der letzte Ritter' (The Last Knight), a nod both to his heritage and his character.

De Beaufort, who won Le Mans in 1957, believed that the closer the relationship between driver and mechanic, the faster the car, and that the extraneous workings of a team, sponsorship deals and factory visits, only detracted from that. He was a privateer who owned the car he drove at Grands Prix and knew it probably better than anyone else.

'My way is different from theirs,' he would say of the corporate factory-backed teams he raced against. 'I go to the factory and tell them exactly what I want.

'On my return from a race I'll tell them all my stories and show the guys my time sheets and the photographs I took. In the evenings, I'll take them out to dinner. And in case they need to work late, I'll buy them a crate of beer and bring along a pile of food.'

He would help out too, and he was well respected by the Porsche mechanics whom he often fed. So it was a moment of almost universal celebration when De Beaufort became the first ever Dutchman to score a Formula One World Championship point, and on home soil too. At the 1962 Dutch Grand Prix, better remembered for being Graham Hill's first ever race win, De Beaufort brought his Porsche home in sixth place for a single point and revelled in having beaten Jo Bonnier, one of the works drivers 'who has never been to the factory' and had 'no meaningful contact' with their mechanics. He also pointed to his timing sheets, where his lap times almost all began with one minute, 42 seconds.

'That's how I've managed to become the fastest Porsche of the race. That's my style, to be fast and consistent during the entire race.'

The story of De Beaufort's career ends in a sadly familiar fashion though. He had brushes with death throughout racing, some due to his own recklessness and others due to the nature of the era. Even on that day in 1962 when he first scored a point, it was tinged with sadness. His friend Ben Pon, whom he had put into a second, newer Porsche for the race, started nervously and having been passed by De Beaufort, was desperate to impress by re-passing his team's leader. He spun off and was thrown out of the car.

'When I passed the wreck, I was worried he hadn't made it,' De Beaufort said afterwards. Miraculously, he had – but swore never to race single-seater cars ever again. He was one of the lucky ones. His friend was not.

De Beaufort had, later in his career, developed a reputation for safety. Despite some of the reckless pranks of his younger days, Alfonso de Portago's fatal 1957 crash at the Mille Miglia, after which the Spaniard's body was found in two pieces and nine others were killed, he started to be called Veilige Careltje

('Safe Wee Carel') because of his caution on the racetrack. His demise then was perhaps all the more tragic.

De Beaufort died after an accident at the Nürburgring in 1964. During practice, he had worn a Beatles wig to entertain spectators during his early laps, but then decided to start trying to find some pace. On his fifth lap, the car veered off into the trees and he was thrown out, suffering broken bones in his thigh, chest and crucially skull. He was moved to a neurological centre but after two days of medical attention, he was pronounced dead on the Sunday evening. The likes of Graham Hill and Ben Pon carried his coffin at the funeral on the Maarsbergen estate, where he was subsequently buried at the age of just 30.

While he had made a lasting impression on the motor racing world, the Netherlands was struggling to catch up with the rest of Europe. The Dutch Grand Prix appeared to be under serial threat despite having apparently overcome the financial challenges of the 1950s, and Zandvoort was far from immune from the dangers of a deadly era. Piet Alders would not be the only person to lose their life there. Piers Courage crashed during the 1970 Dutch Grand Prix after his steering broke on the notorious Tunnel Oost bump and rolled up one of the dunes. His own front wheel struck his head and removed his helmet before the chassis burst into flames.

Courage's death, combined with the substandard facilities at Zandvoort, saw the race removed from the calendar at the behest of the drivers in 1972, and there was an overhaul of the safety structures in place. There was an extra corner added to reduce speed in the final sector, new asphalt and a new race control tower, but key areas, such as the flimsily attached Armco barriers, went undeveloped, marshals remained perilously underequipped and the pit lane was still regarded as too narrow, but the race was reinstated nevertheless after passing its inspection.

That made it all the more gut-wrenching when just eight laps into the return of the Dutch Grand Prix at Zandvoort in 1973, disaster struck again with the eyes of the world watching.

Roger Williamson had won consecutive Formula Three titles and been offered a drive by BRM for the 1973 season, only to turn it down and drive for March instead. He was just 25 and racing in F1 for the second time when he suffered a suspected tyre failure at high speed on the Hondenvlak right-hander and flew into the fencing, before rebounding across the track. His car rolled and the fuel tank burst, engulfing it in flames.

What followed is one of the most shocking pieces of footage in the archive of F1, and a scene hopefully condemned to time gone by. Another British driver David Purley, a former paratrooper, pulled over and ran to the flaming wreckage. He desperately tried to turn the car over, knowing that Williamson was still alive because he could hear the driver's screams. Marshals rushed to his aid but, unlike him, were not wearing fireproof suits and were therefore unable to assist other than deploying a fire extinguisher from a distance, which Purley soon grabbed from them and tried in vain to put out the fire, alternating between the fire extinguisher and trying to roll the heavy car to the point of exhaustion. He was awarded the George Medal for bravery, but Williamson could not be saved.

Staggeringly, the car was not removed, even once the fire had gone out. The race continued with the car covered by a blanket. After the race finished, a recovery crew, the police and a judge arrived. In possibly the most morose scene ever witnessed on a racetrack, Williamson's body was taken out of the cockpit and placed straight into a coffin. 'Better safe than sorry' is not one of Holland's most used proverbs.

The track was later adapted again to reduce the speed in the segment of the track that had claimed two lives in four years, but as writer Mattijs Diepraam put it when recalling the incident years later for the excellent 8W encyclopedia of racing history, it rather felt like 'filling up the well after the cow has drowned'.

In total, Williamson was the seventh racer to lose his life at Zandvoort and six more have since followed, even with a number of significant alterations. It will never be forgotten in that part of Holland that for all the passion in motor racing, it remains an intrinsically dangerous sport.

De Beaufort had been Holland's biggest motor racing star in the early years of F1, having won Le Mans and scored points – in an era when only the top six finishers scored points – on four occasions, but doubtless that figure would have grown higher were it not for his untimely demise. Gijs van Lennep was probably the next one to make much of a mark, arriving in F1 having won Le Mans in 1971 with Helmut Marko, the man who now helps run the Red Bull Racing teams, but he struggled to make much of an impact, jumping in and out of the Williams and twice scoring points, but ultimately failing to race more than eight times. He went on to win Le Mans again in 1976 but was not highly regarded.

Like Van Lennep, Jan Lammers won Le Mans, albeit he did so in 1988 when already 32 years old. He had started racing early, born in Zandvoort in 1956 and learning his trade at the school run by Rob Slotemaker, another Dutchman who dipped his toe in F1 but another who lost his life on the Zandvoort circuit in the late seventies.

Before even gaining his road licence, Lammers had become the youngest touring car champion in Dutch history, and while still a teenager turned his attention to single-seaters. He soon moved to England to drive in European Formula Three for Hawke, but the car was uncompetitive and he returned to his home country a year later.

He joined Racing Team Holland, one of the very few homegrown teams in the Netherlands and one for which both Slotemaker and Van Lennep had raced in junior series, and won titles, just as Lammers did following in their footsteps. He won the 1978 European Formula Three title and earned a seat in F1 after impressing Shadow's team manager Joe Ramirez during a test at Silverstone. Sadly for Lammers, it was his only full season with the same team.

Lammers was a multi-talented driver, having started in touring cars and then switched relatively late to single-seaters, and proved as much during a special Zandvoort event before his first F1 season, when he won three different races on the same day in three quite different cars. Lammers had brought the cash-strapped Shadow sponsorship money too thanks to a deal with Samson, a Dutch shag tobacco company, but he could not change the fact that even then his pockets were far shallower and the Shadow was a glorified shopping trolley. His ninth-place finish in Canada was a minor miracle, although it was telling that while news of his success did sneak on to the back pages, being the best result for a Dutchman in F1 for some years, the news of cyclist Joop Zoetemelk's move from Mercier to join Dutch team TI-Raleigh garnered far more column inches and prominence. Lammers sneaked on as an aside at the bottom of *De Telegraaf*'s sports splash.

For the most part, motor racing and F1 seemed to remain a secondary or tertiary concern in the Dutch sporting calendar; although Zandvoort was a picturesque and exciting highlight, it had turned into a commercial failure. The attendances that had topped 60,000 had dwindled away, not helped by the absence of a hometown hero. (Lammers, born in Zandvoort, raced there just once and retired from F1 in 1982.) Bernie Ecclestone, then in charge of the sport, gave a typically brutal assessment of the situation in a TV interview during the 1985 Dutch Grand Prix, by which point the hapless but well-backed Huub Rothengatter was the only Dutchman on the grid and a rise in ticket prices had seen crowd numbers fall further.

'If you see 15,000 or 20,000 at the race, will that be sufficient for you [to keep the race next year]?' asks a hopeful Dutch presenter.

Ecclestone looks him dead in the eye, pauses, and then just says: 'No.'

Pressed, he suggests he is looking for a number closer to 45,000.

'And that is a financial success?' he asks again.

Ecclestone, showing almost no emotion, produces a brutal one-liner.

'No, then it's not quite such a big failure.'

Ecclestone half-smiles at his own jibe and then realises he should probably show a little deference to the people whose livelihoods depend on the Dutch Grand Prix.

He adds: 'We've been supporting this race for five or six years financially and it's about time it stood on its own two feet.'

His sparring partner suggests that the Dutch character is not so predisposed to money-making ('maybe we are not so penny wise and pound foolish') and implies that the race is about more than that. Ecclestone, the ultimate business pragmatist, baulks at the suggestion.

Over the three days, 56,000 people turned up at Zandvoort, but with more than 25 applications for races in 1986, Ecclestone was no longer prepared to pour millions of pounds into the circuit. They left, and would not be back for more than 35 years.

Compare those numbers to the 2 million who regularly tune in to Ziggo Sport's coverage of a Grand Prix on Sunday or the million who applied for tickets for the ill-fated 2020 Dutch Grand Prix, and it is a sign of how strong the appetite for F1 could have been.

For all the financial arguments, the fact is that a talented Dutch driver winning races is what brought F1 back to the Netherlands for the 2020 season, albeit a race that never went ahead because of the coronavirus pandemic, and that had one been in circulation at the time, it might have been a far easier sell to the public and to Ecclestone. However, they had to wait another decade for the arrival of Jos Verstappen, who clearly had the talent to win races but never quite managed to become the first Dutch race winner.

Verstappen's accession to F1 though did seem to indicate a shift in mentality and racing culture in the Netherlands. Previously, as suggested by Ecclestone's interviewer, there was an air of naivety to the Dutch approach, particularly in the cut-throat world of F1. Drivers and teams had success in more junior formulas but what was required for success at the highest level – a potent cocktail of speed, racecraft, sponsorship and pragmatism, on and off the track – seemed somehow lacking. The Dutch contribution to F1, as detailed above, features some thrilling stories that provide great texture, but rarely end happily.

Verstappen though had a bit of an ace up his sleeve, and although some might regard him as more of a wild card, Huub Rothengatter was perhaps exactly what Dutch motor sport needed.

Rothengatter had raced in F1 30 times in the mid-1980s but never scored a point. He was notorious for finding ways of poaching drives from other drivers, although always in substandard cars, and had a penchant for guerrilla marketing techniques that earned him a reputation in the paddock. His origin story involves a huge crash that should have been career-ending, but it seemed to only strengthen his resolve to reach F1 by hook or by crook.

So when he took on a second career as a manager, he seemed born for it. He spotted and attached himself to Jos Verstappen and was soon soliciting offers from a number of top teams, that grew to just about the entire grid by the time he had completed an impressive Arrows test in Portugal.

Rothengatter's ambition and eagerness for Jos though is sometimes seen as his downfall by those who believe that Verstappen would have been Holland's first race winner if he had trod a different path.

When every man and his dog came calling in 1993, Rothengatter and Verstappen plumped for Benetton, predominantly because they were offering him a two-year deal. The plan was not for him to race in 1994 alongside Michael Schumacher but JJ Lehto's heavy crash in pre-season testing and subsequent broken neck gifted him a debut, and he grabbed back-to-back podiums in Hungary and Belgium. He was still a reckless, 'pass first, ask questions later' driver though and had not mastered the finer points of F1. Perhaps, had he accepted the McLaren test offer and ended up debuting for them in 1995, things would have been different. Perhaps, had Rothengatter not started to issue large financial demands for his client's services in 1995, Flavio Briatore would not have opted against re-signing him. And perhaps they should not have got into a contract holdout with Jordan in 1998 that left Verstappen without an F1 drive when they plumped for Heinz-Harald Frentzen instead.

What Rothengatter did do was get Verstappen from karting to F1 in double time, as he raced just 52 times in any sort of race car before making his debut in an era when most drivers took far more to earn a place in the fastest series, but by his own admission, Jos was not ready. The people of Holland though absolutely were. Even before he made his debut, the famous fan club with its annual membership of £20 and its magazine entitled *Jos the Boss* was growing strong. Starved of Grand Prix action since Zandvoort lost its race nine years earlier, Verstappen's meteoric rise and his first podium in Hungary was huge news back home. His home town of Montfort exploded in celebration. His 71-year-old grandfather Sef was quoted in *De Telegraaf* as saying, 'Give him one or two years and he will be a world champion.' It was dubbed a 'historic race' on the front page, where Verstappen was pictured celebrating with teammate Schumacher. It was not clear at that point which of them would reach greater heights, certainly not in Holland.

Four years later, Max was born, but over the border in Belgium. Jos had moved to Monaco at the start of his career but returned to northern Europe and in a small, secretive wedding married Sophie Kumpen, Max's mother, in the Belgian city of Hasselt, where they settled down. Hasselt, capital of the Belgian province of Limburg, is a Flemish city about an hour's drive from the town of Montfort where Jos had grown up and where his father still lived, not far from the border. Max grew up in

Belgium, travels on a Belgian passport and lived in Belgium all his life until he moved to Monaco in 2015.

Despite the strong Belgian influence in his life though, Max races under a Dutch super licence which means that when he stands on the top step of the podium, it is 'Wilhelmus' that is played rather than 'La Brabançonne', and when Max's fans pack out grandstands across Europe, it is bright orange that marks them out rather than anything that a Red Devil might wear.

'I have lived in Belgium all my life, but I feel more Dutch,' Max himself said back in 2015. 'Because of all that karting, I spend more time with my father than with my mother. I'm just always among the Dutch.

'I actually only lived in Belgium to sleep, but during the day I went to the Netherlands and had my friends there too. I was raised as a Dutch person and that is how I feel.' It is from an early age too. A picture of father and son taken not long before the 2006 FIFA World Cup shows them posing with their go-kart, the whole vehicle painted orange while Jos holds an orange football and the front wing bears the message 'Hup Holland hup'!

Like so many things, in Max's head it is very clear. Racing drivers often have this quality that can be mistaken for arrogance or stubbornness, but it is a product of their profession. When you are doing 200 miles an hour and have to brake for a corner, there is no grey area. You cannot have a debate about it or hedge your bets; you must brake once and hard, otherwise you are in the gravel or the wall. So that bleeds over into life.

Limburg though is about as Dutch as Belgium gets. The Dutch-speaking Flemish province was one entity, until Belgium became independent in 1839 and part of the area was designated on the Belgian side of the border. Now there are two separate provinces, both called Limburg, one of which Max was born in (the Belgian one) and the other which was Jos' hometown (Montfort). Many people will choose to live on the Belgian side of the border because of the more favourable tax arrangements and generally cheaper housing. So understandably, in that part of Flanders, there is a little fluidity on national identity.

Belgium, you might argue, has a more successful motor racing history than the Netherlands. Max's mother Sophie was born into a family packed with racing talent. Her father Robert, who passed away in 2020 after a fifteen-year battle with cancer at the age of 69, was a successful go-karter in his own right before turning to entrepreneurship and was also chairman of the football club in Genk, but would still organise go-kart races in which his daughter and his nephew Anthony would race – partially to appease Anthony's mother who was fed up with him driving his go-kart round the garden and destroying her flower beds. His brother Paul, Anthony's father, was the Belgian national rallycross champion in 1987 and later founded his own race team. He even appeared on Belgium's version of *Dancing with the Stars* (he was voted out just three weeks in). Anthony went on to race too, competing for his father's PK Carsport team in a European stock car series and twice winning the title, before moving upstairs in 2018 after failing a drugs test during the 24-hour race at Zolder, an event he had won six times in his younger days.

Sophie too was no slouch, although never progressed to professional racing, even though the Kumpen group run by her uncle, which includes a multimillion dollar construction company, an American real estate investment wing and previously shares in Belgium's biggest bicycle manufacturer Ridley, could easily have helped fund her through it. She had shown the talent to earn it by beating plenty of drivers who went on to reach the heights of F1; the man who is now her son's boss at Red Bull,

Christian Horner, raced against her in 1989 at the Junior World Kart Championships.

'In that race were some super talented drivers: Jan Magnussen, Jarno Trulli, Giancarlo Fisichella, Dario Franchitti. She was top ten in the world, for sure,' Horner says.

When she won the prestigious Andrea Margutti Trophy in 1995, the field included yet more drivers who would go on to race in F1 – but Sophie gave it up when she met Jos. His career had already taken off and in 1997 Max was born.

'I sometimes still talk to my mum about it and it's nice to see some old pictures of her racing,' Verstappen told the *Financial Times* in 2018. 'My dad got to know my mum because of racing. Definitely, when I was very young, we were always talking about it when we were at home.'

If Sophie had her way, Max would probably be racing under Belgian colours rather than Dutch ones too. When Max was still seventeen, and her name had to be on all the paperwork as he was still underage, she told a Belgian tabloid: 'The only identification that Max has is Belgian. He turns eighteen on 30 September, and on that date, and not before, he can opt for Dutch nationality. In the meantime, he is Belgian and nothing else.'

Max though was already racing on a Dutch super licence and was planning to leave Belgium and move to Monaco shortly after his eighteenth birthday. The gift of two jet skis from his father Jos and manager Raymond made it clear his future did not lie in Flanders, more than 100 miles from the sea.

'Actually not much has changed,' Max insisted after moving to Monaco. 'Because I travel constantly. And at any time I can go back home to Belgium [to visit].'

It was perhaps the final nail in the coffin of any slim hopes the Belgians had of 'reclaiming' the man born on their soil.

The strange thing is that Belgium has a far greater track record when it comes to motor sport, particularly in F1. Antonio Ascari won the first Belgian Grand Prix back in 1925, thirteen years before Henri van Alphen threw down a few hay bales in Zandvoort town centre, and the race has been a familiar part of the F1 calendar ever since the war.

That is not to say that Grand Prix racing in Belgium was an instant success. Spa-Francorchamps, the circuit to have hosted the first and the majority of Belgian Grands Prix, was originally designed in 1920 to host a revival of the pre-World War I La Meuse Cup on public roads, but the inaugural Spa race in 1921 had to be cancelled after just one car entered. Instead, 23 motorbikes raced around the circuit. A year later, an event run by the Royal Automobile Club of Belgium (RACB) broke in the circuit for four-wheeled vehicles in what became known as the first Belgian Grand Prix.

The track became notorious as one of the toughest and most exciting, with elevation changes through the forests that remain to this day, but also as one of the most deadly. In total over the course of its history, Spa has claimed the lives of 48 drivers or riders, including the shocking death of Frenchman Anthoine Hubert during the F2 race in 2019. The circuit was revised and rebuilt a number of times over the years for safety reasons and at just 4.3 miles is now less than half the length of its original layout.

Nevertheless it has remained a profitable and popular race, which has doubtless helped cement F1 into the Belgian national sporting psyche, but they also had one of the best racers of the 1960s and 1970s to get behind.

Jacky Ickx's father had been a motoring journalist and had taken his son to races as a child, but the youngster showed little interest until he bought him a small motorbike. Ickx appeared to be a natural and was soon national champion and went on to win European honours too before swapping two wheels for four and entering touring car racing with Lotus.

In 1967, he won the European Formula Two Championship with Tyrrell and appeared for both them and Cooper in Formula One, but his title in the second tier earned him a full-time drive with Ferrari the next season. In just his fifth outing for Scuderia, having already bagged his first podium on home soil a month before, he became the first Belgian to win a Grand Prix when driving through treacherously wet conditions in Rouen. The Pathé newsreel report though focuses on the incident for which the race is more commonly remembered, the second-lap crash that led to the death of French driver Jo Schlesser after his experimental Honda, with its magnesium-based chassis, burst into flames. Ickx, standing on the top step of the podium for the first time, barely acknowledged his victory. It is a mark of what kind of a challenge F1 represented in its early days that Ickx's first two victories were both overshadowed by the death of a colleague. By the time Ickx won his third race in Canada in 1969, he was racing for Brabham in a battle for second place in the championship; Jackie Stewart had already sealed the title. The win took Ickx past Bruce McLaren and clear of Graham Hill into a second place he would retain until the end of the season.

Having been reinstated by Ferrari, Ickx managed the same feat behind Jochen Rindt, who lost his life halfway through the season but scored enough points to be awarded the title, and it seemed certain that the Belgian would at some point win a world championship. Second though was the closest he ever got – he also finished fourth on three separate occasions.

His career was not without laurels though. Between 1969 and 1982, he won the 24 Hours of Le Mans on six separate occasions before he retired in 1985 after being shaken by his involvement in yet another motor racing fatality, this time Germany's Stefan Bellof who died after a collision with Ickx during a World Sportscar Championship race at Spa. Nevertheless, Ickx is known in Belgium and the world over as one of the greatest drivers never to win an F1 world title, and even raced in the Paris–Dakar Rally until the age of 55. He was also inducted into the International Motorsports Hall of Fame and remained involved in the sport as a clerk of the course in Monaco.

He was followed by Thierry Boutsen who managed three race wins and fifteen podiums in his 164 Grands Prix career, but like neighbours Holland, Belgium is still without a world champion and is crying out for one. However, even if Max Verstappen does not raise the Belgian flag on the podium, the country gains from his success. Its relative proximity to Germany meant that selling tickets for the Michael Schumacher show was rarely a problem in the early 2000s, but the race went fifteen years without a sell-out before Max's arrival on the scene started an annual migration across the border for what was then the closest thing he had to a home race. In 2016, Verstappen's second year in F1, an estimated 25,000 Dutch fans headed for Spa to watch him race. A year later, that number is thought to have tripled as the race was reinvigorated with around a quarter of a million people now turning out every year in Belgium. Verstappen regularly cites it as his favourite race, partially down to the Orange Wall that assembles alongside the Kemmel straight every year to watch him.

It is orange though, and not the crimson red of Belgium. Much as they might relish his presence, Verstappen will always be the Flying Dutchman.

3

DAD, THE WORST BOSS IN THE WORLD

'I never had any surprises in F1 because no one was as hard on me as my dad.'

Certainly, Jos has always known how to get through to his son.

In 2012, they had been at a karting world championship event that Max describes as what should have been 'one of the easiest weekends of my career', so dominant was he over the field. However, he had burned the clutch out during a heat on Friday forcing him to retire and giving his father plenty of work to do to get the go-kart back into shape for the pre-final. He did though – being Max's mechanic was his full-time job at this point – and after starting in tenth in the pre-final, Verstappen made up eight places on the opening lap and won the race by four seconds.

It put him on pole for the final, with a driver by the name of Daniel Bray starting next to him on the front row. Bray was a relative no-name. It was his first World Cup event, and he even recalls one press officer coming up to him and asking: 'Who ARE you? And where did you come from?' He and Max had been the fastest drivers all weekend and the final was to be a showdown between the two. Even Bray knew though that, in all likelihood, he was racing for second.

'Everybody up and down the grid knew Max basically had the thing in the bag,' says Bray, who now runs his own go-karting team in New Zealand and uses his time spent in Europe to help other Kiwis make the difficult and often expensive move to the international circuit.

'A very good friend of mine, Josh Hart, a world champion go-karter, was talking to me before the race and he said, "So you got any for him?" and I said, "I don't think I've got anything for him". But we came up with a plan which was basically: if he passed you, just pass him back, just keep in front. Don't let him run away, basically.

'We got off the line, did a lap, and I got a good draft and I passed Max into the corner.'

The way the track was laid out that weekend made it one of the fastest in the world. The go-karts were hitting speeds of close to 110 miles an hour on the main straight and slip-streaming was extremely powerful. Even in qualifying, it was virtually impossible to set a competitive time without teaming up with someone for drafting down the main straight and the whole field was covered by about eight tenths of a second.

It made overtaking on the main straight relatively simple, and breaking 'the tow' (i.e. getting far enough ahead that you could not be overtaken again a lap later) would not be easy. In the pre-final, Max had overtaken nine drivers so he knew it was not a track where passing was hard.

'We'd already pulled out quite a long way on the field and that was how I thought it was going to be because we were the two fastest karts all weekend long,' Bray adds.

'And then we come back around the track and come down to the corner in front of the pits there. It was a super-fast right-hander so you were fifth gear and then just dropped to fourth. You hardly even took any speed off the go-kart.'

There were no speed guns trained on the corner but cars were routinely taking it at more than 80 miles an hour.

'No one all weekend had made a pass through there. At that speed, the apex comes in that fast, you're looking that far in the distance, you flick down the gear and turn in.'

It was an impossible place to pass, but with Jos' words of chastisement for his mistake with the clutch ringing in his ears, Max was impetuous. He dived down the inside and his front left tyre slipped under Bray's right rear. The New Zealander never saw him coming.

'It was a stupid pass,' says Bray, who saw his hopes of a podium at his first ever World Cup race dashed by the incident.

'Realistically, for the speed that he had, all he had to do was wait three more corners, then we were back onto the straight where he passed me and he would have done the exact same thing I did, draft past me. And then I would have done the same thing and tried to hook it and draft back past him. Just like cycle racing.'

Bray shrugged off the disappointment, pleased just to have made the final and proved himself in an elite international field. Max's mother came straight over to apologise for the incident. An elite go-kart driver herself, it was clear who had been at fault. Jos did too, although he waited half an hour to do so. He needed time to calm down. He conceded that it was Max's fault and apologised, but was no less angry.

In fact, Jos was furious. Of all the pieces of advice he has given Max over the years, many of them are about being calm and patient, conscious of his own impetuosity that had often cost him in his racing career – not to mention the fact that he had sweated blood to get the car in shape for the finale of the weekend.

He lost his temper and packed up his kit in the van. Max asked him to help getting the kart from the track to the van after the race. 'Do it yourself,' Jos replied angrily. With the help of a friend, he loaded it up and the pair set off on the long road home.

Max, true to his character, wanted to resolve things. He kept trying to talk to his dad about what had happened – but Jos couldn't even look at him. Eventually, they stopped at a petrol station and Jos told him to get out, before driving off into the distance.

He insists now that he knew Max's mother was not far behind them and could pick him up, but Jos' reputation precedes him. As it was, Jos turned around and came back for his son, but the retribution was not finished. They drove the 1,100 miles home, painful for anyone but particularly Max, an instinctive appeaser.

Later, in a 2020 podcast appearance for Aston Martin, the pair discussed the incident at length. Max said that he was upset after the race but that his father was that worst of all parental emotions: disappointed. Disappointed was probably an understatement. Jos didn't speak to him for a week – until eventually he explained himself.

'To me it felt he did everything too relaxed. You know, it was all very easy for him,' Jos said.

'But I really wanted him to feel the pain. Because he had to think what he was doing. That was the last race of that season and the season afterwards we won everything. Because of what happened at that race, it made him a better driver.'

In the same year, Jos 'really smashed' his son on the crash helmet during a race weekend, in the middle of the paddock, because of how Max had performed during a practice session.

'What are you doing?' Jos recalls saying. 'We're here, it's the world championships and I think we can win it.'

Max admits he was driving 'like a potato' and that the bang on the head was a wake-up call that worked – he went on to win all the heats, the pre-final and the final that weekend – but it had not gone unnoticed. Nearby mechanics were baffled by the incident. Max was still a child, albeit a prodigious one, and while Jos was his father and karting dads are famously tough on their charges, it seemed he was close to the line on more than one occasion.

'"You retarded bastard, stupid pig, you're never going to make it," that sort of thing,' Max recalls his father saying to him.

'That sums up that time [during go-karting] very well. My father was always very strict with me when things didn't go as well.'

There is often a feeling in elite sport that the ends justify the means, and that young athletes are pushed harder than 'normal' children. There are plenty who feel that even the ends – winning the 2021 world title – were not justified by the means by which Jos chose to help his son achieve it. Even Helmut Marko, one of F1's hardest taskmasters, thought Verstappen was 'more than hard' on his son. Jos was certainly not the perfect father – but he was completely committed to their joint goal, both in terms of time and finances.

Mercedes team boss and part-owner Toto Wolff, who having also run a driver management agency knows more than most exactly how expensive it can be to get to the top, recently took a stab at the numbers.

'If somebody is talented, very talented, you probably need to spend €1 million in karting through junior, senior and international races,' says Wolff. 'You need at least a season in F4 or Formula Renault which is another €350,000 if you do it properly.

'You need €650,000 for an F3 season so we are at €2 million. You probably need another season of F3 so you are at €2.6 million or €2.7 million and then you haven't done any GP2 or World Series. So let's say you are at €3 million if you are an extraordinary talent.

'GP2 is another €1.5 million so probably, if you want to be on the safe side, you are around €4.5 million and €5 million and you have only done one year of GP2. You are on the verge of getting into Formula One but you are not in there. You need another €2 million to €3 million to get the drive. So you are talking about €7 million to €8 million.'

At a certain point, a driver will hope to cover some if not all of these fees and costs through sponsorship, but that kicks in exponentially as they climb the ladder. At the very start, you're going to need someone with a six- or seven-figure sum burning a hole in their pocket and a decent amount of knowledge of the sport in terms of how to spend it.

The driver academy system, where teams like Ferrari, Renault, Mercedes or McLaren scout talent in the junior series and try to fast-track them and fund them through to the top, is marginally more meritocratic, but even then most drivers they pick up will have already spent hundreds of thousands on their career.

It was not always thus. Take one of the first great Formula One champions, Argentina's Juan Manuel Fangio. He dropped out of school at a young age and started working in a mechanic's garage before being enlisted in the army, where his driving skills were noticed and enhanced. When he returned to civilian life, he cobbled together enough money to build a race car himself. His parents, a housekeeper and a stonemason by trade, let him use their garden shed. Such a story was unremarkable in the early decades of F1, with an engineering background one thing that tended to unite the drivers on the grid. Some had parents with oil on their hands like John Surtees whose father Jack was a motorcycle champion and dealer, but others like Jim Clark had actively defied the wishes of his farming family by going into motor sport.

The modern pathway is perhaps more diverse but no more meritocratic, perhaps even less so; family ties to the sport are commonplace and with the sport so prohibitively expensive to break into, so it helps if you have a parent who is a driver, or a millionaire, or preferably both.

As always, there are exceptions that prove the rule. Damon Hill was the first son of a world champion to win a world championship, although his father and two-time world champion Graham was tragically killed in a plane crash before seeing his son, then fifteen, make it all the way to F1. Curiously though, Damon never expressed much of an interest in motor racing until after the death of his father. While someone like Verstappen would have taken a pre-school drive if the FIA had sanctioned an under-fives series, Damon spent years doing other things. His first love was motorbikes, which he found more aesthetically pleasing. He felt that cars looked uncomfortable going round corners, which in the 1970s they were, and that even so you couldn't see all the work the driver was doing. On a motorbike, you saw the rider wrapped around the machine, miraculously clinging on for dear life and pouring it through high-speed corners, all the while wrestling over its back like a vine wrapped around a drainpipe. He did afford a nod to his father, racing in helmet design that was almost identical to Graham's, a dark navy blue background with white oar blades (his father had been a rower before a racing driver) adorning it around the crown.

Despite an obvious love for the sport, he took a laissez-faire approach to being successful. He was racing at a relatively low level and would not bother with practice, instead simply turning up and expecting to win. He couldn't even start it sometimes.

'I spent most of my time pushing the bike and then everyone else had gone!' Hill said in a 2019 interview.

'I had no idea. I didn't have someone telling me what I was supposed to be doing. So I had to learn the hard way.

'I had bitten off more than I could chew.'

The talent was there, somehow. He had been exposed to racing his whole life, met just about every living world champion, scampered around the paddock as a child and watched his father win two world titles, yet always said he was just a spectator with little understanding of what was going on. Unlike others, he had no discernible passion for racing, not in the first instance at least.

He later indicated it came down to an eminently relatable emotional string: a fear of disappointing his father.

'When he died, the spotlight was turned off and I had the chance to be myself. There was this sense of relief,' he wrote in his 2016 autobiography. 'I didn't have to worry about whether my dad approved of what I was doing. It was a complicated feeling of freedom, at the cost of his life.

'By racing, I was resurrecting my dad. My performances were mine, but they inevitably contained some legacy of my dad's racing career and honoured his memory.

'In some senses, it was a way of getting to know him as an adult that I couldn't have done any other way.'

Hill Sr had won the World Drivers' Championship in 1962 and 1968 and when Damon Hill achieved the same feat three decades later in 1996, the legendary F1 commentator Murray

Walker uttered the immortal words: 'I've got to stop because I've got a lump in my throat.'

A moment of dead air followed, a real rarity for a commentator who generally tried to talk as fast as the cars he was describing. Some said Walker had been biased against Hill's title rival Jacques Villeneuve during the season, something the broadcaster strongly denied, but if a little favouritism had crept in, you could have forgiven him.

Being a British racing driver in the 1980s was not an easy living to carve out. Money rolled into motor sport from Continental Europe, often Italy, but it rarely made it over the Channel. Instead, drivers would have to scrap for every and any sponsorship they could and drives were not easy to come by as a result. Having worked in motor sport since the 1940s, he had known Damon almost his entire life and been the sort of ally that his father would have been.

Hill had encountered the difficulties of racing without that father figure during his days on two wheels, but he also cited it as partially the making of him. Once he was left to do it entirely on his own because his results saw his sponsors melt away, he seemed to learn the value of what he was doing. Having started from the ground up, things started to click and the speed followed. He says he won every race he entered in 1984.

Reality then struck however. Bike racing had a poor prognosis. All the reasons for which Damon loved it – the balance, the exposure of the rider to the elements, the high speed – came with the caveat that most were racing injured and that voluntary retirement was a luxury that most riders did not have. Injury or even death was a far more likely outcome, and the financial benefits of the sport compared to its four-wheeled cousins were not the same.

Money was a serious issue. Not only was it difficult to attract sponsors, but Hill's family had been close to bankrupted by his father's death. He had been flying back from the south of France following a testing session with a race team he was running under his own name. There were five others in the plane with him – designer Andy Smallman, manager Ray Brimble and two mechanics, Tony Alcock and Terry Richards – all of whom perished in the crash. It transpired later that Hill's paperwork was not in order and the plane's insurance was invalidated. There was no payout for Hill's family and the relatives of the other five dead men made claims against the Hill estate. The luxurious 25-room mansion in Hertfordshire, where the parties hosting the great and the good of the Grand Prix world had become legendary, was no longer viable. His widow Bette and the three children Damon, Brigitte and Samantha were effectively flat broke.

So while Hill has never quite said as much, the idea of the family losing another member and without even the prospect of significant remuneration because of the risk was not a sensible one and the opportunity to drive racing cars had presented itself. Bette convinced him to go to the Winfield Racing School in France where he started to show some natural aptitude.

Progress though was slow. Hill had not been through go-karting or professional race car driving in the same way as his rivals. At 24 he was a late starter, and by his own admission was a little slow on the uptake of racing culture. When he talks about the horse-trading he was involved in later on in his career, he openly admits to having no real business acumen, hating contracts and never really understanding the political side of things.

'When my dad was doing it, I was just hanging around. I knew what my dad's attitude was to things and that he was a very hard worker and incredibly determined but the more I learned about my dad, he tried too hard in certain areas and didn't delegate enough to people – which is the real talent.

'Racing drivers tend to be a one-man band and slot into a team. In car racing, you had to be part of the team and you let those people give you the equipment and you just drove it. With my bike, I did everything myself. What I wasn't terribly good at understanding was that you had to get the right people around you.'

When he did make his breakthrough, having picked up scraps of drives at Le Mans, in Touring Cars and in Formula Three and 3000, he got the job as a test driver at Williams. After six or seven years in the lower echelons of motor sport, he had started to pick up the scent of a promising drive and actually approached Williams before they approached him. The team was the making of him, giving him 18,000 miles of experience over two years and toughening him to the physical and political challenges of F1. Nevertheless, that insecurity still haunted him.

'I felt like I was always trying to convince people that I was any good because there had been so much press around me starting and quite a lot of scepticism,' Hill said.

'I never really felt like I was regarded as a proper driver.'

That scepticism increased when he was surprisingly promoted to partner Alain Prost in 1993 when there were other more experienced drivers available. The team had taken a chance on him, although cynics might say it was because team boss Frank Williams knew he could pay Hill next to nothing compared to some of the others on the market. He did pay them back and then some, finishing third in his debut season and then second twice before triumphing in 1996 – after which he was unceremoniously dumped for Heinz-Harald Frentzen.

It is a tragic hangover from an era when driver safety was an afterthought, rather than a priority, that Damon Hill's story of parental loss through motor racing is not a unique one. By a quirk of fate, Hill's teammate Villeneuve had also lost his father, another former F1 driver, as a child. Jacques had just turned eleven when Gilles, never a world champion but the 1979 runner-up to Jody Scheckter, crashed during qualifying for the Belgian Grand Prix at Zolder. He hit the back of Jochen Mass's car at more than 125 miles an hour and the car was launched into the air for 100 metres before Villeneuve himself was thrown out of the car and broke his neck. He was kept on life support long enough for his wife, Jacques' mother Joann, to get to hospital but he died soon after aged just 32.

Jacques had actually already been somewhat estranged from his father, sent away to live with another family at the age of nine because 'the energy at home wasn't good'. It meant he had a slightly different vision of his father, one that was shared by many in the paddock. Rival Niki Lauda once described him as 'the craziest devil I ever came across', something to which Jacques' short but complicated relationship with his father is a testament.

'The way I was brought up, when I was with him, he was always doing crazy, stupid stuff, either in a helicopter, a 4x4 or on the roads. That's the only image I had of him, as a racer and not as a dad,' Jacques said in 2019.

He thinks it was deliberate – not the absentee fathering but the exposure to speed and adrenaline.

Jacques added: 'I don't have many memories of my dad, but all I know is that he was wanting his son to race. There was no doubt in his mind.'

For Gilles' first year of Formula One, his family would travel around the world with him, camping out at Grand Prix circuits in the motorhome, before school became a little more important and family life seemingly more complicated.

It's possible that Gilles' eagerness for Jacques to become a racer, although more likely his absence, pushed him away from it, at least to begin with. He did not start go-karting until the age of fourteen but, he claims thanks to having become an extremely accomplished skier while at boarding school in Switzerland, he had a natural aptitude that his instructors back in Canada had never seen before.

He retained that daredevil spirit of his father's too. When he would ski with friends, they would go jumping off cliffs. Jacques would always find the biggest one to jump off because he knew they would not have the guts to follow him. In F1, he was going flat out through Eau Rouge, the famous and dangerous corner complex at Spa, even though it didn't actually prove to gain him any lap time. It was about doing it because he could.

Nevertheless Formula One was always his ultimate goal and he went one better than his father when he beat teammate Heinz-Harald Frentzen to the world title in 1997 having lost out to Hill the year before. Like his former Williams teammate, he was often left having to prove that he was a genuine racing driver and more than just a surname. The two could have been firm friends with so much in common but the awkwardness of being teammates and battling for a world title at the same time created too much friction. Both describe their relationship as utterly 'professional' – a word that almost all drivers use as a diplomatic term as an alternative to saying 'we weren't friends' – and in the end they were only together for a single season.

Some things have changed a great deal in F1 since the 1990s, but the presence of names on the grid that echo through the sport's history has not. Along with Verstappen, we have watched Nico Rosberg, son of 1982 world champion Keke, Kazuki Nakajima whose father Satoru was Japan's first ever full-time F1 driver, three-time champion Nelson Piquet's son Nelson Jr, Jan Magnussen's son Kevin and Jonathan Palmer's son Jolyon all add their names into the F1 history books along with their parents with varying degrees of success.

In fact it is almost impossible to reach the dizzy heights of Formula One unless your parents have at least a passing interesting in motor sport. It is not like football or tennis where you can pay your fee, drop them off at nine and then pick them up at five having spent the day being taught all the skills. As a parent to a budding speedster, you need to be a sponsor, a chauffeur, an engineer and a strategist. Fortunately, Jos was able to be all those things and more to Max, but he also wanted to make sure he could coach his son in the right way. He had in his mind that, the way his career was panning out, he would have more time to spend working with him once he reached the age of six. By then Jos would be into his thirties and perhaps on his way out of F1, so that's when he had planned to buy him his first go-kart. Max though, as he so often has in his life, wanted to get on with things.

Jos says: 'He was with his mum at a go-kart track near Genk and he called me crying because he saw a younger boy driving and he said he wanted to do it as well.

'So when I came home – I had been in Canada for a race – I bought him a go-kart. That's how it started. He was four and a half.'

Max himself tends to tell the story, because it is a well-rehearsed bit for both men by now, a little differently, suggesting Jos did not relent so easily. He had seen one of his friends, who was indeed younger than him and remains a friend to this day, driving at the track near Genk. His initial tearful pleas fell on deaf ears when he rang his father to ask him. 'Wait until you're six,' he replied, sticking to his plan. Max though cried for days and his mother, who bore the brunt of his campaign, was the one who rang Jos this time and said: 'I think we need to buy him a kart. Now.'

Jos often tries to insist that he would have let the little boy do whatever he wanted, but in a racing family he also knew very little else and vehicles were his first and only love. After that, Jos would have been, even he admits, frustrated if Max had given up later in childhood, once it became clear how talented he was.

For Carlos Sainz Jr, who would go on to be Max's teammate at Toro Rosso, there were also some serious parental expectations. His father Carlos Sr was a two-time rally champion and the two young men would have had plenty in common when they joined forces.

Like all racing fathers, Carlos Sr was away a lot when his son was growing up and as seems to be inevitable, Carlos Jr became obsessed with driving from a very early age. When he was two years old, he had been bought a small battery-powered car and when his father returned from a race one day, he saw his son driving around the garden. He was sliding the car around, doing doughnuts and even the 'Scandinavian flick', a technique used in rally driving to get the car around corners in low-grip conditions.

'Who the hell taught him to do that?' Carlos asked. His wife shrugged. No one had. Somehow, the skills were in his blood.

As he grew older, Carlos Jr quickly developed into go-karting. His father owned an indoor centre in the Latina district of Madrid, not far from the Vicente Calderón where Atlético Madrid played football at the time before moving to the new

Wanda Metropolitano Stadium on the other side of town. At the karting complex, Carlos Jr showed prodigious talent that suggested he might be more interested in racing on smooth tarmac than the dirt, dust and snow that his father had practically made his own.

His career could have gone either way, but then a chance meeting decided things for him. At the age of ten, the two Sainz boys went to Barcelona for the Spanish Grand Prix, where Carlos Sr's name opened many doors. One of those was the Renault hospitality tent, where world championship leader and Spanish hero Fernando Alonso was sitting. They went over to meet him and Carlos Jr was so nervous and excited he could hardly speak. Fernando remembers that his father told him that Junior only wanted to race on circuits, and he was desperate to put him in a rally car. The meeting with Fernando sealed it. When they got back to Madrid, Carlos told his family he wanted to be just like Fernando Alonso. They probably didn't believe that ten years later, he would be racing wheel to wheel with him.

Like Carlos, Max was strong-willed and knew his own mind. One New Year Jos took his family to Norway on holiday, along with his manager and close friend Raymond Vermeulen and his family. They stayed near Michael Schumacher's holiday home there, and the three families spent time together. It is indicative of the familial nature of F1 that five-year-old Max was not the only future racing driver present; Michael's son Mick was two years younger. Max was five years old and Jos bought him a week of expensive skiing lessons; by the end of it he still preferred sledging down the mountain shouting 'a sled like this goes nice and fast and is much easier than two of those long skis'. In the evenings – because it gets dark at 4pm in Norway at that time of year – they would head over to the Schumachers' chalet and play board games. It was doubtless extremely competitive. Jos and Michael talked constantly about Formula One, about the changes to FIA regulations and, as Jos joked at the time, 'whether they would apply to him or not'. Clearly, Jos' availability was regularly mentioned, just in case Michael could put in a good word somewhere.

So when he bought Max that first go-kart, Jos had by no means given up on F1 even though he wanted to be the one to teach him what to do with it. He was without a full-time drive admittedly, but would still attend almost every race weekend at some point to meet with sponsors and team principals, to keep his name in the hat for whatever drives might be going. It paid off too, because he did bag a drive with Minardi, although it would turn out to be his last and a rather limp way to end his own F1 career: he finished in the top ten just twice in the 2003 season and in his last race in Japan, he was two laps down by the end and was the penultimate finisher. His mentoring of Max had already started by that point, and of others for that matter. Jos clearly felt he had much he could pass on, was still occasionally karting competitively and had Giedo van der Garde, who would go on to drive in F1, racing one of his go-karts in the world championship. Giedo though was a teenager. Max was just a child, barely a toddler, and Jos did his best not to be too involved until later. Fortunately, Max was a natural.

'I didn't really coach him much in the beginning. I just let him have fun and drive – but I never really had to tell him the racing lines or things like that. He knew because he was watching all the time.'

When Jos did start to get closer to his son's career and take a more active role, he did not hold back. The pieces were already in place for Jos to work through some of the regrets and problems he had encountered in his own career and ensure that Max would not encounter them in the same way.

'My career all helped to make his career what it is. I learned a lot from my career. You learn the most from the mistakes you make,' Jos said in 2019. 'I looked in the mirror and I knew exactly what I did wrong or didn't do right and I tried to teach him only the good things.'

Quite apart from the technical, practical skills that Jos was able to impart upon Max, he was also able to put him in the right place at the right time, more often than not, and a man who was instrumental in doing that was Raymond Vermeulen.

In the mid-1990s, an insurance broker from nearby Roermond was in 'De Rotonde' in Montfort, a regular haunt of his, and got chatting to the owner, Max's grandfather Frans. Raymond mentioned that he was keen on go-karting at the weekends and asked if Frans had an engine he could buy for his go-kart. As it happened, Frans had one in mind – but it would need installing and tuning for Raymond's kart. Being something of an amateur, he asked whether Frans might have someone who could help him do it, and Frans recommended his son Jos.

'I got to know Jos basically because of my complete lack of racing talent,' Vermeulen jokes in an interview with local newspaper *Limburgs Dagblad*. The pair quickly became firm friends and Jos started to get Raymond involved in his career to the point that he was effectively Huub Rothengatter's number two. As the paddock's patience with Rothengatter wore thin – he was often painted as a stubborn and duplicitous negotiator – Raymond became more involved. Whereas Huub ruled with an iron fist, the media and the teams felt they could do business with the more malleable Vermeulen. When it came to Max signing for Red Bull, the only people present were his family and Raymond. He remains the man who separates the world from Max, who keeps the pack at bay. After Jos, Raymond is Max's closest confidant. In fact, Raymond has become part of the family. Max's mother calls him 'a listening ear for the whole family'.

'He is actually the common thread through our life,' she says. 'He always has a solution.'

Even Red Bull's irascible supremo Helmut Marko has allowed him into the inner circle – not that he had much choice in the matter.

'Normally we don't work much with managers,' he said. 'But with the Verstappen situation, you have a package: it's Jos and Raymond.'

Sometimes both men are seen at races, sometimes neither, but usually one or the other. Vermeulen says he often finds it more practical and productive not to attend race weekends when it comes to getting business done, which is his primary concern. These days, Jos seems to have resumed his role as father now that there are great armies of people to attend to his son's sporting needs. It is probably for the best. There are countless examples of sports people reaching breaking point with their familial business links. Just a few doors down, if Max wanted to ask, he could hear a cautionary tale from Lewis Hamilton, whose father Anthony was similarly all-encompassing during his early career and helped him make his first waves in F1 – until the pair split professionally in 2010. It was billed as a mutual split at the time but three years later Anthony revealed that his son was 'fed up listening' to his father and 'decided he wanted to be his own man'. It was a damaging period.

'In the search for success, with the pressure it put on us all, we were so immersed in the drive to succeed that we lost sight of what was most important – our relationship,' Lewis told the BBC.

'Over time, we lost that father-son bond and it has been something we have both wanted back for so long.'

Jos has often spoken of learning from his own mistakes. Perhaps he learns from other people's too. When Max moved to Monaco, it was to give himself an independent life. On a Grand Prix weekend, he remains independent – but Jos is never far away for a word of advice.

'Max's success has changed our whole family's life. I have more time for my private life that I didn't have for the previous 25 years. It changed my life, it changed my daughter's life a lot, it changed his mum's life. It changed everything.

'We [with Raymond] make the decisions, we always talk, we always have the conversation: every deal we always discuss together. The three of us get along very well and it's so good to have the right people in the right place.'

4

A VIDEO GAMER IN REAL LIFE

When the coronavirus pandemic took hold of the sporting world, Formula One very nearly got away with it. Or so they thought.

The virus appeared in the Far East in December, when the sport was just preparing to go into hibernation for winter ahead of what was then to be the last season under current regulations. No one could have predicted what would follow, but F1 seemed to spend a significant amount of time in denial. It is famously the most international sport in the world with drivers from around the globe and fans in every corner, yet they believed they could somehow continue to run their sport, perhaps with the concession of delaying the Shanghai-based Chinese Grand Prix until later in the year.

Teams were forced to change their plans, with flights being rerouted to avoid Covid-19 hotspots like China or Singapore on their way to Australia, but optimism still abounded, even among teams like Ferrari and AlphaTauri who would be travelling from northern Italy, the epicentre of the outbreak in Europe. Australia did not have a travel ban on those arriving from Italy and all teams were able to travel to Melbourne. Incredibly, the Australian

Grand Prix, the traditional March curtain-raiser on the modern F1 calendar, got within hours of kicking off on Friday morning before the authorities were forced to abandon it after a member of the McLaren crew tested positive for coronavirus and a whole host of others were forced to self-isolate as a result of contact with them.

Every hour it seemed, another race would be postponed or cancelled as the scale of the pandemic gradually sapped the optimism of organisers. Within a week, the season had been pushed back three months until the beginning of June. In fact it would be 5 July when racing finally got under way in Austria under scrupulous and strange conditions, with no fans, team-based bubbles within bubbles and bi-weekly testing for all those on site. In the meantime, the sport was desperate to retain some sort of presence. Fortunately, F1 prides itself on being the one of innovation and quickly the wheels were put in motion to take racing off-track and online. They would not be championship events, naturally, but they would involve a number of the grid and utilise the official Formula One game to create a form of racing that viewers could still enjoy.

'We very quickly put together a virtual Grand Prix series where we had our real-life F1 drivers, we had the past F1 drivers, up-and-coming drivers and then wider celebrities,' says Dr Julian Tan, the head of eSports at F1 and digital business initiatives, the man who helped launch the sport head first into the world of professional video gaming in 2017. Alongside some of those who had been present at its birth, F1 managed to attract a number of the current grid including the likes of Lando Norris and Nicholas Latifi, as well as footballer Thibaut Courtois, golfer Ian Poulter and international music superstar Liam Payne. Existing eSports

F1 teams, a project all ten of the real-life grid's competitors have bought into, also took part.

'We had a very diverse group of celebrities who participated, but at its core it was really around the F1 drivers themselves racing against each other on the official F1 video game to continue to bring racing entertainment to our fans because we weren't able to put on real world racing entertainment by getting our cars on the tarmac.

'But we were still able to deliver live racing through eSports over lockdown and also in that similar vein continue to deliver value for sponsors and content for our broadcast partners who were really in a very unique situation.

'Everything had gone dark so it was really important for us that we could still continue to keep the lights on through eSports.

'I think [2020 was] a really big year that has continued to show that eSports really has a big role to play as we look towards transforming the sport of Formula One and what it means to engage with or become a fan of Formula One.'

The takeover of F1 by Liberty Media, an American company with a large media and sports portfolio, saw Bernie Ecclestone finally removed from control of the sport after decades in charge. A global, multibillion dollar sport (the total buyout was worth $4.4 billion) had been run by Bernie and a few staff members from a small office in London. If you wanted a pass to the paddock at an F1 weekend, he would have to personally sign it off. He was the ultimate micromanager and a brutal businessman, but one who had seen F1's overall viewing figures decline in the 21st century. The central challenge for Formula One's new owners was to rectify that slump and, the holy grail for almost every sport, reach a younger audience.

Dr Tan himself is a far younger man than Bernie would ever have considered hiring in a senior role, for starters. An Oxford, Cambridge and Harvard Business School graduate but with no motor sport experience per se, he probably wouldn't have given his CV a second glance. Instead though, the former consultant has masterminded a remarkable expansion, arguably the most successful one by a sport, into the eSports world.

'When we entered [eSports] in 2017, the main objective and the main emphasis of us actually doing that was that there was a wider appreciation that as a sport we had an ageing fan base,' Dr Tan says.

'So it was really important that as we were going through that transformation, where as a sport we were transforming across a lot of different facets, we wanted to be bold and we wanted to experiment on new initiatives that can help us build that pipeline of fans into Formula One. At the time eSports was growing rapidly as an industry so it caught our attention.

'We knew there was a burgeoning industry and one that helped us talk to the younger generation and reach out to them. So, we jumped head first into eSports in 2017 and honestly I think [when] we did it, we didn't fully understand the industry. We took the plunge regardless because we felt it was an important thing to do.

'And, as a company I think as part of the Liberty acquisition we've taken on a little bit more of an entrepreneurial, or risk-taking, sort of approach in terms of finding out new areas to play in.'

It was not an uncalculated risk, much as Dr Tan might play down its significance. Liberty's takeover had brought with it new ideas and coincided with the arrival of a new breed of driver whose experience of racing was not simply limited to the real world, many of whom were involved with eSports and sim racing at a serious level.

In 2015, Max had signed up with Team Redline, a sim racing team founded back in 2000, but even by that point already had his own racing seat, wheel, pedals and three curved screens – all Red Bull branded of course – complete with a high-speed internet connection to allow him to turn his Monaco flat into anywhere in the world. It was a testament to his belief in the system that he joined the virtual team during his first year in F1 and that he said he planned to continue sim racing alongside his other career. Red Bull were keen to encourage it too, designing a custom livery for him online that inverted the colours from their real-world cars. They let Team Redline handle the simulator though, hooking him up with a new rig which was 'even more realistic'.

'If I could, I would have a full professional simulator at home but my current set-up is pretty close to real life,' Max says after his first month using the Redline rig, noting that Red Bull's one in Milton Keynes is still significantly more advanced.

'That thing is ten times the size!'

Max is pretty instantly competitive, but even still he is aware that sim racing, where testing is effectively free and drivers can put in hundreds of hours a month if they want to, has a very high ceiling.

'You can compare sim racing to starting in go-karts age four,' he adds. 'If you drive them for ten or fifteen years, you're going to be very good at it. It's the same with sim racing. So it's very hard to bridge that experience gap.'

The results, in terms of adding extra elements to his on-track skill set, seem to be immediate. The first race after the four-week summer break was in Belgium, Max's first ever home Grand Prix. Unfortunately, he has to start from eighteenth on the grid after an engine penalty and has to fight his way through the pack. After ten laps, he is already up to twelfth and closing fast on Sauber's Felipe Nasr. He catches the Brazilian just before the two high-speed right-handers at Blanchimont, corners taken at around 180 miles an hour on race day. Ordinarily, it is not an overtaking spot, but the seventeen-year-old Verstappen hangs it around the outside through both corners, remaining level with Nasr before completing the move at the Bus Stop Chicane and taking eleventh place. He would go on to finish ninth.

Afterwards, he is relatively nonchalant about the move while the TV commentators rave to him about the move. 'No one overtakes there, but you did,' says David Coulthard to him.

'I started so far back but I thought I would try it. There was a bit of run-off [beyond the kerb] but it was a tricky move,' Max replies, laughing to himself. 'I had the soft tyre on so I was pushing like hell so definitely I wanted to try.'

This was Max's first ever Grand Prix at Spa-Francorchamps, only his eleventh lap around that corner in race conditions, and yet he handled it like a pro. As it transpired, perhaps his Redline deal had something to do with it, as a few days later some footage emerged of him in training at the virtual Spa. He had been practising overtaking Atze Kerkhof, a Redline teammate and F3 driver, at that exact corner, just a week before. He even tweeted footage of the session with the caption 'people say I have been practising overtaking on the outside of Blanchimont'. The subtext seems to be 'this was not a reckless fluke that just happened to come off, this is the kind of stuff I'm going to be doing all the time now'. If he had not had the chance to do it in the simulator, he might never have tried it with hundreds of thousands of pounds and plenty of man hours of repair, not to mention his safety, at risk.

It is the obvious advantage of sim racing over live action: that mistakes will never cost time, money or in the worst cases lives.

'The drivers, because it is an eSports race where if they were to crash they just press the restart button and it's not going to be hundreds of thousands of dollars of damage, are more risk-taking as a consequence of that,' Dr Tan says of just one of the benefits he has been able to harness by bringing F1 into the eSports world.

'In our F1 eSports races, all of the cars are equalised which is one thing that's very different from the real world so you're able to kind of create a very different dynamic. You get scenarios where a Williams overtakes Mercedes which probably wouldn't happen in the real world too often.

'But it happens quite often in eSports and it gives the Williams fans, for example, something else to cheer about. It is still racing; it's maybe different, but it's still racing at the end of the day.'

The first racing simulation games were built in the early 1980s as arcade-style games that are still seen alongside shoot-em-ups, air hockey and Pac-Man in modern, albeit somewhat retro, arcades of the 21st century. With primitive graphics and limited realism, they bear little resemblance to the modern equivalents, but the concept was the same: to build a game where a player could sit in a seat, turn a wheel and push a pedal, just like the real thing. Initially, the emphasis was on entertainment, given that the mass market appeal would be to people who would want to have fun with it, rather than train for a racing job. However, towards the end of the 1980s, 'Indianapolis 500: The Simulation' was released, seemingly the first genuine effort to make a true-to-life racing experience. David Kaemmer, one of the designers, came from a flight simulator background and essentially made a track version of that. Even he admitted twenty years later that his business partner 'humoured me by letting me write racing sims', despite the fact that the market interest in oval-racing simulation was practically non-existent.

'Just as Flight Simulator let you climb into a Cessna and see what it was like to be a private pilot, I wanted to make a program that would show someone, as much as possible, what it was like to drive a race car,' Kaemmer said.

As it was, they got lucky and a small San Francisco-based firm named Electronic Arts, the precursor to the organisation that is now the second-largest gaming company in the Western world, picked them up to develop an Indy 500 simulation game for PC. In the UK, Geoff Crammond was busy designing something similar for open-wheel racers on the Commodore 64. Even if there wasn't a consumer-side market for the product quite yet, there was clearly a developer-led thirst for realism. The two franchises developed apace – IndyCar and Crammond's Formula One Grand Prix game – with developers admiring and competing with each other's work.

The real breakthrough for sim racing came in 1994, when NASCAR Racing from Kaemmer's Papyrus studio hit the shelves and became the first game of its type to sell more than a million copies. The game also had a networked capability, meaning players could use their phone lines to dial in to races with others around the country. Those phone bills sometimes ran into the hundreds or thousands of dollars, and were the signs of things to come.

Formula One, seeing the success of the American and indeed British versions, licensed its own game for the first time in 1996 and released it on PlayStation, arguably the market leader at the time, and later on PC. It featured 35 different drivers, seventeen drivable tracks and commentary from the great Murray Walker. The early 3D graphics of late 1990s consoles left something to be desired though and contemporary reviews complained that while the aesthetics and liveries were true to life, the actual gameplay and driving skills required were basic and too easily mastered. Only really when 'force feedback' technology, that would give users a sense of feel in the controller through vibrations and movement, became more advanced and online racing more usable and affordable did sim racing really start to take off in the civilian market in the late 2000s, perfect timing for the pre-teen Max Verstappen.

Even then, his first experiences with simulated F1 racing were much like anybody else's playing the early console games with primitive controllers, but as he got older and his dad remained a prominent figure in and around F1, especially in the Netherlands, developers were keen to get the game in their hands. In November 2009, when Codemasters had just released their first game licensed by the sport officially, having taken over from Sony to produce the franchise, Max and Jos raced against each other at a promotional event. The Nintendo Wii's motion software and wheel controller extension made it a good fit for the game and the pair faced off in front of a crowd of photographers, journalists and race fans crammed into a small back room in Breda, in southern Holland. Never short of confidence, Max tells the assembled crowd he is expecting to win the Grand Prix, despite the fact he is racing his father, a veteran of more than 100 actual F1 races and still an active racing driver. Max though has had the game early and been practising on his Wii at home.

Largely by coincidence, they race at Sepang, the circuit where Max had his first experience of an F1 weekend as a toddler. Jos is nervous.

'Those jitters were indeed there, even when driving a virtual car,' Jos says pre-race. 'It's also very realistic, almost real.'

Jos is in the McLaren of Lewis Hamilton but Max, in the Renault of Fernando Alonso, drives off into the distance and in a three-lap race beats his father by 26 seconds.

'Actually I expected this,' says Jos while his son grins smugly. 'While practising, I have not seen anything else from Max. Nobody wants to lose to their own son, but children have more feeling with such a game computer.'

It may have been something that sparked a lifelong passion for gaming but Max was already well hooked. He was not the only one either. Hamilton, whose car his father drove on the Wii, made reference to Crammond's 1994 game 'Grand Prix 2', made with the blessing albeit not under the auspices of F1 officially. After equalling Michael Schumacher's 91-win record in Germany in 2020, Hamilton admitted it was surreal to have emulated a childhood hero whom he had played as on the video game.

'When you grow up watching someone you generally idolise them in terms of the quality of the driver they are but also what they are able to continuously do race on race, year on year, week on week,' Hamilton said.

'There was a game called "Grand Prix 2" and I remember playing as Michael and seeing his dominance for so long I don't think anyone, especially me, could imagine that I'd be anywhere near Michael in terms of records.'

Had it not been for a life-changing skiing accident in 2013 and six subsequent months in a coma, Schumacher would perhaps be able to return the favour on a far more advanced version of the game.

Of course when Hamilton was playing in the 1990s and early 2000s, the level of simulation was nowhere near what it is now, and in real terms it bore limited relation to the kind of racing that would make him a multimillionaire. When Ron Dennis took him under his wing and signed him as a thirteen-year-old, it was not on the basis of his performances on a video game, it was because he was a champion go-karter, something his father Anthony had made huge financial sacrifices to facilitate. In fact, Hamilton was one of the least well-funded drivers on the grid, because even before reaching teenage years, it costs six-figure sums to put someone through karting.

The rise of eSports though is changing that. Jean-Eric Vergne, a former Red Bull F1 driver and a two-time Formula E world champion, saw the potent combination racing and gaming was forming early on, co-founding Veloce, one of the first and biggest teams in eSports back in 2015. Even with his years of racing pedigree, he cannot keep up with the men and women he now helps manage at the top of eSports.

'It's probably more difficult to be the best eSports sim driver in the world than being the best – well I wouldn't say the best Formula One driver because it obviously takes a lot more than just skills, but it is quite similar [in terms of level],' Vergne says.

'The guy that is the best in any area [of eSports is the best] out of millions of gamers [so that] is extremely difficult. Unfortunately, because motor sport is an expensive sport, not all the kids can [gain] access to the top.

'You have to do karting and then you need to go to single-seater. And even then you need to always be in the top team, to be able to try and win races, so it's extremely difficult to be successful in motor sport.

'But to me sim racing is a little bit like football: you just need to buy a pair of shoes and the ball and you can start from the favelas and be one of the greatest football players of all time.

As long as the kids can afford a good enough computer and a steering wheel, they can race against thousands and thousands of gamers online.'

The idea that F1 team bosses might look to a driver's results online to inform their decision about promotion and contracts, something Vergne says he has always believed will eventually be the case, is already not so far-fetched. Japanese-born Brazilian driver Igor Fraga was a finalist at Formula One's first eSports Series in 2017. He had been playing racing game 'Gran Turismo' since the age of three and go-karting not long after, but struggled to make his way through single-seaters when he was older due to the sheer financial strain. Then he won the Nations Cup world final of the Gran Turismo Sport Championship, one of the first FIA-recognised eSports series, in 2018 – now he has a drive in F3, just two tiers away in theory from F1. There is still a long way to go, but Fraga, who was signed by the Red Bull junior team in 2020, is much closer than he was even two years ago.

'I don't think that it's necessarily going to be a short-to-medium-term thing,' says Dr Tan of the idea that gamers could become racers. 'It is a longer term journey, but I think you're really starting to see the impact of opening up that funnel and getting more and more people access into motor sport just more generally, and then into Formula One.

'But I do think that the journey of graduating from one level to the next before you get to Formula One is still really important because we're talking about the pinnacle of motor sport, but I think that already just opening up the funnel is really such a big step for a sport like Formula One.

'There are still inherent challenges to progress up the ladder. I think there's obviously the element of physicality which is not accounted for when you're sim racing, but beyond that there is an entire ladder which gets you into F1 and that journey is still a relevant one. You still sort of need to go through that journey before you graduate from F3 to F2 to F1.'

The physicality though can be built and worked. Sim racers apply themselves with the same dedication to repeating laps and learning circuits as racing drivers do to the gym to keep themselves trim, light and able to withstand the G-forces involved in F1.

Vergne says: 'When we win a race to win a championship [in sim racing] it requires more or less the same thing as winning the race or championship, but in real life you need to handle the pressure and you need to play hard.

'Winning something requires a lot of work, dedication, talents, also a bit of luck. And if you are able to win something so complicated, if you are given the right tools in motor sport, if you have the talent, then yeah, why not, of course they can make it.'

In 2017, McLaren decided to try to harness some of these burgeoning online talents and give them a chance to drive in the real world. They ran a competition searching for the World's Fastest Gamer, with qualification events on all the most popular platforms to cast as wide a net as possible. It was basically an F1 talent show, with a contract as a McLaren simulator driver at the end of it.

The 2019 winner was James Baldwin, a 22-year-old from Buckinghamshire. He had been a national level go-karter whose family agreed to give single-seater racing a go, entering him in two Formula Ford races. The process almost bankrupted them and James got a low-level job making parts for aeroplanes with an eye on a degree in mechanical engineering. Then he won the World's Fastest Gamer, offering him a moonshot into motor racing.

Three years later, his work with McLaren had got him a drive in British GT3, a real car on a real racetrack for a team owned by none other than former F1 world champion Jenson Button. The realities of not driving in a simulator were pressed home to him ahead of Baldwin's first race. Even in 2020, there was plenty of scepticism about how the gamers would fare on track.

'You're driving a very expensive car,' Baldwin said in an interview with the *i* newspaper. 'I had several briefings across the weekend of 'please don't crash, the front bumper alone is £40,000'. It's not nice to hear before you go out, especially on a track like Oulton Park where there's no real run-off and if you go off, you're going to hit the wall.

'I think a few of the drivers think that I won't know how to race wheel to wheel and I had a couple of drivers come up to me before race one and chat to me, saying, "Just be careful," like they were worried I was going to do something crazy. I think subconsciously they do get a little bit worried because the stuff you learn in sim racing takes you to a whole new limit.'

To everyone's surprise, Baldwin and teammate Michael O'Brien won on their first outing for Jenson Team Rocket RJN and just as crucially kept the car in one piece, finally finishing fourth in the truncated 2020 championship. The future for Baldwin remains slightly uncertain given the global economy, but he is confident that eSports and gaming has given him a leg-up that nothing else could have done.

'My dream growing up was to be in Formula One but that's not going to happen I don't think,' he added. 'People getting into F1 now are eighteen, nineteen and I'm already 22, and they have huge, huge budgets. But I've always wanted to be a racing driver so I've ticked that off the list, but I've always wanted to be one of the best racing drivers in the world, and you can be that without being in F1. You could be winning Le Mans, Formula E or IndyCar so that would be a real goal, to get a factory drive with a manufacturer like McLaren or someone like that.'

Baldwin has veered from the single-seater route with his foray into sports car racing but there will be those, F1's eSports aficionados included, who will hold up his story as an example of how it can work, and he earned that drive even before the pandemic afforded virtual racing an extended day in the sun.

F1 had already convinced all ten teams to take part – even Ferrari eventually joined – in their eSports series when they started trying to arrange races online to fill the void that Covid-19 had created. Some remained steadfastly against it, seeing it only as an opportunity for embarrassment rather than growth, but on the whole the grid embraced the chance. For racers like Max Verstappen, Lando Norris and Charles Leclerc, already accomplished sim racers and streamers in their own right, it was a gift.

Although Max had signed for Redline in 2015 and spent the summer training with Atze Kerkhof, he did not have much time to race competitively. As has already been pointed out, to race at the top level requires hours of dedication that a rookie F1 driver probably did not have to give. However, after the 2018 season, Max started to sim race more seriously again, perhaps because the reality of the F1 campaign just past was that he had been blown away by Mercedes and there was not much he could do about it. Whatever the reason, he spent much of the winter on iRacing, his preferred platform due to its handling model being more like a car, with Team Redline, and in February 2019 he took part in a twelve-hour race with Lando Norris, Kerkhof and BMW factory driver Nicky Catsburg.

In the end, the race was bust as Max only managed a lap before an earlier crash ended their entry, but the spark had been reignited and over the summer break in 2019, he was once again in competition with Norris as one of his teammates, joined by two other drivers named Max, Germany's Benecke and Wenig. They drove the 24 Hours of Spa in a virtual format, at a full length, and dominated as you might expect a team with two full-time F1 drivers to do. It was not without its scares though, especially when the brake pedal in Max's simulator failed with fifteen minutes to go. Fortunately, he was able to stop without crashing and change driver, allowing Norris to see out the win by 30 seconds, but the fear in the voices of the two drivers as the incident played out live on streaming platform Twitch is testament to the commitment they both gave to the race.

So when the F1 World Championship effectively went online in 2020, and CEO of Torque eSports Darren Cox decided to organise 'The Race – All-Star Esports Battle', Max was obviously the big fish for the organisers, but they also knew he would not be an easy one to lure. He was an iRacing man through and through and the organisers had chosen to use rival platform rFactor, one used by most F1 teams for their factory simulators, which would weaken Max's advantage. He didn't even know if his flight back to Europe would get him back to Monaco in time to take part, having been convinced by one of his friends – Rudy van Buren, another World's Fastest Gamer winner – to give it a go.

'They wanted more real-world drivers than sim drivers to draw the viewers,' Max said. 'I'd raced some of them back in F3, go-karting or F1 – quite a few big names.

'It's the first time I drove [the 2012 handling model used]. Even if you're good in real life, you don't just jump in the simulator and be automatically quick. The sim guys had more knowledge of how to drive it.'

Max qualified from the heats in ninth place, despite beating all the other real-world drivers, a stark illustration of the specialist skills in sim racing, and then collided at the first corner to spin to the back of the field. He fought his way back through the pack to eleventh.

With no racing going on for four months, Max was a near-constant presence on the iRacing servers. His anger at the malfunctioning of certain platforms or technology, inevitable gremlins even at the highest level, were almost indistinguishable from what he calls his 'radio rants' to his engineer during Grands Prix. The only difference was that he did not have to scream over the engine.

Anger of course is easier to contain in an F1 car, where lashing out or losing control has very serious consequences. From the comfort of one's own home, you are an easier target. With such a famous name playing video games online, even within iRacing's well-policed licensing system where the top races only have top racers in them, Max would find himself as flypaper for trolls, often resorting to fighting fire with fire when other players attempted to push him off the track or just attack his car for attention. By the time interest had exploded in online racing over lockdown, Max had to some extent retreated a little, refusing to take part in the virtual Grands Prix on the official F1 game because of concerns about the gameplay and using a pseudonym on the iRacing servers while 'grinding his rating', i.e. working on his lap times online. Nothing though, even the persistent trolling of the world of motor-sport gaming, would stop Max racing online.

'I like sim racing, but I love real racing more,' Max says, somewhat stating the obvious.

'Maybe at one point I'll combine them in my schedule, but I'll never swap it.'

It's not just pride and enjoyment either. When racing returned in summer 2020, every driver who had participated in the virtual Grands Prix was faster than their teammate. And there's money too. Vergne says the top guys are making $3 million a year in eSports racing, and even full-time F1 driver Lando Norris has been impressed by the prize money coming into the virtual sport.

'You look at the NASCAR World Championship Series presented by Coca-Cola, it's a $300,000 prize pool, which is like pretty incredible for sim racers,' he said in April 2020.

'Porsche just put together a $250,000 or $200,000 prize pool for their championship, so the money is starting to get pretty huge in sim racing.

'People are starting to make a living, more so than honestly a lot of real race car drivers are getting paid. It's pretty insane, the top guys.'

ESports is not going away, and the money is only getting bigger. Max could become the first person ever to win world titles on track and online – although one will always be bigger than the other.

5

LIKE A DUCK TO WATER

Nothing in life is inevitable, but you can usually make some educated guesses, and if you had met Max at the age of one and looked at his family tree, you would have guessed that he would pretty likely be a go-karting fanatic. His paternal grandfather Frans ran a team, his maternal grandfather Robert used to put on public races and his parents both raced karts to an international level. 'If you can see it, you can be it,' goes a popular aphorism about role models. Max could see little else.

Jos had tried to put off getting Max behind the wheel but the famous tearful phone call, and subsequent petition from his wife Sophie, left him no option. His father remembers well the first time he put his son into a go-kart at a public rental circuit in Genk. It was a moment that had the potential for disaster, to end in tears and create a traumatic memory for Jos to recall in an embarrassing wedding speech or at a 21st birthday party. This was no normal four-year-old boy though. Max already had two years of flying around on his quad bike in all weathers to rely on. He was like a duck to water and had no hesitation in going as quickly as he could. While other fathers might have been nervous, Jos was unsurprised when Max took the whole track flat out in his first run.

'He had some experience with speed and knew how to steer,' Jos told Max's Red Bull colleagues on a show called 'Talking Bull' in 2020. 'We had done quite a lot of things already before we put him in a go-kart.' For all Jos' insistence that he just let Max get on with it, every step, even as a toddler, was taken with something else in mind.

Max drove this tiny kart so fast that the vibrations broke the carburettor; go-karts of this size were designed for drivers who, at that age, were not brave enough or even able to drive with such commitment. Just days after buying Max his first kart, Jos went out and bought him his second one, a bigger, sturdier model. That first one now hangs on the wall of the Verstappen megastore in Swalmen in the Netherlands, near the German border, a seminal piece of motor racing history.

Jos himself was still heavily involved in karting in all senses. When Max was still agitating for a kart of his own, Jos was mentoring Dutch hopefuls through karting. Giedo van der Garde was his star pupil, winning the Formula Super A World Championship in 2002. He was already seventeen and it earned him a move to Van Amersfoort Racing in a junior formula, no doubt with a good word from Jos, and Giedo still cites Jos as, apart from his own father, the man who taught him the most in the world. When he started to be touted around the F1 paddock a few years later, Jos was not short of an opinion.

'Motor sport is not all about talent,' wrote Jos in a 2010 column for *De Telegraaf*, clearly alluding to his own reputation as a supremely skilled but ultimately unsuccessful F1 driver. 'There is a lot more to it and it remains to be seen how Giedo and the people around him will handle that.

'I hope for him that he will be able to find a home with one of the teams in the midfield, so that he can at least show something as a driver.'

As it was, Van der Garde spent another two years in GP2, now known as F2, before being promoted by Caterham to their F1 team. Sadly, the car was little more than a backmarker and Van der Garde lasted just one season, never finishing higher than fifteenth. Giedo remains close to the Verstappens – when he is not busy racing in the World Endurance Championship he can sometimes be spotted in the Red Bull garage chatting to Max – and jokes that when people ask him what he does, he has to introduce himself as 'the Dutch F1 driver before Max', even at home in the Netherlands.

He was not the only driver Jos had his eye on in the early 2000s, hoping his go-karting team would become a hotbed of young talent that might learn from his mistakes, particularly Dutch drivers under his tutelage like Randy Bakker or Pascal Westerhof, but none ever reached the heights even of Van der Garde, never mind Max Verstappen. They had success in Formula Super A though, something Verstappen Sr was always keen to stress was not just a means to an end, a gateway to the next stage.

'It's a tough class, this Super A. The best 32 karters in the world drive around here,' Verstappen would say. 'It's not just young guys. There are still guys driving around that I used to be go-karting against myself. These guys are professionals in karting.' The implication being that if Jos used to race them, they must be good.

Jos himself was not afraid of jumping back into a go-kart either, while still angling for a way back into F1, although not always with such positive outcomes. Shortly before Christmas

2002, he participated in the Winter Cup in Kerpen, near Cologne, the track where Michael Schumacher first started karting. It had existed even before the famous German came to prominence but the Schumacher association gave it a prestige that could not be bought and the event still runs to this day. In 2002, Michael's former teammate Jos was keen to make his mark, particularly with seats for the 2003 season still up for grabs. A go-kart win would not do much but it might spark the odd idea in a team principal's head, and the event was a good excuse to shake hands with the great and the good of motor racing.

Things did not go well for Jos. The first two races were in the larger 125cc karts, and he broke a chain in his first heat before spinning out of the second after contact with a rival. In the smaller 100cc machines, Jos managed to finish sixth in the first race and was leading the second before another competitor collided with him from behind and broke his exhaust. One can imagine muffled sniggers in the paddock and the phrase 'same old Jos Vercrashen' being muttered into coffee cups, and there was more to come. In the final race of the day, Verstappen came together with the same driver twice more, with the second clash leaving him parked at the side of the track. If there had been sniggers before, now there were open catcalls and shouts in his direction. Jos' short temper flared and he got into what might generously be termed an altercation with the driver's team manager, one Peter de Bruijn.

Jos and Peter were no strangers. Peter was a legend of karting in Holland, having won the world title way back in 1980 and then helped Jos himself to a series of major successes that would help catapult him into the upper echelons of motor sport. Peter was effectively Jos' mentor, which perhaps afforded him greater licence to be critical when he saw his former protégé fifteen years later getting punted off the track in a karting race by Peter's son, as it transpired to be. The Dutch media naturally seized upon the fight which Jos claimed was blown out of all proportion.

'Tall trees catch a lot of wind,' he said of the tabloid media's reaction, quoting an old Dutch proverb. 'It was actually nothing more than a fierce exchange of words, call it "in the heat of the moment".

'For me racing is 100 per cent commitment, then the adrenaline pumps through my body. And then I sometimes react not completely rationally. Then there is some shouting from the side and, well. Afterwards you can say: you had better first be able to count to ten.

'But still, maybe I let myself go a little too much. Look, I am a driver with passion. If I go for something, then I give it all. Even with a race like that, yes. Otherwise I might as well stay at home.'

He promised he would soon be having coffee again with De Bruijn, and that they had already laughed about it, but his comments portray much of the man. When it came to racing, he was fully committed, something that would become increasingly clear in his son's career.

Karting remained and still remains just about the only way into F1. Of the modern grid, none have not go-karted at some level. You could hardly put an eight-year-old in a road car, so karting is a the most practical way of learning the skills required to get a racing car around a track in the shortest time possible, especially in low-grip conditions because go-karts, with their narrow, slick tyres, are on the limit of grip even at low speed. Ayrton Senna was perhaps the greatest go-kart driver ever to have lived and described it as 'the purest driving experience', preferring it even to F1. He continued to race them during his professional career, as did the Schumachers and a number of others.

De Bruijn though, who still runs his own karting team in the Netherlands, believes 'the golden age of karting is behind us'.

'It is unclear if today's drivers are as good as those of the past because there are many different categories, so comparing talent is not easy. But I am convinced that early transition to cars for top prospects has consequences on the general level,' he said in a 2014 interview, bemoaning drivers not spending more time in karting before moving up. 'The case of Max Verstappen is an exception, but I remember when Kimi Raikkonen was with us, he was not fantastic at sixteen. He became very good at eighteen. It was the same for Fernando Alonso.

'I also think that attitudes changed at the start of the 2000s. In the early days and into the nineties, drivers drove almost every weekend, rain or shine, because they were passionate about it and it was not very expensive. With a mechanic, often a friend or family member, you could do it if you were not afraid of getting your hands dirty!

'Nowadays, drivers want comfort, beautiful awnings, professional mechanics, an attentive staff. A taste for effort has disappeared, while the services have become more expensive.'

That might certainly be true of Max, who was fortunate to have one of the best kart tuners around for a father and by his own admission have much interest in working on the engine. Driving interested him the most, although he did try to understand what was going on with the machinery.

Max had plenty of feeling though. Those years spent power-sliding his quad bike around the garden paid off when it came to go-karting, and everyone could see it. Jos noticed it when he entered him in his first serious race at Emmen. Max was seven years old, as young as racers are allowed to be by the regulations.

'[My dad] was far more nervous than me, which was very funny,' Max told the *Guardian* in 2018. 'I saw him next to the fence, holding tight, and you can see from the body language he was really tense and worried.'

It is interesting to note when Jos is actively anxious and when he is not, and says a lot about his and Max's drive. Children are acutely sensitive to their parents' feelings, often more so than the parents themselves. Jos was not nervous when he plonked four-year-old Max into a go-kart for the first time, or when Sophie or other family members would take him to the track as a youngster in Genk when Jos was away. He was immune to the fear of speed or crashes that civilians would naturally experience, having been in motor sport his whole life, where injury and even death are part and parcel of the profession.

'I always say going to school on a bicycle is more dangerous than what he's doing,' Jos said in a TV interview when Max was eleven. 'If you hit someone from behind with those speeds, you can do some nice somersaults. But you can see they have spoilers on the front and back, which offers reasonable protection.' However, when it came to competing on the track, putting his skills up against the others and trying to win, that is when Jos' nerves kicked in. His competitive spirit and edge, much as he might try to paint a more chilled-out picture now that he is an older, wiser man, was always there.

That race in Emmen was hardly round the corner either. They had driven more than three hours up to the north of Holland to take part at a rather desolate karting track, sandwiched in between the peat farms of Drenthe. It was a significant undertaking to go up for the race, but one for which Jos was more than prepared. By this point, he was starting to realise he might have driven his last race in F1. He was testing for Fittipaldi Racing and the HVM team, both of which competed in the Champ Cars series, a US-based single-seater series that was a successor to Championship Auto Racing Teams (CART). He was struggling to raise enough sponsorship to find a seat at the top level though, despite concerted efforts to do so. His focus was beginning to switch, and his nerves at Emmen may have been magnified by the prospect that his son's racing might soon be his biggest stake in motor sport. Fortunately, he was not disappointed.

'We got pole and won both races,' Max recalls. 'It was perfect – but I spoke to my dad after the first race. I said: 'I saw you were very nervous.' He said: "Of course. It's your first race." But I was just enjoying it and driving as fast as I could.'

His manager, chief mechanic, chauffeur (and father) put his emotions aside to analyse the performance, and was pleased. The one-man team said: 'Then I saw that he had talent.

'The racecraft stood out. When he went out for a race on cold tyres, his first lap was always a second quicker than anybody else. So when he had the lead at Turn One after the start, the first time he came over the start-finish line, he had a second lead and they are running on colder tyres. For me, that's talent. That's feeling and what you also see in the wet where you have very little grip; that's where he is fast.'

That summer, Jos booked a holiday in the south of France, but it was not an opportunity for him to turn down his intensity. Jos does not do two weeks relaxing by the pool and never has, which was convenient for a man with a son about to turn eight, a bundle of energy and eagerness. He took their go-karts with them and deliberately booked the family in near to a go-karting track. 'We want to stay in shape, Max and me,' he told his fan club in one of his fortnightly updates. 'We can turn it into a sporty holiday.'

Jos was also trying to get himself back into shape having been signed up by the Dutch team for the new A1 Grand Prix series, which had massive backing from the wonderfully named Sheikh Maktoum Hasher Maktoum Al Maktoum, a member of the ruling family of Dubai who therefore did not require Jos to bring a significant portfolio of sponsorship with him, although the Dutch team were only able to run one car. So the two Verstappen boys cycled, ran and crucially raced their way round the south of France, both in their own way doing a pre-season training. (The selling point of A1 was that every car was equal, and far less electronic than F1, which was supposed to leave it down to driver skill alone, a huge boon for Jos who still believed he could beat almost anyone on the track, all other things being equal.)

After just a year of competitive karting, and with Jos still in the middle of his A1 season, the father is unable to contain the pride in his son. While Mick Schumacher raced under a false name to avoid the spotlight, the Verstappens seem to relish being marked men. 'We are watched with suspicion, but fuck them,' Jos told a local Dutch newspaper when Max's first success at the age of eight began to draw media attention. 'It never interested me what others think about me. I had to work hard to get this far and Max will have to do that too.'

Few could think that, with Jos as a taskmaster, Max had it easy, although jealousy is an ugly emotion, especially in junior sport. Jos though is not shy about the advantages Max has.

'[Max] sees himself driving a Formula One car one day. Because he grew up with that, it goes without saying. Does he know how difficult it is to get that far? Still I think it is his dream.

'He started racing four years earlier than me. I was eight years old when I first got behind the wheel. This already gives Max a great lead. He has talent, the right attitude and, not unimportant in Formula One, because of my own career, we have many contacts in that world.'

Max's family, not just his father, were extraordinarily supportive. His little sister Victoria, a keen go-karter herself, held the bouquet of flowers and posed for photos while Max grasped the trophy after his first ever championship win in 2005. The series, Belgian VAS, was a spec one, meaning all the cars and tyres were the same, but it was free rein on set-up and in Jos, Max had an expert engineer who had been tuning karts his whole life, and a mechanic in his ear before races whose racing experience was not remembered but real and present.

'That can save a second per lap,' Jos says at the time. 'Of course Max benefits from that, but it is also the perfect learning experience for him. I prepare him for what is to come. It is wonderful to see him in the race doing things that we have discussed in advance.'

Even on the day he sealed that very first title, the talents of the Max Verstappen that we have come to know at the highest level of motor sport were clear. The first two races of the day were in the dry and Max dominated. In the afternoon, it rained. Others might have seen it as an opportunity to depose the morning's dominant force. Anyone who knew Max would have realised it was likely quite the opposite. He romped to a third win, assuring a championship victory that was particularly sweet because had he not sealed it there, Jos would have missed the next race in Estoril. Instead, the track in Genk just a few miles from home was where they popped the champagne corks for the first time.

'The very first year and then already champion. That's amazing! I have to let that sink in first,' Jos says, all a fluster with excitement and pride.

As if to illustrate the hectic nature of the Verstappen lifestyle, in the space of a month they are celebrating Max's win in Genk, racing again in Portugal, and then flying out to Australia with Jos for the A1 Grand Prix. Max is eight and Victoria has just turned six when the three of them are snapped in the Dutch garage while Jos fires up the car, fingers in their ears to protect them from the noise. Max has his hair spiked up with gel, wearing a fashionable watch and a silver necklace, while his sister smiles excitedly for the camera in her patterned dress. Behind them stands Sophie, less enamoured with the situation than the children, so it seems. She and Jos divorced less than a year later, and two years after that he would appear in court to be found guilty of breaching a restraining order and sending threatening text messages.

The children split as well as their parents. Victoria went to live with her mother while Max, who was spending just about every weekend racing, lived with his father in Maaseik. Max and Victoria remained close though and still do; Max's 2020 helmet was designed by Victoria – or Victoria Jane Verstappen as she is known professionally – with the symbol of her clothing line 'Unleash The Lion' on top of it and she previously worked for Red Bull Netherlands in a design and marketing capacity. In 2020, she gave birth to a son Luka, making Max a doting – if necessarily distant – uncle for the first time. A year later, Luka was joined by Lio. Despite their close relationship, the Verstappen siblings say they rarely talk about their childhood. The divorce was, at the time at least, bitter and both of them remember a lot of arguing. When the decision was taken that Victoria would go and live with her mother and Max with his father, it was not easy to handle.

'I let Max go because I knew that if he wanted to make a career, he would have to go with Jos,' his mother said.

'That was very emotional for me, because you're letting go of your child. I would take Victoria to school and Jos would take Max. At a certain point, I didn't really know Max as a teenager.'

It was still his father who was, literally, the driving force behind his career. The pair began covering thousands of miles across Europe to races, with trips to Italy usually involving a nine- or ten-hour drive each way. They even had a favourite service station in Austria that they would stop at on the way down and on the way home, preferred because it did the best food of anywhere by the side of a European motorway. Before Max was old enough to compete internationally though, they had to conquer the races closer to home.

In that very first season, there were times when Jos couldn't be there, but in just Max's second full season of karting, he essentially had his father working for him full-time. He had left the Dutch A1 Grand Prix team run by Jan Lammers after just a season with financial problems once again at the heart of the split – Verstappen was reputedly only paid for the first season shortly before the second one began – and would never have a full-time drive again. He would still enter one-off races, such as the 24 Hours of Le Mans and kept his go-kart, winning the last race of the Belgian championship in 2006, but he had seen enough of his son to believe that he was worthy of being his main focus now.

'The way he overtakes, his insight, the drive he radiates: it is exactly his father, only he drives more elegantly. I was much wilder on the track in my childhood.' This, of his eight-year-old son, suggests Jos already knew that Max could be better than he ever was.

They were now living together just the two of them but they were not alone in their racing endeavours. Raymond Vermeulen remained a close friend and business associate, while another family friend helped them with workshop space. It was Stan Pex, a year younger than Max, whose karting exploits had triggered his tantrum at not being considered old enough to race and the Pex family owned a workshop at the back of their roofing business, Pex Dakbedekkingen. They were keen karters, Stan and Jorrit racing at the national level at which their father Richard had also competed, but Jos and Max made a corner, and soon more, of that workshop their own. The van was their home from home, but the back of the Pexs' warehouse was where father tried to teach son everything he had learned working for his own father Frans and then throughout his racing career about the machines themselves.

The age restrictions stopped the Verstappens straying too far from home but they travelled round the Benelux (Belgium, Netherlands and Luxembourg) region, picking up trophy after trophy. Max dominated Belgian karting, winning national title after national title and when he went up to Amsterdam for the Dutch championship in 2007, he started on pole. Just as he had in Belgium, he pulled a second clear of the pack on his opening lap and then controlled the race. He was scarcely ten years old and already the karting king of two countries. Jos knew they would soon be able to go bigger. European and world championships were beckoning.

However, Max was also at an age where he had to start thinking about secondary education, which would clash with mammoth journeys across the Continent to karting venues in Italy, where many of the best races took place. School was a sore point for Max, as it often is for racing drivers and their parents who see little point in learning about literature or soil filtration rates when their son or daughter is focused entirely on racing.

For Max, clearly missing out on school paid off but there are many for whom it does not. Adrian Newey, one of F1's most respected aerodynamicists and a man given much of the credit for Red Bull's four world titles with Sebastian Vettel, warned about the impact of the culture of not schooling young drivers back in 2014.

'A lot of the drivers in karting and in junior formulas frankly just aren't going to school. They don't go to school at all,' Newey said in a technical chiefs press conference at the Belgian Grand Prix, coincidentally just a few weeks before Max's first test session at an F1 race weekend for the team's junior outfit Toro Rosso, which would take place just after his seventeenth birthday.

'The parents then hide behind that by saying that they have private tutors but I think in many cases – not all, I'm sure, but in many cases – that's actually a complete sham and I think if you asked a lot of those kids to sit their baccalaureate or GCSEs or whatever it might be that the results would tell a fairly depressing story, which means that the few kids that do get through, fantastic.

'Being at a motor race and so forth, the kids do learn in a different way – not an academic way but they learn in other ways – but I think for many of those children that don't quite make the grade, they have spent all that time not going to school, not having a proper tuition and then what happens to them afterwards is altogether another question. It's something which motor racing as an industry urgently needs to look at, because personally I think we're being irresponsible allowing that.'

Max dropped out of school at the age of fifteen to be tutored privately, having attended St Ursula's in Maaseik where he was joined by his sister Victoria. By the time he left, attended was hardly the word; he was in the country every third week and was constantly behind, desperately trying to catch up.

Jos, in answer to Newey's point, did repeatedly encourage Max to do well at school. If he did not achieve the grades expected of him, they would not let him leave to go racing, a deal that was enough of a motivation for an energetic but not academically engaged young boy. And if he did not show such talent on the racetrack, Jos says he would have kicked him all the way to school. Fortunately, he did not need to. What he did need to do though was compete with some of go-karting's elite. Max could do it on the track but Jos was a one-man band trying to outdo factory teams that were funded by larger organisations than the Verstappen family.

'We did everything ourselves from the chassis set-up to the engine as well,' Jos said. 'We had our own dyno to put the engines on, so we were always well prepared when we went racing. We knew exactly which engine was the best and which one to use during qualifying.

'Everything was already sorted, so Max only had to set up the carburettor; that is a feeling a driver needs to have. I think Max was very good at that. He was very precise on what he liked to have on his go-kart.'

Despite his apparent ability to specify what he needed and wanted from a kart, Max did not have a huge hand in the technical side; motor racing has moved on from the days of Fangio cobbling together his own car in his parents' shed. Jos recognised the importance of hard work and would make Max meticulously clean the kart after every race, but before it he would stand and watch his father work on it, trying to understand what was going on, but he rarely got a spanner in his hand himself. The important thing from his perspective was to understand what was going on under him on the track, and what it felt like rather than how to fix it when it broke.

Jos was highly skilled though and the kart did not break often. The Verstappen boys were effectively privateers but well-financed ones, with Jos having made good money in Formula One and having sold his karting team to focus on Max. Most series they raced in were spec, so they could not buy their way to the front, but money was rarely a problem, despite the fact that Jos spent around half a million pounds in total on Max's karting career.

With Jos having faded from the limelight as an F1 driver, there was a vacuum in the Dutch media that had become used to writing and reporting on stories about him. Christijan Albers and Robert Doornbos both made it into F1 with Jos' old team Minardi, but neither were seen as having the same level of talent. Already, columnists would regularly write, 'We are waiting for Max.'

6

EMERGING FROM HIS FATHER'S SHADOW

When Max was eleven, he appeared on Dutch TV with his father for an interview with Wilfried de Jong on a show called *Holland Sport*. The interviewer initially engages with Max, quizzing him about his recent results (all victories, naturally). Max looks relaxed, laughing along with De Jong while his father next to him stares into the middle distance, pushing his fingertips together anxiously. The dynamic is becoming a theme of their role at major events. In every interview you can find with young Max, he is staggeringly self-assured compared to other boys of his age.

When Jos is called upon to answer at last, he takes a moment to re-engage before trotting out the story about Max crying about Stan Pex being allowed to go-karting before he was. De Jong probes him about his own career and joshes him with a gag about being good at 'parking'. It is clear now though, if it were not before, what Jos' hopes for the future are.

'I did Le Mans last year, and I would like to do it again. I still have contact with some people so I have hopes for that,' Jos says.

'I've been driving since I was eight, so 29 years now, but if your own kid is racing, you're more proud of what he's doing than what I ever did.'

Jos mentions that Max has won 49 out of 50 races, the one blemish coming after spinning out because he hit a wet spot on the track. The incident took place in Eindhoven, where he had won the first two heats of the day in dry conditions. There was one corner though in the third and final race that had got wet and Max failed to spot it, spinning and damaging his tyres before colliding with another driver while re-entering the track. From the back of the pack and in a less than healthy kart, he made up seven places in the last six laps to finish fourteenth and salvage third overall from the day.

'It seems that the way he drove forward after he was in the back was insane. One setback is okay,' Jos said on the day. 'I think things like this only make him better.'

Publicly, Jos was calm about the mistake, but as Max grew up and began to talk about their relationship more, it seems clear that the error would have been discussed at length and with few words minced. Mistakes were to be learned from, naturally, but certainly not repeated. As such, the slip at Eindhoven was a rare blip. He had already won the first two rounds, albeit with Jos away testing elsewhere, and he went on to take the Belgium Minimax title by 37 points. While Max was clearly talented, he benefited from having grown up on many of the tracks used for major races. In Genk, he was close to unbeatable. In 2008 he sealed the Benelux Karting Series at the Horensbergdam where he knew just about every inch of road. Even though they had resurfaced it shortly before the crucial weekend, he and Jos had been down on the Wednesday to make sure they knew what they were working with. Having been caught out a few weeks previously in Eindhoven, the pair were all the more determined to get it right. It is hard to think of go-karting as punishment for Max, but the extra training session was certainly partially motivated by the pain of that defeat. As it was, the new asphalt was smoother and it seemed to suit Max more. When Saturday came, he took pole position and won both races, although he came under pressure from Joel Affolter, who was able to hang on to his coat-tails, but never quite overtake him.

'That was exciting, wasn't it?' Max shouted afterwards. 'Joel was fast. He was able to keep up with me because he was in the slipstream. I drove defensive lines so he couldn't overtake me.'

The second win ensured he could not be caught in the championship standings but he returned on Sunday to rack up two more victories and lift yet another title in style, demonstrating exactly why his Pex Racing Team Kart bore the number one. He had won eleven of the Benelux Series' twelve races, and yet the one which he failed to win sticks in the mind of the team. It is not perfectionism necessarily, rather a raw competitiveness that will not be shifted.

The name Pex and Verstappen were quickly becoming closely linked. Max and Richard Pex's sons Jorrit and Stan were all rising stars of the karting world and their fathers, both living out a second career through them, were happy to keep supporting them. Although Max often raced on an entry of 'Verstappen Racing' or 'Jos Verstappen', he had been part of the Pex Racing Team for much of his early success, in an invaluable support network. While Jos often paints their story as him and Max against the world, he would be on the viewing platform with Richard Pex and a few others, all decked out in the same uniform. Jos of course was focused on Max, but he wasn't afraid to give other drivers help and mentoring along the way. He was a father first and a teacher second, but he would not confine his advice to his son. He was painfully aware that his career was not as successful as it perhaps should have been, and that if his own father Frans – strict, hard-working but not ultimately from racing stock – had had at his disposal the kind of financial backing and contacts that Jos would later accumulate, he might have ended up going about things a very different way. When he was still running his own karting team, he would talk up his Dutch drivers but preface almost every comment with 'but to get to F1 it's not only about talent', as if to reinforce the fact that he was good enough, just not savvy enough, to succeed in the sport. He would auction off karting masterclasses for charity and was never shy about singing the praises of Robert Doornbos or Christijan Albers, or later Giedo van der Garde, whom he had mentored more personally.

With Max though, he was often trying to play down his talents, even though the utter dominance of his results was hard to hide, and the Verstappen fan club was slowly drifting from reports about Jos' career and commentary on motor sport, to detailed reports of Max's progress.

At the end of 2008, Jos wrote a column in *De Telegraaf* about how he was considering a year of rest, a sabbatical from motor racing. He would perhaps do Le Mans – and he did indeed go on to race with Anthony Davidson and Darren Turner for Aston Martin – but otherwise it was a good moment to step back from full-time racing, especially with the financial crash having a contracting effect on the motor industry as a whole.

In truth, Jos' career had probably been over for some time as he found it harder and harder to force his way into seats. There was a time when Huub Rothengatter or latterly Raymond Vermeulen could usually magic something up, with a couple of weighty Dutch sponsors and a timely reminder that Verstappen did have raw speed that few others possessed. But by Christmas 2008, Jos was 36 years old and had not driven in a full-time series for five years. His son would soon be starting secondary school (some of the time) and had an extremely promising motor racing career, which Jos kept missing parts of to do fairly menial testing or small-series racing jobs. The credit crunch may have come at just the right time for him to use it as a smokescreen to duck out.

With his focus squarely on Max, it becomes apparent that he is no longer learning much from winning the Belgian and Benelux karting championships, however much that might do for his confidence. The only overtaking he does is in practice, because he invariably takes pole, drives a second faster than the field on the first lap and then controls the race from there. Jos insists that Max is 'self-motivated enough to want to stay at the front' and those behind him are more than motivated enough to try to claw him back. With Max now retaining titles he had won in 2008, the rest of the karting scene was starting to sit up and take notice. While the term 'hater' had not been coined, they had certainly been born and were out in force. At race weekends, there would be whispered accusations that Max had bought his success. Some fathers of Max's rivals even rang in anonymously to the local and national newspapers that had started to report on his success with claims that he was driving an illegal go-kart. There was never any evidence of it, and if anything it was a testament to Max's ability and Jos' tuning that those parents felt they had to. Jos hinted at the accusations in one interview where he mentioned that the karts 'had to be checked over again at the end', so they could not possibly be cheating. Indeed if they were cheating, they were far better at it than anyone had been previously and they kept doing it all the way to Formula One. It seems unlikely.

Jos was rather used to the criticism and already had a chip on his shoulder about never quite becoming the F1 driver he and others thought he should have been. Max meanwhile seemed oblivious to it, whether by choice or by accident. He was living his dream and en route to the goal he had established before he could even really express it: driving in Formula One.

There were other bumps in the road too, not just the ugly, baseless suspicions of rival teams predicated exclusively on the fact that Max was faster than them. Verstappen.nl published a column entitled 'Value for Money' by Frits van Eldik in the summer of 2009 about sponsorship and the value of spending a relatively small sum sponsoring the likes of Max, and the return it might give you when he found himself in F1 a few years later. Frits, a Dutch motor sport photographer, had known Max since he was just a week old and had been snapping Jos since the early days, so was hardly a neutral in the matter, but it is indicative of what the Verstappens knew was coming. They would have to start travelling around Europe, racing and servicing bigger karts, and that was going to start becoming very expensive. Not only that, but if they wanted to attract the interest of senior teams, it would help to have a slew of sponsors to back them up. That was what held Jos back later in his career, and he did not want history to repeat itself.

By chance, Max started to face challenges on the track even before they made the switch to international racing. At Spa-Francorchamps, on a tight karting track on the infield on the approach to the famous, high-speed Blanchimont corner, Max struggled for grip on the bumpy track, as all the CRG-produced machines seemed to. He persevered and won both races on

Saturday, but when they returned on Sunday, Denmark's Nicklas Nielsen in his Tony Kart, the chassis of which handled the surface better, beat him twice, but Max still won the title. Any individual outside elite sport though will look at what happened, an eleven-year-old winning yet another national title, and triumphing in two of the four races in a weekend, and think there is some cause for celebration. Not so.

Max had won all ten of the previous races, and his two second places on Sunday confirmed he was once again Belgian champion, this time in a class of thirteen-year-olds when he had not yet turned twelve. He ended the weekend on the top step of the podium with yet another trophy – but not with the admiration of his father, who was furious that Max had been passed on the last lap of the final race.

'I was very disappointed! Even in my own career I have not been so disappointed after an incident,' Jos said. 'He was disappointed, but when he saw my angry face after the race, he couldn't do anything else.

'Max has never experienced this. So it was not only the loss, but also very strange. That's why. I think it's good that he once lived through this and happy it happened now.'

It would be easy to see these incidents through the lens Jos wishes us to: that everything is a learning experience and that everything was sunshine and roses afterwards, that it might be written off as 'only a game', that he was as philosophical with Max as he is on reflection with reporters or the Verstappen fan club staff, but time and again we see Jos' temper and competitive spirit spill over into one another. Remember that Max has said openly that the transition into F1 was easy because no one would ever be as hard on him as his father was. Even the famously irascible and brutal Dr Helmut Marko pales by comparison.

Working under Jos cannot always have made for a pleasant weekend, even when Max was mostly winning.

The wheels were in motion though to move Max further up the ladder. The karting regulations, the same ones that had kept him from racing until he was seven, stopped him from racing internationally, which must have frustrated him. That same anger that had him crying down the phone to Jos for a go-kart at four years old probably returned when his father went to Italy for the world championships as a mechanic for Jorrit Pex, while Max was still too young to race. Max was faster than Jorrit, and he knew it, but he just wasn't old enough. Previously in the karting world, it had never really been a problem, but Max was breaking the mould at every opportunity.

The summer of 2009, once Jos had got his Aston Martin Le Mans drive out of the way (they finished a disappointing thirteenth), was spent testing factory karts in Germany, a chance for Max to prove he was not just the best driver in Belgium; in between they would still be crushing the Belgian karting scene, as well as the odd race in Holland or France. Since it was the summer holidays, Max could pretty much drive every day. One race, a rare trip to race abroad albeit still as part of a Belgian series, stands out.

In July, they had headed to Ostricourt, only a two-hour drive just over the border into France. A carburettor problem in the first race saw Max shoot to the back of the pack, a lap down on the whole field and he inevitably finished last. What followed might have been the performance that set in motion the rest of his career. Starting last for the second race in a rolling start, Max has to fight his way through the pack, something he has rarely had to do in his entire career. The eyes of the paddock were all on him. They had watched this prodigious talent dominate from the front of the pack, stroll through qualifying and races, but if there were any doubts, it would be about whether he could fight.

By the end of the seventh lap, he led the race. A camera mounted on his engine allows us to live every metre with him.

As the race started, he had stolen a few extra yards of tarmac on the right-hand side to sneak past four of the backmarkers and when they return to the start-finish straight after one lap, he has picked off two more and is eyeing up another. It is Stan Pex, the boy whom he had seen racing in Genk and forced his parents to buy him a go-kart. The two are teammates and friends but that means little on the track. Max, having got his tyres up to temperature quicker in signature style, takes a wide entry into the first corner and switches back with superior grip to overtake Pex. He cannot resist a little wave as he does so. Even he knows that was a well-executed move, and that the rest of the pack are unlikely to cause him too many problems. Sure enough, he made short work of the top ten and crossed the line a comfortable winner.

Over the summer, Max seemed to have made a significant leap forward with his driving. At his home track in Genk, a flatter, simpler track, his rivals could stay at least in touch with him, although beating him remained out of the question. Elsewhere, such as when they headed to Schumacher country in Kerpen, Verstappen was sensationally dominant. The gaps to the field behind him were getting bigger and bigger every week, and combined with the behind-the-scenes testing results and the race-day performances, one of the big names of European karting had seen enough to back Max in the coming season. In November, just a few months after turning twelve, he signed his first major deal to become a factory driver for CRG in the 2010 season. The Italian company in their press release were keen to stress Max's racing pedigree, listing Jos' achievements above those of the boy they had just signed.

That is not because CRG wanted a piece of Jos. They were fully invested in Max, although his father's connections helped. CRG's team in Netherlands was run by Michel Vacirca, for whom Jos had built engines and who had already been supporting Max's karting efforts. In Italy, where CRG were based, founder and owner Giancarlo Tinini had been keeping an eye on his progress and, with the benefit of hindsight, admits the signing of him was a no-brainer.

'In reality, Max is not my discovery! Anyone who was not blind could see how strong he was!' said Tinini years later.

'The first time I saw him was [at testing] in Muro Leccese, in 2009, I think. I did not know who he was, only that he drove a CRG kart and that I liked, like in a crazy way, the way he drove.

'I immediately went to talk to him and told him that, as soon as he reached the right age, I wanted Max on my team.'

For Jos this must have started to feel like the early 1990s all over again, when his career took off and every Formula One boss worth his salt was on the phone to Huub Rothengatter, desperate to get this young Dutch tearaway into their car. It was not the only similarity. Everyone knew that Jos was, to say the least, a forthright driver and Max, as Tinini says, drove in a 'crazy way' that attracted him.

'Many times they have asked me what his main characteristic was,' Tinini added. 'For me, it was his absolute mastery of the kart. Even with cold tyres at the start of the race, he makes the kart do what he wants.

'You see it immediately, as very few racers are able to make the difference in the first two laps of a race. One of them was

Danilo Rossi [who raced against Jos in karting], who did not win five world karting championships by chance.

'Another distinctive trait is the aggressive full-on racing style, certainly inherited by the paternal DNA, as Jos was the typical 'bad boy' that nobody liked racing against.

'Max has the same determination and, compared to him, I think he is faster. Let's just say that he is a great mix of dad and mom Sophie Kumpen, who in her own rights is also a great and successful kart and car driver.

'Furthermore, Max has an innate desire to win, even when he drives a rental kart. In this he reminds me of Hamilton, one who wanted to be first even if it was a question of going down the stairs.'

Despite the move to a factory role, where CRG would supply Max with all the karts he would need, he continued to race with his father as the chief mechanic, with the freedom to adjust and tune the karts as they needed to. Jos after all had experienced this level before and backed himself to do a better job than any CRG factory mechanic. He also seemed unconcerned about how Max would handle the significant step up in quality at international level. In January 2010 they travelled to Lonato in Italy, at the southern tip of Lake Garda – with a stop at their favourite service station on the way – for a testing session. The lap times confirmed what Jos had suspected, that Max would more than be able to handle himself among Europe's top karting talents. When they returned a month later for the first race of the season though, it was not so straightforward. The Dunlop tyres, a harder version than previous years, proved troublesome and the cold, wet conditions, usually a strong point for Max, were making it harder to find a consistent set-up that would work. Jos was mystified. Everything was in place. It was even raining, Max's speciality. Practice had not gone well.

Fortunately, Max's fortunes picked up in the afternoon and he qualified fourth fastest for the first of a series of races that would whittle the 108 drivers down to the seventeen that would contest the final. The Friday afternoon race would be one of a series of five against the same group of drivers. Max laid down a marker. He won, in the words of his father, 'by a street'. Lunch had not tasted particularly good but the Verstappens slept well on Friday night.

Saturday went well too and by the time they lined up for Sunday's final, Max had seen off every other CRG factory driver. He started second on the grid, usually a position that would virtually guarantee him victory. This though was a higher level. He was virtually the youngest person on the racetrack and pole-sitter Egor Orudzhev was two years older than him. Try as he might, Max could not find a way past and when the chequered flag came down he came across the line just three tenths of a second behind the Russian in second place. Behind him were names that would become familiar friends and foe over the coming years: Alex Albon was in third, Esteban Ocon was in seventh and Pierre Gasly in ninth. Charles Leclerc did not even make the final. All four would race against Max at the highest level of motor sport years later.

What is interesting is that even at such a young age, these fellow racers are already on the radar of top teams. Leclerc is racing for Maranello, and would soon be snapped up by the management company owned by Nicolas Todt, whose father Jean ran Ferrari for many years. Albon stands on the podium next to Verstappen in a Red Bull-branded race suit. Ocon, like Max, says he felt it was just himself and his father fighting against the big teams in their first year in international karting. His own father Laurent was a mechanic by trade but had none of the race experience that Jos boasted.

Max, and Esteban for that matter, would soon be attracting attention of his own, but for now he still had much to prove. In pictures, he stands on the second step of the podium, unfamiliar territory to say the least, and smiles for the cameras. It is a start, but nothing more.

'Sometimes you win, sometimes you lose,' his father concedes. 'Let's face it, Max is only twelve.'

In what is becoming a running theme, Max's years did not hold him back. Two weeks later, at the testing track where he had caught the eye of Tinini in Muro Leccese, he secured his first win at international level. Standing on the top step of the podium, the two boys next to him still tower over him while he can barely lift the trophy, not that it matters of course; all that matters is that he can handle the go-kart, and there's no question he can do that.

He arrives at Genk for the penultimate round of the Euro Series with the KF3 title within his grasp. To do it on the track where he grew up, with so many friends and family watching, would be sweet. Standing in his way are two men who would go on to be his teammates at Red Bull. Starting third in the final knowing only a win would seal the title, he overtook Gasly off the line, before a huge crash further back saw the race neutralised by yellow flags.

'I was just sliding,' Max says afterwards. 'The tyres were already quite worn this morning and it was difficult to keep them warm.'

Nevertheless, he desperately tries to overtake Albon. With no threat from behind, he can focus on the overtake and a first title in front of a home crowd. Each lap he gets closer and closer, until he feels the engine start to give up. It is not giving him the same power, and his tyres are sliding everywhere. Max keeps his cool though. He makes an adjustment to give the engine more power in the low and high revs and it seems to iron out the problem. He is back on Albon's tail, but just can't find a way past. The Red Bull driver is Max's main rival for the title, and the Dutchman has a 77-point lead. Winning this final heat would put him clear – but crashing out would cut his lead in half if Albon goes on to win the race. The twelve-year-old puts away the impetuous streak he inherited from his father and drives for the points, showing maturity beyond his tender years. A month later, he wraps up the WSK Euro Series (KF3 class) in southern Italy. It is confirmation, if any further were needed, that Max had more than enough to dominate KF3, the first level of international karting, and he is already talking about Super KF, although he will not be allowed to race at that level until he is fourteen.

He is not peerless though. Albon pushed him all the way in the Euro Series and when they clashed again in the World Cup in Portugal, the British-Thai driver with nearly two years more experience got the better of him. 'I will not celebrate my thirteenth birthday until next week so this is not so bad,' Max says philosophically afterwards.

There is no Albon when they travel to Egypt for the finale of the World Series at Sharm El-Sheikh, but again Max hits a setback. In the pre-final, he clashes with Robert Visoiu, defending his position on the straight by switching to the inside before the Romanian made contact with him from behind. The stewards warned Max, rather than Visoiu, for dangerous driving and the pair started the final on the front row. This time, it was Verstappen chasing Visoiu and in an almost identical incident but the other way round, Max was the one who made contact. This time though, the stewards penalised the rearmost driver and excluded Max from the results of the race after his second warning of the weekend. He is understandably crestfallen initially, but has still garnered enough points to take the World Series title. That though is scant consolation for Jos. Up until now, his son seems to have taken defeat with good grace, humility and maturity, seeing the bigger picture most of the time. For Jos, the bigger picture is one of inequality, of siege mentality.

'If this is how it's going to be, we will no longer participate in WSK championships,' Jos says angrily to his press team. 'I try to race my son, to give life the important values and honesty is also part of that. But it is hard to find here.

'Every action of Max is under a magnifying glass. They try to slow him down that way, because that's the only way left. Hardly anyone on the track can follow Max.'

While the conspiracy theory may be far-fetched, he is not wrong about the competition on track. Albon is the only one to have consistently challenged him, and at the CRG awards ceremony at the end of the year, he receives a gold medal from owner Giancarlo Tinini for winning the World Series title. At the wider WSK ceremony a month later, he and Jos pick up three trophies for the three titles he cleaned up.

Age restrictions mean he must remain in the same category for the 2011 season but it proves to be no cakewalk for Verstappen. The fickle gods of karting and the weather play a significant role in forcing him to show off his overtaking skills in the early part of the season, as he spins in consecutive finals after contact but on both occasions fights his way back on to the podium. Esteban Ocon, now in his second year of KF3 like Max, proves to be his main rival, although future F1 driver

George Russell is also extremely fast, but Verstappen's ability to rescue points from difficult weekends is vital, and he builds a significant points cushion in the Euro Series. When they head to La Conca in southern Italy for the penultimate race of the series, Max is already in position to secure the title with a weekend to spare. Then, yet more disaster strikes. For the first time in his young career, Max finds himself physically unable to race. After practice on Wednesday, he emerges from the kart complaining of a sore rib. Jos flies a physio in from home to look at him and he does not drive on Thursday at all to see if the pain will die down. Bravely, he tries to drive on Friday, but manages only four laps. With the chance to win the title, both father and son are determined to push the pain barrier. On Saturday though, it becomes too much and five laps into qualifying, Max returns to the pits. He cannot go any further. His ribs and now his back are screaming with pain through every corner. They have to pull out.

After scans back home show no serious damage has been done, Max recovers in time for the European Championship, only for what he calls a 'bumper cars' race to break out and Max can only finish fourteenth after multiple collisions while George Russell takes victory. At least the week after he is able to seal the Euro Series title despite having missed one of the four race weekends through injury and a major engine problem. His return to the World Cup where Albon had beaten him in 2010 saw him clash with another future F1 rival when Charles Leclerc overtook him and clipped his front wheel on the way through. 'It seemed as if he did it on purpose,' said Max afterwards. In truth, Max's pace had been off all weekend and Jos blamed himself for getting the set-up wrong. Max tries to sleep on the way home from Italy in an effort to be ready for school in the morning, but the frustrations of the day make it tough. Nevertheless, Max may not be winning quite so many races, but the consistency of his results is enough to show anyone caring to take an interest that he is good enough for all-comers. There was no shortage of people taking an interest either. The Intrepid Driver Programme, who already had the likes of Albon, Leclerc and Russell on their books, had been chasing Max ever since he signed for CRG, and at the end of the 2011 season the Verstappens finally relented. He would now be in the same karts as some of his biggest karting rivals after arguably the most challenging year of his career. He had clearly been doing something right, and would now be able to prove once and for all he was more than just his father's son.

7

FROM TEENAGE ANGST TO SINGLE-SEATERS

In go-karting, Jos and Max probably learned more about each other and bonded more than at any other stage of their relationship. They would spend hours on the road together and talk about everything and anything, something not every teenage boy has with either parent. When it came to interviews, which they would often find themselves doing together, they would appear open about each other and not afraid to discuss the other's flaws, an attitude many elite strategists feel is crucial to moving forward in a team. And that's what they are, in the end. Motor racing is an individual sport in one sense but it is very much a team environment; the driver gets over the line but without a team of, at the top level, hundreds or even thousands, they cannot even get off the grid.

Intrepid were, in Jos' mind, another stepping stone towards F1, but they also offered an element of driver focus that he believed to be important. When he was asked whether he had any regrets about his racing career in 2018, he insisted he had none. It didn't ring true though, and he quickly followed with an explanation.

'I would have done things differently, prepared better physically, got a proper trainer, built things up,' Jos says. 'It was all good for me. I made money, and then in 2003 I stopped and I put it all into the guy who is racing now, so it all worked out.'

Jos himself, by the standards of the day, rushed from karting to Formula One and was a green young driver. Although his son was technically moving far quicker than him in terms of age, Jos was making sure that he was not being rushed and was getting the right support at the right time.

Intrepid had a proven record of being a springboard for drivers who ended up in F1 too. Sébastien Buemi and Jaime Alguersuari were both graduates of the programme and had already spent several years in F1. Jules Bianchi and Will Stevens would soon follow. In Max's cohort, Intrepid already had a group bursting with talent: Charles Leclerc had won the 2011 KF3 title and George Russell the European Championship. It seemed like a perfect fit – at first. From the beginning though, Max's path in 2012 was not clear, with Jos wanting to race in KF1 but also mentioning that they would only do so if the field was right, and that they also wanted to get Max into the KZ2, a step up to gear-shifting karts, at some point.

Things started to get complicated, however. In January, Jos was arrested on suspicion of deliberately hitting his then-girlfriend Kelly van der Waal with his car. He strenuously denied the charges but was held in pre-trial detention for two weeks before his lawyers successfully got the attempted murder charges dropped and he was released. It meant that Jos missed Max's trip to Italy for the Intrepid Kart and Race Fair, where the new boy met many of his teammates and took part in a three-day test. At fourteen he probably relished the time to spread his own wings a little, but it was hardly an ideal situation.

Jos also recognised that apart from his own troubles, Max was at a delicate age. He had grown significantly, as fourteen-year-old boys often do, and with that growth spurt came the possibility that he could develop other interests outside the motor-sport obsession that had been with him since before he could walk.

'If he wakes up one morning and doesn't feel like it any more, that's it,' Jos said of his teenage son. 'I would of course think it would be a shame, especially with all the energy I put into it, but it remains his choice, his life; only if it is so, [I prefer] that he tells me now and not just in five years, because then I can go on vacation tomorrow.'

Perhaps it is teenage angst, the step-up in quality or the issues that would make his Intrepid stint last such a short period of time, but 2012 was far from a perfect year for Max. He starts strongly, winning the Winter Cup in Lonato on his Intrepid debut, with his new mechanics taking a lead role in preparation. Jos was still part of the team, tuning the engine and helping wherever he could, but he was not as in charge as he was at Pex or CRG. Max was growing up, but things were not getting easier. In Leclerc, now an ART driver, he had found a rival truly worthy of taking him on. The pair were neck and neck in the KF2 Euro Series and things came to a head at Val d'Argenton in western France.

Max was now another step up the karting ladder, and the interest had intensified a little more. The karting community were beginning to get the sense that this was a golden generation of racers. As such, when Leclerc and Verstappen collide during a wet qualifying session, both boys have a microphone shoved in their face before they can even get warm and dry.

'He's just unfair! I'm leading, he wants to pass, he pushes me, I push him back and after he pushed me off the track. It's not fair, uh?' Max says angrily, cheeks flushed and his father marching off ahead of him similarly peeved but wisely the man with the microphone goes for the younger of the two Verstappens. The Italian interviewer runs off excitedly to find Charles, sensing a big story between two up-and-coming stars.

'Just a racing incident,' Leclerc says, brushing it off. His team boss parrots his answer. Nothing to see here. The stewards disagree and disqualify both drivers from qualifying.

Max gets caught up in two more incidents over the weekend and it proves a costly trip as he picks up just three points and now trails Leclerc 50 to 122 in the title race. The weekend sticks firmly in the memory of both men. Eight years later, Leclerc still insists he is innocent.

'He ended up on the grass but only because he got distracted while I was side by side with him to complain about his previous move,' Leclerc says in 2020.

'His kart went in such a deep puddle that only his helmet was sticking out of the water. He was furious, but now thinking about that episode makes me laugh a lot.'

Max has yet to laugh it off.

Not only was he being challenged in KF2, but Jos was pushing him forwards and upwards. He entered the KF1 World Championship, a two-round affair in Japan and Macau with the races some five months apart. Max showed glimpses of his talent, picking up two podiums across the eight heats, but could only finish eighth. The racing was harder and without his dominant speed, combined with reliability issues that started to make him think the world was against him, it became almost impossible to win. Even when he did manage to cross the line first, triumphing at the European Championship in England, the victory was eventually taken away from him on a stewards' appeal and awarded to British driver Ben Barnicoat. A counter-appeal was lodged but dismissed, Jos claimed, on a technicality, something about paperwork they were never told they needed not being filed on time. Both men were fuming and 2012 was fast turning into an *annus horribilis*.

Jos acted decisively to change their fortunes. In July, he announced that Max was moving team again, citing the departure of Intrepid founder Mirko Sguerzoni in murky circumstances, the lack of money available for development and the fear of stagnation. He intimated that Intrepid were going broke. They join a team called Chiesa Corsa to race in Zanardi karts, a move that would take them back under the auspices of the Tinini group, owners of CRG and much more familiar territory for Max. Within a few weeks, he was back in a CRG kart with KF2 and several gear-shifting KZ2 entries on his calendar. Switching team mid-season though was not easy, especially doing so twice, no matter how familiar the kart you end up in or how talented the driver. His pace was generally impressive but his cursed year continued: at the Karting World Cup in Sarno near Naples, he dominated the KZ2 category in all bar one of the races before the final, the one slip-up coming when he burned out the clutch, a clumsy error, forcing him to start the pre-final in tenth place, which he won anyway. When it came to the final, he was desperate to grab his biggest win of the year and spying a slim but makeable opportunity to overtake Daniel Bray, who had just taken the lead from him, at a high-speed, fourth-gear corner, he made the move. The pair collided and Max was forced to retire.

Afterwards, he admitted his mistake, knowing he would have passed Bray eventually with his significant speed advantage, but perhaps the first part of the year spent in an inferior kart had clouded his mindset.

The mistake in Sarno was a seminal moment, as it resulted in the now-famous incident in which Max was abandoned, briefly, at a petrol station. Max, who would turn fifteen a few weeks later, should have been world champion in the KZ2 class, in more advanced gear-shifting karts, an accolade that would have been a huge two fingers to those who had stymied his progress and questioned his various moves over the summer. Instead, they were making the lengthy journey back to Belgium without any silverware in the van as their third different kart of the year rattled around in the back. Perhaps Jos was beginning to think of the summer as a microcosm of his own career, almost constantly moving teams trying to make things work and eventually never really achieving enough. When he left Max at a service station, it must have been a shocking moment of realisation for both of them: for Max, about the depth of his father's passion and anger and for Jos, about how far he would go to teach his son a lesson. He seemed to feel that Max had not taken that defeat – and all the other struggles of the year so far – to heart enough, even though he was deeply upset not to have won. It had the desired impact. Max is many things, but a good loser he is not. 'Show me a good loser and I'll show you a loser,' American football coach Vince Lombardi is supposed to have once said, a phrase that might as well have been painted on the inside of the Verstappens' van. When Daniel Ricciardo accused him once of being a 'sore loser' over the team radio after a 2017 collision, he probably would not have denied it.

After the galling disappointment of Sarno, Max's schedule for the rest of the year changed somewhat. After taking second at a World Cup event in Spain, beaten only by CRG teammate Felice Tiene, the Verstappens went chasing bigger prizes at a higher level, buoyed by the speed shown against the KZ2 class. Max pulled out of a number of WSK events and travelled to the United States for Superkarts in Las Vegas for the KZ2 race there. There was a conscientious push to make up for lost time. Even still, it felt as though they could not catch a break. In Macau, Max caught an infection that left him bedridden – but he still drove fastest in the practice sessions. After a few paracetamol and many hours of sleep, he managed to finish second in the first race but a technical problem retired him from the lead of the second race. In Las Vegas, a broken spark plug stopped him winning the final after once again cruising through the earlier rounds. Two trips across the planet with nothing to show for it other than a lot of jet lag and a few stamps in his passport. However, both team and driver asserted that Max would be at CRG next year. The dalliance away from the team where he had won so much had not worked. Now they would push Max into KZ1 and the KF classes, the highest series of karts with manual and automatic gearboxes respectively.

When they sat down and mapped out their year, featuring sixteen race weekends and a number of testing sessions, it became clear that Max would not be spending much time in Belgium, never mind at school. He was never that keen on it anyway, school that is rather than Belgium, and had only been achieving decent grades because his father had struck a deal that if he did, the school would give him the time off he needed to race internationally. Pretty soon, even that was not enough.

'I stopped school when I was fifteen and a half; after that it was just difficult to combine. I was two weeks away, one week at school, so it was very hard to catch up,' Max said in a 2017 interview with crash.net.

'But it's a risk. I've had a lot of people in racing who did the same, and eventually it doesn't work out and you need to go back to school and study again, and that was my motivation to try to do well, so I didn't have to go back to school afterwards.'

Jos, as many racing parents did, paid for a private tutor instead to try to keep Max's academics up, knowing that in just twelve months' time they would be leaving karts behind and moving up to cars, if they could make the finances work. Then the world would start to become a whole lot bigger for Max and it was a point at which, as the boy himself put it, it might not work out, so he stuck at his online tutoring.

The dangers of a growing boy abandoning his childhood passion were real and present too. He was no longer dwarfed in podium pictures. In fact he was almost as tall as his father, and a few spots were starting to appear on his chin and forehead, an inevitability of teenage years. Jos was wary. When he was eight and the other drivers were playing football in the paddock while Max tried to understand why his kart was sliding from his dad, it was easy to keep him engaged. Now he was nearly sixteen and the distractions were altogether more significant. There was a change in dynamic within the team too, as mechanic René Heesen became more prominent and Jos, as he would go on to do so many times in Max's career, tried to step back from being quite so involved in the karts. René had been working with Jos on and off for years, having guided Giedo van der Garde to a karting world title, and then Nico Hülkenberg. Max though, he thought, might be better than both of them, and at last, after the difficulties of 2012, things seemed to be coming together again.

'It was all so incredibly easy,' Max says after dominating the KZ2 category in the opening race of the season in Italy. Even Jos was impressed.

'With a KZ kart you drive angular and with a KF, with an automatic gearbox, a bit rounder,' he says.

'But Max now drives that smoothly with a KZ and therefore takes a lot of speed out of the corners, which is not normal. Max is doing amazingly well; it is going really well. He always goes fast and is very good everywhere. I am very proud of Max. His way of driving is just insane. I can't say anything else.'

You can almost sense the relief in his high praise, the like of which he has not aired publicly for some time. With another Winter Cup victory under his belt, he headed back to La Conca for the first round of the Euro Series, where there is a familiar and famous name on the start sheet: Michael Schumacher. The 44-year-old German was a part-owner of Tony Kart, one of CRG's major rivals, and his son Mick was also competing in the junior series. Max was racing in KZ1, where there are no privateers, only dedicated factory drivers, and there are no punches pulled. 'Schumi' too should have been in this category but pulled out of the event after a couple of practice sessions. His times, some said, were as much as a second slower than Max's. Alas there was no great showdown between Jos' former teammate and go-karting's hottest young prospect, and tragically Schumacher's skiing accident suffered a few months later means there may never be, although Jos would have been glad that his old friend got the chance to see Max, who had been on family holidays with the Schumachers, karting at the highest level up close and personal.

Max was peerless once again in southern Italy, taking maximum points and a commanding lead in the Euro Series over teammate and friend Jorrit Pex. By mid-summer, he had wrapped up the title, sealing it with a patient, thoughtful drive that ensured he finished with enough points to see off contender Ben Hanley and wrap up the trophy on Saturday in Genk, allowing him to enjoy Sunday's race on his home track without too much pressure on his shoulders. He won the European Championship in the KZ class and the KF a month later, before adding the first half of the KF World Championship in England in September. The hype, which had been slowed by the difficulties in 2012, was starting to take shape again. Tentative phone calls were starting to be made. Scouts were starting to arrive at race weekends. Agent Raymond Vermeulen was becoming a busier man by the day. Even Huub Rothengatter, Raymond's predecessor, was intrigued. When Max arrived at the KZ World Championship final in Varennes-sur-Allier, he could not resist the trip.

'I heard all kinds of stories and saw great results this season. That made me want to see with my own eyes what Max was doing,' Rothengatter said.

'So together with Raymond we just decided to get in the car very early in the morning on Friday and drive to Varennes. I can tell you, and this is an understatement, that Max does not disappoint me at all. It is fantastic what he has shown here in France!'

He impressed everyone that weekend: Rothengatter, Charles Leclerc whom he battled repeatedly, even himself. Seven years later in an interview with German online publication *Speedweek*, he would cite the final as one of his best races.

'This race will always be with me,' he said. 'I left the field behind me and was never really under pressure.

'We had worked very hard all weekend; that's why this victory was so satisfying. The icing on the cake was that my father had prepared my kart.'

Max had not yet turned sixteen years old and there was no more karting world left to conquer. He was hardly weeping though. He was giddy with excitement as to what lay next, just like those team principals trying to recruit him. Just like Jos all those years ago, Verstappen was the name on everyone's lips, but his father was determined that things would be different.

What many who watched him win that KZ title and perhaps nudged a fellow bystander to suggest he should be in a racing car fairly soon did not know was that Max had already had his first taste of single-seater driving in a secret summer session.

Not many people outside of the world of motor racing may be able to find Pembrey on a map; it is probably better known these days for its dry ski slope and enormous caravan park. However, the small Welsh village, and more specifically its converted airfield, has played a significant role in the folklore of a number of drivers. Because of the lack of noise restrictions, it was often used as a testing circuit by F1 teams in the eighties and nineties, with McLaren decamping there on several occasions. In fact, a famous Ron Dennis-led summit between warring drivers Alain Prost and Ayrton Senna is said to have taken place there during the very height of their epic internal strife. More than twenty years later though, the track was still in use for testing of GT and minor formula cars, including Formula Renault. Eric Boullier was CEO of Gravity Sport Management, a company owned by Genii Capital, and when they bought into the Renault F1 team, he was installed as team boss. When Renault pulled out and the team was renamed Lotus, Boullier remained, but he was still working on scouting young talent, especially in the French engine manufacturer's junior series. Gravity had already contacted the Verstappens and made some progress earlier in the year (Boullier even name-dropped Max in a 2013 interview as a talent he 'had') so it was no coincidence that Max was given the chance to test a Formula Renault 2.0 car there in August 2013, albeit under the auspices of a Dutch team. It was kept under wraps though, with Max's father making sure that few people were aware of it.

'Because many eyes are on Max, we decided not to publicise it further,' Jos wrote in a column a few months later, by which time his son had already been given a third shot at a day in a single-seater. 'I wanted Max to be able to learn the first things at his leisure without pressure and without people looking along the track. It is a very big step from karts to a car.'

Jos was so cautious because of his own first F1 test and the media attention that had pushed him into that first move to Benetton, the seat next to Michael Schumacher and a path he could not reverse back up, much as he wanted to.

The night before the test, Jos sat up with Frits van Eldik, a photographer who had been snapping him since his own racing days and who had become a close friend. Frits first met Max when he was one day old, taking the first picture of the Verstappen family after his birth. They discussed what might happen the next day with some anxiety. In the end, they took the same thought to bed to manage their expectations and worries: 'We will see tomorrow.' They knew that it could be the start of something, or it could be nothing. In the end, Frits would describe it as one of the most memorable moments of his life.

Perhaps predictably, given that Pembrey is not far from the UK's wettest city Swansea, Max's first ever day in a single-seater racing car – Wednesday 14 August 2013 – took place in soaking conditions. Nevertheless the Dutch Manor MP Motorsport team put the wet tyres on, and tentatively sent out a fifteen-year-old in their bright orange car for his first ever laps, probably expecting to have to retrieve him from a puddle a few minutes later.

'Of course before you jump in the car you don't know what to expect,' Max said. 'But after I did a few laps, I started to feel comfortable. You start to feel the limits a bit.

'It's completely different to go-karts. I mean, the braking pedal, the throttle application, how you sit in the car, the view. That was the main difference really.'

Max astounded Manor mechanics. Within half an hour, when he was still supposed to be taking things easy, he was going full throttle. The team had told him that anything close to 58 seconds on the short testing track would be a decent start, based on previous data in the wet. By the end, Max's fastest wet time was a 56.1. On Thursday, when the rain relented, he set the fastest time of anyone in a 2013 spec car of the kind he was driving. If Manor could have signed him on the spot, no doubt they would have done, but this would not be a rushed decision.

There was another significant difference: Jos was not tuning his engine, warming it up and training him for the track. For a man who has lived and breathed his son's career just about every day for the last decade, it was a strange feeling. He had relaxed the reins with René in tow, but now he really would have to be more of a father, and less of everything else.

In October, two months after that first test, Jos was sitting at Alcarras, a small Spanish circuit not even watching his son fly round in his third Formula Renault 2.0 test, this time for Finnish team Koiranen. The Welsh rain was far away and Max was able to rack up the miles. He and Raymond were mulling over the offers of various teams in a number of series, desperate to make the right decision with the agony of so much choice. Jos wrote his monthly column in Alcarras, this one entitled 'Time to let go of Max'.

'For me, the step from karts to cars means that I will soon no longer have any influence on Max's performance, after years of doing his karts,' he says.

'So far I have no problem letting go of that. I notice that I even like it. It is nice to be able to take it a bit slower than the past few years.'

There is not much self-awareness though in his next sentence.

'I will still go to all tests and races for now. That is nice for Max.'

Doubtless, he would be glad of his father's counsel, but there was also a sizeable possibility of overreach. He was sixteen now and was, as he has always been, an old head on young shoulders. As he now began his professional career in earnest, he may not have been so happy to have his old man peering over his shoulder, quite literally at times.

First, he had to get there though and there were contracts and relationships to sort out. In a spec series where all the cars were the same, testing with different teams was even more important.

'We will base the choice of the team where we will drive on our feelings,' said Jos.

'It is important that Max can work together with the engineer.'

The subtext of course was that the engineer must be able to work with all the Verstappens, not just Max. At Koiranen, he noted that the Finns are not men of many words, a cliché given credence by the likes of Kimi Raikkonen and Mika Hakkinen, although the latter's post-racing career as a pundit has started to buck that trend.

Max tested with KTR, run by Belgian Kurt Mollekens, a former rival of Jos', and impressed round Hockenheim. After the two-day test Mollekens sang his praises, saying that he should be targeting Formula One and that he should go through Formula Renault 2.0 to get there, preferably with KTR. When the rookie test at Barcelona came around, where 33 drivers in total set times, it is KTR whose car Max drives.

He set impressive times for a rookie in the morning, going third fastest behind Gustav Malja and George Russell, the future Williams F1 driver, but ended the session in the gravel after losing control. He blamed a pedal problem that also limited his running in the afternoon, when most drivers set their quickest time, and he finished the day down in eighth place. He was still the second-fastest rookie, but it was a frustrating day to hit trouble after being invited by Renault to take part. It was even more frustrating when he tested with Tech 1 in Hungary a week later and set a track record for Formula Renault 2.0, narrowly beating Alex Albon for fastest time of the day. At least he had shown his true colours on a day when there were other drivers present to provide a benchmark, especially one like Albon who had proven a worthy rival in karting and already had two seasons of Formula Renault under his belt. At Spa, he went fastest of a nineteen-driver, two-day test, this time working with Josef Kaufmann Racing. He beat the field in wet and dry conditions.

Still no decisions were made and no team with whom Max tested withdrew their interest, understandably, because he was fast becoming junior formula racing's hottest property. Even Max admitted that he was faced with a difficult decision for next year, while also having to keep his karting eye in, because the KF World Championship final race in Bahrain did not take place until the end of November. When it did, Max was excluded after a collision the stewards deemed to be his fault. After a season in which he had won a total of six titles though and was almost assured a racing car drive next year, it was hard to be disappointed – although the controversy was the talk of the tables when Max picked up his haul of awards at a dinner a few weeks later.

'It was the best season ever and we have made history in karting by winning two European and one world title in the same season and in two different categories,' Max said. 'Now is the time to look forward to a new challenge.'

Even as late as December, Max was expecting that challenge to come in FR 2.0, the series he had tested repeatedly in and three times now for French team Tech 1, who won the 2013 title with Pierre Gasly taking individual honours. Then came an opportunity he could not turn down. After his ninth FR 2.0 test, at which his father happened not to be present ('I was fine, even without Jos,' he laughed when asked if it affected him), he was offered the chance to drive a Formula Three car for the first time. F3, as it is now known, is just two tiers below Formula One and a series mostly populated by drivers with two or three years of racing driving at least. Max would be the ultimate rookie, but Team Motopark, who were operating under a Lotus name and livery, were reliably informed that they could do a lot worse than give this youngster two days in their car.

Jos flew out to Valencia for the test, which was still regarded as an exploratory rather than preparatory one. No one expected Max to excel in an F3 car, given he was driving an automatic go-kart less than a month ago. Again, they underestimated him. Actually, Max again shocked himself when in his first 45 minutes in an F3 car, at a circuit he had never driven before, he was the fastest man on the track.

'I did not expect that I would be the fastest,' he said after an exhilarating first day in which he broke the lap record. 'That surprised me. The car fits me very well, so I can easily adapt.'

His dad had one word for it: 'Genius.'

The man who had given Jos his break in the early 1990s in F3, Frits van Amersfoort, was watching on. 'Within ten minutes I knew what sort of driver we had in the cockpit.'

On the second day, he broke the record again, and was even quick when the rain came down in the final hour of the day, his last piece of driving for 2013. Two days earlier, Max had insisted that he would still be in an FR 2.0 car next year. Now, he was not so sure.

'No decision has been taken yet about next year, but I hope to get clarity soon.'

Things were moving very fast, on and off the track, and they were only going to start moving faster.

8

CATCHING THE EYES OF THE F1 GRID

Motor sport started 2014 under a cloud. Michael Schumacher, Jos Verstappen's former teammate and a seven-time world champion, was in a coma after a skiing accident that doctors say would have been fatal were it not for his helmet. He remained in a critical but stable condition, and the Schumacher family were fighting fiercely to protect his privacy. Even to this day, little is known about his condition after he was brought out of a coma in the summer of 2014 and moved to his home three months later.

Meanwhile his former team Ferrari were trying to firm up their own future by securing the best motor racing talent in the world, and in doing so they fired the starter pistol on the race for Max's signature. The majority of talented drivers around him have already been recruited to one talent programme or another, and it was surprising but no accident that he had not. Jos was constantly trying to avoid the pitfalls of his own career and Max was not ready to ignore him. However, when Ferrari come calling, it was a hard summons to ignore. So when Luca Baldisserri, who had worked as a strategist for Schumacher at Ferrari but now ran the driver academy, invited Max to the United States for January's inaugural Florida Winter Series, he leaped at the opportunity.

The series was only four races long and organised by Ferrari essentially to get a better look at drivers they were considering for their programme. The cars used were not far off Formula Three specifications and had the same safety regulations as F3, making them ideal for someone at Max's stage looking to amass mileage at that level. There was though the small matter of a €95,000 fee. For other competitors such as Lance Stroll or Nicholas Latifi, their billionaire fathers would have no problem footing the bill. Jos had done well in F1 but had already spent a huge amount of money in karting and with a season in car racing to come, could not cover the whole lot. He was calling on the old sponsors from his own racing days to help out, and plenty were helpful, even though the Florida series was a favour rather than a genuine marketing opportunity. (The finances for Team Verstappen were always somewhat precarious during his first year in car racing, despite the best efforts of Jos and Raymond, and without the support of Dutch supermarket Jumbo, Max's very first sponsor in car racing, his career might never have got off the ground. Max even approached Michel Perridon, a star of the Dutch version of *Dragons' Den* and a former investor in Jos, to pitch him for sponsorship personally at a race weekend, pointing out that his mother was already wearing a hat bearing Perridon's Trust brand. It was as bold a move as one of Max's signature overtakes, although unlike those, it did not come off.)

The Florida Series, Ferrari stressed, was not a championship – there was no big trophy at the end – but a competitive winter training exercise at a time of year when there was little other racing going on. Ferrari would spread their engineers across cars, run seminars for the young drivers on various aspects of racing and allow them to rack up around 3,000 kilometres of driving. Each race weekend would consist of four hours of practice, two qualifying sessions of 30 minutes and then three 30-minute races. Jos would travel too as Max's 'coach' now that he cannot really be his engineer or mechanic any more and Sophie also flew over to support her son. For Max, it was a chance to make his racing debut and gain invaluable experience, as well as a chance to further advance his reputation; he still had not put pen to paper for the 2014 season and every passing week and fastest lap only broadened his choice. If he could beat either of the Ferrari Driver Academy members expected to participate – Jules Bianchi and Antonio Fuoco – he would make some serious waves.

As a true rookie, having never completed a race in a single-seater racing car, Verstappen was certainly at a disadvantage. There were four drivers who had spent the previous season in European F3 and two more from Formula Renault. Only four of the eleven drivers due to complete the whole four-race series had come up from karting that year, one of them being Max, and some of that inexperience showed with an inauspicious start in testing; he crashed into the back of Antonio Fuoco in the pit lane and broke his front left suspension, losing him some track time and more than a little pride. Perhaps there was some exuberance and excitement getting the better of him. In his first race too, there were moments of impetuosity that stood him apart from the others, as well as pace that did the same. Despite having chosen to jet out to Florida for some January sunshine, the opening race of the series started behind the safety car because of the rain. From third place, Max's skills in wet conditions were quickly on show as he set fastest sector after fastest sector, overtaking fellow Dutchman Dennis van de Laar and Ferrari's own Fuoco, an old karting rival, to take the lead of his first ever race in a car on the first lap. At the front, he tried to push on and build a gap, but in his eagerness overheated the tyres and he was slowly reeled back in. With three laps to go, Max made a mistake on the final corner and lost three places. 'I was so angry,' he reflected after the race.

Fortunately, he quickly put that anger aside to set the fastest lap of the race, worth no points but enough to cement fourth place. There were more lessons to learn in races two and three. In the first, he rear-ended Ben Anderson and lost his front wing to end his race after he braked much earlier than expected. He left the mechanics racing against time to get his car ready for race three. They managed to do so – but then he was penalised for a false start from pole position. There were good moments and bad moments, no less or no more than you would expect from a rookie. However, this was a Verstappen and a bit more was expected.

He would have to wait until a week later for his first victory. It was another date to mark in one's diary – 5 February 2014 – as the day Max claimed his maiden victory in cars. If you had tried to predict it, you would not have picked the Palm Beach race based on Monday's practice session. The rain came and went, the asphalt was incredibly rough and would wear the tyres out too quickly for any meaningful running. Max was struggling to reproduce the form that had earned him pole position at Sebring. He complained about the circuit since there were not many corners where he felt he could make a difference, not to mention the track surface that made pushing very difficult. He finished the day eight tenths off the podium. The next day featured two qualifying sessions and the first of the three races, and Max only got better as the day wore on. The overnight set-up changes seemed to have worked and he took pole position for

Sophie Kumpen and Jos Verstappen at Rockingham Motor Speedway, Corby, England, 2003 (Motorsport Images).

Max with Jos after finishing second in the 2010 Winter Cup, South Garda Karting, Lonato. 21 February 2010 (Kartpix.net/Alamy Stock Photo).

Jos & Max Verstappen at the WSK Euro Series KF3,
La Conca, Italy, 7 March 2010 (Kartpix.net/Alamy Stock Photo).

Christian Horner (L) walks with Red Bull team advisor Helmet Marko
ahead of the third practice session for the Chinese Grand Prix in
Shanghai, 13 April 2013 (Mark Baker/AP/Shutterstock).

16-year-old Max in conversation with his father before the Masters of Formula 3 at Zandvoort in the Netherlands ...
(Sander Koning/EPA/Shutterstock).

... and celebrating after winning the event, 6 July 2014
(Sander Koning/EPA/Shutterstock).

Zandvoort racing circuit, Netherlands (Hollandse Hoogte/Shutterstock).

Max celebrates with the Red Bull Racing team after winning the Spanish Grand Prix at Circuit de Barcelona-Catalunya in Montmeló, 15 May 2016 (Toni Albir/EPA/Shutterstock).

Max and his Scuderia Toro Rosso teammate Carlos Sainz at the Albert
Park Circuit in Melbourne, Australia, 15 March 2015
(Srdjan Suki/EPA/Shutterstock).

Daniel Ricciardo (R) celebrates victory alongside second placed Verstappen
on the podium at the Malaysian Grand Prix in Sepang,
2 October 2016 (Fazry Ismail/EPA/Shutterstock).

Max talks with manager Raymond Vermeulen in the garage during practice for the Formula One Grand Prix of China at Shanghai International Circuit, 7 April 2017 (Mark Thompson / Getty Images).

Christian Horner (L) embraces Max Verstappen after winning the Austrian Grand Prix, 2 July 2018 (APA Picturedesk Gmbh/Shutterstock).

A colourful Dutch contingent watches on as Max competes in the Austrian Grand Prix at the Red Bull Ring, Spielberg, 30 June 2019 (Pixathlon/Shutterstock).

Max Verstappen celebrates winning the Austria Grand Prix flanked by second placed Charles Leclerc (L) and third placed Valtteri Bottas, 30 June 2019 (VALDRIN XHEMAJ/EPA-EFE/Shutterstock).

Verstappen and Hamilton crash at the Italian Grand Prix,
12 September 2021 (Dppi/LiveMedia/Shutterstock).

Max celebrates after winning the Abu Dhabi Grand Prix,
12 December 2021 (Xinhua/Shutterstock).

Wednesday's last race with not just the fastest but the two fastest laps of the day. In Race 1, he started third and overtook Latifi for second in the early stages, but could not reel in Fuoco on a track where following and overtaking was no mean feat. He took his place on the podium for the first time, and immediately gave the trophy away: he wanted to thank the mechanics who worked tirelessly the week before to fix the car he had broken. It now sits in the Prema Powerteam factory, with Max's signature on it. Clearly, they knew it might be worth something one day.

The next day, Max started from the front with a mass of more experienced drivers behind him. Fuoco is the reigning FR 2.0 Alps champion, British driver Ed Jones won the European F3 Open title, and Max was driving his second ever race weekend in cars. However the sixteen-year-old pulled away nervelessly and never gave up his lead. Jones overtook Fuoco and got within a few tenths of second but Verstappen never faltered, even with a damaged gearbox that threatened to give up at any moment. Perhaps had a late safety car not been deployed and the race ended early due to an incoming storm, his car might not have held on, but nevertheless enough laps had been completed to declare him the winner. Max was still seven months away from his seventeenth birthday and he was already a winner in race car driving. He had given away the small glass trophy he had won on Tuesday. 'This one I'll keep,' he said after stepping off the top step.

In the aftermath of the win, with virtually no crowd present but a keen Dutch fan base following the timing screens avidly from back home, the Verstappen PR machine rolled into action. Within 24 hours, his website had published two pieces: one with quotes from Jos playing down the mistakes Max had made in the first two rounds and playing up his learning from them, and one explaining that there were three different series, never mind teams, vying for his presence for the 2014 season. They claimed that Formula Renault 2.0, German Formula Three and European Formula Three were all championships under consideration. The message to suitors was clear: make your next offer a better one. More directly, Jos tried to point to Max's gradient as much as his peak, understanding that one race win in a meaningless training series would not butter many parsnips.

'See how much progress Max has made from one week to the next, that's great. That's why it's good that Max makes those mistakes,' Jos says, a deft propagandist.

'When you see how he recovers afterwards and finishes a first race second and then wins the third race, even with a technical problem when shifting the gearbox, you see that he picks up very important things very quickly.'

While his future remained up in the air, Max headed to Miami and the Homestead Speedway for the last two rounds of the series. Competition was getting stiff, even though there was no title at stake. Fuoco and Verstappen had raced together plenty in karting and both had burgeoning reputations. Neither wanted to be outdone, and when they collided in race two, Max was not happy. He had dived down the outside of a corner as both men were trying to work their way through the field of the reverse-grid race.

'I steered to the left to overtake him on the outside, and wanted to take the corner right in front of him to the right when Fuoco suddenly went full throttle again and rammed my right rear wheel,' Max said angrily.

'That broke off and then my race was over.'

Again, Max was forced to rely on the mechanics to get his car in shape for the final race of the round, and even then he was beaten by Fuoco and Latifi, the two other drivers who had emerged as the front runners from the series ahead of the final round. Fuoco had already been confirmed as Prema's driver in European F3 for 2014 while Latifi was soon to join him; it was a statement of intent and a proof of pace that Verstappen was willing and able to match them in equalised machinery. Max finished with a bang too, winning the twelfth and final race of the series by less than a hundredth of a second, pipping Nicholas Latifi on the line on a circuit layout where slipstreaming, rather than pure racing, was the key. He had spent much of the race overtaking the Canadian, only to be passed again on the straight, and eventually he out-strategised his more experienced opponent to be the first over the line – although with a margin of four thousandths of a second, it was as much down to fortune as proper planning.

Jos, Sophie and Max flew home from Florida mostly satisfied with their work, with plenty of lessons learned and probably feeling they had not wasted a six-figure sum on the trip. Certainly, they had made much progress since crashing into the back of Fuoco in the pit lane and of their three options for the 2014 season, they chose the toughest. European Formula Three and Van Amersfoort Racing would be their next port of call.

It was a decision taken, seemingly, for many of the right reasons. While European F3 would be unfamiliar territory, VAR would not be. Jos himself had driven for them in the 1990s on his journey to F1 and Frits van Amersfoort, who had founded the team in 1975 and been in charge of Verstappen Sr, was still running things more than twenty years later. The team were also based in Holland, Max's engineer would be Dutchman Rik Vernooij and the team operated in Dutch, something his new team boss had played up in negotiations.

'It's good for a kid to act in his first season of car racing in a team that speaks his own language,' Van Amersfoort said, despite Max speaking excellent English even at the age of sixteen. 'He will make some mistakes but that's what he can learn from, and it will help if he can talk them through in Dutch.'

Expectations were being managed. Once again, Jos was conscious of his own errors two decades before and was trying to dampen his son's progress, publicly at least, for his own good if possible. The team boss at VAR was singing from the same hymn sheet too.

'In motor sport you get a lot less time on the track than in karting,' Van Amersfoort adds.

'My experience has taught me that many karters encounter this in the beginning and Max will also have to get used to it. Everything has to fall into place in the twenty minutes of qualifying. You effectively get only two or three laps to set your fastest time.

'The racing will be fine. Max has already had an awful lot of competitions and that part is at least as well developed as with Jos. The great pressure and emphasis will be on qualifying.'

In what was an inherently risky decision in which Max could end up looking out of his depth, they had chosen the safety net of working with a Dutch team based close to home and a team that had finished seventh in the constructors' standings the year before in a series to which they were relatively new. There would be some even bigger decisions to make a little further down the line, although how soon they could not possibly predict. It was revealing, especially when you consider what criteria Jos set up for the decision to move to F1 further down the line, to read what engineer Rik Vernooij had to say on the eve of Max's debut too.

'Van Amersfoort Racing is definitely an underdog within the European Formula Three field if you look at the championship teams where there is an infinite amount of money and opportunities,' he says.

'But I really have the feeling that the best people are with us. Our way of working is mainly aimed at young drivers. I think we are really good at coaching and directing a rider, who of course has to be talented. In the last eight years that I have been working at Van Amersfoort Racing, we try to build that up. The average age within our team is low.'

Even for VAR though, Max is young and would have to prove himself once again. He had to show that his F3 test in Valencia at the end of 2013 was no fluke, nor his strong performances in Florida or testing. Both Fuoco and Latifi were driving for Prema Powerteam, the Ferrari outfit who won the title the year before, along with familiar face Esteban Ocon, a Lotus F1 junior driver, and Dennis van de Laar, another Dutch driver whom Max had beaten consistently in the US. Nevertheless, the forums and paddocks were alive with talk that like his father, Max had already taken on too much too young. European F3 was not an entry level championship, after all.

His debut came at the famous Silverstone circuit as part of the 6 Hours of Silverstone World Endurance Championship weekend with plenty of eyes focused on his red-and-white Van Amersfoort Racing car, especially having topped the timing sheets at testing. His early April laps of the Red Bull Ring in testing, despite having never been there before, were nearly two tenths faster than anybody else, and he beat his teammate Gustavo Menezes by nearly a second. In his first race at Silverstone, he hit a clutch problem which forced retirement and he was slow off the line in his second, but fought up from eighth to fifth.

He studied the start closely with his engineer and immediately improved for his third getaway, taking a position off Latifi while Ocon and Fuoco battled it out for the lead. The latter managed to get ahead and pull clear, leaving Ocon to fall into the clutches of Verstappen, who was now setting fastest sectors and lap times and leaving those behind him unable to keep up. The three rookies, on the first weekend of the year, were leaving the rest in their wake.

The F3 cars were not natural overtakers and Silverstone is not a track that necessarily lends itself to passing at the best of times. Ocon made his car as wide as possible and Max was forced to bide his time, struggling for grip so close behind and spending some five laps within a second of the Frenchman, until finally he made a mistake under braking and Verstappen needed no second invitation, skipping through on the inside and quickly pulling away in clean air. Fuoco was by this point too far away to catch him in just eight laps and Max, whose front tyres had suffered badly behind Ocon, had to be content with second place on his first race weekend. Both Jos and Max talked a good game afterwards, but Verstappen's father admitted even he was surprised by the maturity of Max's driving, his overtakes in the third race in particular showing that innate racecraft that he had spotted in his very first race in karting.

'As a father I know him through and through,' Jos wrote in his column for *De Telegraaf*.

'But even so he is further on than I had anticipated.'

It takes a lot for Jos, a father so proud and so confident, to underestimate his son, but Max's racing computer and capacity to learn was what had brought him to this point, racing at a Continental level before his seventeenth birthday, while he was still not allowed to drive himself to events. That first weekend brought challenges – a mechanical failure, a poor start, a track where overtaking is tough – and yet each one he faced, analysed and moved forward. He rarely needed to learn the same lesson twice.

He was not the finished article though. His opening race at Hockenheim was ended on the first lap when he tried to outbrake Tom Blomqvist into the hairpin, and both men ended up braking too late. Blomqvist was able to bail out and avoid contact, but Verstappen on the inside locked up and careered straight into Nicholas Latifi. 'It was my own fault,' Max said. It was a typical rookie move and should be sanctioned, spectators said. The stewards? They did not punish him, perhaps sympathising with the position of it being only Verstappen's sixth career race weekend. Karma caught up with him though when an electrical failure denied him the chance to start on pole in the second race. Any good fortune at avoiding punishment had balanced out quite quickly.

However, when he started the third and final race of the Hockenheim weekend, a track where he had impressed in testing the previous year, on pole position, there was no stopping him. He had worked intensely with Vernooij on his start procedure and was the best off the line of the front-runners. An early safety car was deployed to negate his gap to Ocon, but again his fast learning came to the fore.

'During my races in the Florida Winter Series I had already learned about driving behind a safety car, so that helped me,' he said afterwards.

'In fact, in Formula Three it is easier to lead the way because you know that the competition cannot get too close behind you, because they lose downforce.

'So to be honest it was actually quite a relaxed race for me.'

It was quite a jarring statement, the sixteen-year-old who had just secured his first serious race in single-seaters talking about being relaxed at the front of the field, and such an attitude was often mistaken for arrogance. Even if it were, it would not be misplaced given his talent level. In truth though, Max was relaxed at this level because he had been so meticulously and effectively prepared for this. Some kids might have been intimidated by a historic circuit complex like Hockenheim. Not Max. He had been running and cycling around Formula One paddocks since he was three. Some might have been overwhelmed by the information being thrown at them in a new car with complicated electronics. Not Max. He had been talking to engineers and drivers for as long as he could talk. And some might have started to doubt themselves, when faced with critics who suggest they are too young to compete at this level, but not Max. He had all the proof that he was good enough, and an unshakeable self-belief that it would go on, and on, and on. It seemed appropriate too that the man drenching him in champagne on the podium was Frits van Amersfoort, the same man who did it to Jos twenty years before.

Jos continued to brief privately and publicly that this is 'a learning year', sticking to the traditional path for drivers who want to move through the ranks with two years in each series, one to learn the car and one to challenge for the title, and the early part of the summer brought Team Verstappen down to earth with a bump after his first victory. Ocon was already proving a worthy rival and outdrove him in qualifying on the tricky street circuit in Pau. Street circuits remain something of an unknown quantity to Max, barring a couple of go-kart races in Las Vegas, and while he was close to Ocon and impressed with his ability to push the car to the limit round the extremely tight track, the runaway championship leader was faster. Verstappen managed a podium in the first race, but it went sharply downhill from there. A wet second race started behind the safety car and eleven laps in, Max spun into the barrier from third position. In the drier third race, he got away quickly off the line and pole-sitter Ocon rushed across to defend, clipping his front wing, damage that would lead to his hitting the tyre barriers and retiring in anger again. Ocon insisted he didn't see him but Max, feeling wronged, could not contain his frustration.

'I was already next to his front wing and tyres,' he said of a man who would incur his wrath many times more.

'The rules say you must leave a car's width of space, but he just turned into me.'

A day of testing in Germany helped blow away the anger but his frustration was only compounded in Hungary when he recorded a third straight retirement, this time with a clutch problem. A problem of his own making when he ran wide off the track earned him a drive-through penalty in the second race and by the end of the weekend he had lost more significant ground in the title race. Ocon had won two of the races and finished second in the other to take his total to 232 points. Max had just 80 and was fifth in the standings despite showing pace that suggested he was capable of far more.

What he did not know was that the next few weeks would be the most defining and impactful period of Max's teenage years. Across two race weekends – one in Belgium and one in Germany – he would win every single race and finally convince the F1 teams who had been quietly watching in the shadows and casually chatting to his management that it was time to pull the trigger.

'In Belgium, everything came together: three races, three victories,' Max said a few years later, picking the wins at Spa as one of his favourite ever weekends in racing.

'Moreover, I had a lot of good fights on the track, and I was able to learn a lot from them.'

It should be noted that Verstappen's teammate Gustavo Menezes also ran well at Spa, finishing on the podium with Max twice and finishing sixth in the other race. The low-drag set-up at the high-speed Belgian track was giving them enough pace to stay with and beat the likes of Prema Powerteam, whose drivers Ocon and Fuoco were both ahead of Verstappen in the title race. The fightback started at the top of Eau Rouge when Max challenged for the lead, taking it at the end of the Kemmel straight that just a few years later would be lined with thousands of Oranje chanting his name. Friends and family celebrated in the garage, having made the short trip south to watch him. His rivals clashed and Ocon retired with damage. Ferrari junior Fuoco could not keep up, Red Bull junior Tom Blomqvist was nowhere, and 2013 runner-up Felix Rosenqvist was battling in the midfield. A late safety car once again reduced his lead to nothing but he held off Lucas Auer to claim a second win of his season.

The most impressive drive though came in the third race, when he started from fifth. Once again, he was near-perfect off the line and on one of the shorter runs down to Turn One, known as La Source at Spa, he positioned himself on the inside, praying the gap would open, and indeed it did. Within a few hundred metres of the race starting he was up to third and chasing down the leaders, Ocon and Swede John Bryant-Meisner. A lap later, he slipstreamed his way up to the back of the duelling pair and for the second time in a couple of minutes, Verstappen took two places in one corner. 'Overtaking is an art,' boasted two banners in the relatively sparsely populated stands at Spa. One bore Jos' name, one bore Max's. The younger artist wasn't done yet either. From second position, Ocon could use the slipstream of the

Kemmel straight and twice got ahead of him before the corner. Twice, Verstappen fought back at the corner, once steaming down the inside and on lap four swooping around the outside.

Because of the nature of the track, and just as he had in the second race, he was not able to pull clear of Ocon in second. He would extend his lead in the middle sector of the lap but the enormous straights at the beginning and end would allow the Frenchman to close up again. Even if he had been able to break that tow, he would have been reined in again by yet another safety car. When it pulled into the pit lane with five minutes of racing remaining, Verstappen was in control of the pace.

Safety car restarts are a delicate skill. The leader is never more vulnerable than just as the race starts again, and at Spa, where the slipstream is so powerful, being within as much as a half a second starting the Kemmel straight is enough to make a pass stick. Verstappen backs the field up as far as he can, slowing almost to a stop before slamming on the accelerator and trying to catch Ocon off guard. In the space of just four corners, he has pulled out enough of a gap to prevent the Prema getting past him on the straight. Ocon would only have three more chances to make the same move, while one mistake from Verstappen at any point in the lap would give him enough of an opportunity to close up, wait and make it stick. That mistake never came. Max drove flawlessly to the end and completed the perfect weekend at what was as good as his home track.

It was an impressive set of performances and an exhibition in overtaking, but the Van Amersfoort package had been strong and Spa, in an F3 car, is a place where overtaking is very possible. A week later, his dominance would be even more convincing.

The F3 European circus rolled out of town in Spa to Nuremberg and a unique little circuit, part street, part concrete military parade ground, with a start-finish straight in front of a huge, sandstone grandstand with a dark past; it was the venue for the infamous Nuremberg rallies.

It has since been repurposed as the Norisring and has been used as a racetrack since the late 1940s. The circuit itself is just 1.4 miles long and features technically eight corners, although several are more kinks than braking events. There was not much to it, and little opportunity to make a difference as a driver. In qualifying, the whole field was covered by less than a second, making what followed all the more remarkable. The first race was fairly straightforward, Max utilising the hairpin to great effect to fight up from fifth and claim the win despite multiple safety cars. When the rain came ahead of race two though, he really shone. The race started in mixed conditions, with a dry racing line on the street but damp patches everywhere on a circuit already low on grip. It was reminiscent of Max's karting race in Eindhoven, one his father had not let him forget in a hurry, when he hit a damp patch he had not noticed and skidded off the track.

In Nuremberg, the race was stopped eighteen laps in with Verstappen having retained his lead as the rain began to fall again. As he led the restart, he would have to contend with the fact that all the cars behind him would have slipstream advantage while he had to punch a hole in the air himself. Nevertheless, he was relishing the moisture. The safety car was the only thing that could stop him, as it did repeatedly, and yet after every restart he was instantly able to build a gap to the car behind. Had the race not been stopped so many times, he might have started lapping the field, such was the ease with which he would pull out a gap. From his first pole, he eventually won his fifth straight race. The track began to dry out in the afternoon, but it made no difference. Ocon could not hold a candle to Max's pace. After his early-season mistakes and mechanical issues, 150 points over two weekends closed the gap at the top of the title race to 74. He was still a long way off, but a message had been sent. Whatever gremlins Verstappen and Van Amersfoort had encountered in the early season were gone; this was no longer a learning year, it was a winning year.

9

RED BULL WIN THE RACE FOR MAX

Dr Helmut Marko first met Max Verstappen when he was fifteen years old.

'I usually talk to a driver for about twenty minutes to get a picture of his personality and the whole story, but with Max I sat for an hour and a half,' Marko said in a 2016 interview with German newspaper *Bild*.

'He was a young body, but with a mind that was certainly three to five years ahead. Now his development has slowly levelled off and his age and maturity have come together. And it's far above average.

'[His promotion through the racing ranks] was a daring step and also a not insignificant risk.

'But I saw what maturity he had and how much he had learned in his karting time, and with what commitment he approached his racing.'

If you want to succeed at Red Bull, Marko is the first, and perhaps the only, man you need to impress, and Max managed that from the off.

Marko had been a racer himself. He had grown up with Jochen Rindt, a fellow Austrian who won the 1970 F1 world title posthumously, having been killed in a high-speed crash at Monza. Marko had also raced in F1; in a macabre twist that was typical of the era, he was offered a seat at Rindt's funeral. He only raced ten Grands Prix though before losing his left eye when a stone went through his visor at the 1972 French Grand Prix.

He had by that point though won the 24 Hours of Le Mans for Martini in a Porsche 917 and become a doctor of law; he was well placed to move into an off-track career in motorsport management. He worked with a number of Austrian drivers including Gerhard Berger, through whom Marko came into contact with Dietrich Mateschitz, an Austrian toothpaste salesman who was marketing a new drink known in Thailand as Red Gaur. He changed the recipe and renamed the European version 'Red Bull'. Berger was an early ambassador.

Marko had entered his own cars in races, often driven by his Austrian protégés, since the late 1970s but formed his own team to race in junior formulae, RSM Marko, in the 1980s and Berger was one of its early success stories. The empire continued to grow – Marko opened two successful hotels in Graz as well – and by the mid-1990s, RSM Marko had one of the fastest cars in Formula 3000 and young drivers were fighting over seats, as much for Marko's guidance and commercial contacts as the chance to drive a car with title-winning potential. Eventually, Marko convinced Mateschitz to take a more active role in the team, renaming it the Red Bull Junior Team and using it as a feeder for the Sauber F1 team he had purchased back in 1994. However, that created irresolvable political problems at Sauber; Marko's efforts to force Brazil's Enrique Bernoldi upon Sauber in 2001, and Mateschitz's attempt to back that campaign, did not sit well with Peter Sauber and the partnership broke down. When Red Bull finally did enter F1 as their own entity, it was by buying out the ailing Jaguar outfit in 2004.

By that point, the roster of Red Bull drivers had grown to double figures, and they subsequently bought Minardi too, which they renamed Toro Rosso and used as their own junior team in F1. It would prove crucial to the junior programme, in which Marko had already enrolled what he saw as their first star: Sebastian Vettel.

The German was already a Red Bull Junior Team member of some description but Marko did not get his name on the contract until 2004, when he won the Formula BMW ADAC championship at an absolute canter, winning eighteen of the twenty races. At Hockenheim for the final race of the season, Marko got the seventeen-year-old to put pen to paper. Marko promoted him to F3 where he struggled for the first half of the season.

'The second half was good after quite heavy changes in the team at Sebastian's demand. This showed a lot about his attitude,' Marko said. Famously the straightest talker in F1, it is easy to see what sort of characters tended to catch his eye. His harsh boarding school upbringing had fostered a fiercely independent young man who matured into a manager who did not suffer fools gladly. Win his respect the right way though, and he would back you to the hilt.

He added: '[Vettel] always knew that driving is only part of motor racing and that if you do not have the right knowledge, and the right support of other people, then you will not be a regular winner.'

The similarities with Max are clear to see. When Verstappen Sr picked up the phone and it was Marko on the other end, he was speaking to the man who had guided Vettel from karting to F1 to four world titles in four years. They knew each other well too, having first met at Red Bull headquarters five years previously. Marko was always keen to scout out new talent and Jos was on the ground every week watching it. Further down the line, he would hire Jos to keep a lookout for new drivers coming up the ranks.

Marko was not the only one frantically fishing out Jos' number though. Ferrari were well aware of what he could do. The Prema mechanics had watched first hand as he learned the ropes in Florida and then, knowing how good Esteban Ocon was and how the Frenchman had two more years of car racing under his belt, they had watched Verstappen grow exponentially into the European Formula Three series which he had started to dominate over the summer. Antonio Fuoco, already a member of the Ferrari Driver Academy, had barely figured in the title battle that was quickly becoming a two-horse race, if the Italian team needed any more proof of Verstappen's pace. They had already signalled their intentions of picking up the series champion too.

'The Ferrari Driver Academy is firmly convinced that a Formula Three car, due to the special balance between grip and power, is an excellent car for any driver to drive in a single-seater to learn,' said Luca Baldisserri, the head of the programme who had personally called Max to invite him to the winter series. He did a deal in April to offer the champion of European Formula Three a testing day in a Ferrari F1 car, perhaps hoping or even believing it would be Max. He left too much to chance.

Eric Boullier too, who had already signed Ocon, wanted to include Verstappen in his stable at Lotus but had left the team to join McLaren at the beginning of the year. Mercedes meanwhile had only just returned to F1 in 2009 and had yet to establish their driver development programme in earnest. Pascal Wehrlein signed later in the year as a reserve driver, but they did not believe they could support the teenage Verstappen in the right way.

'At the time, we had no facilities, no structure for juniors. The focus was still on Mercedes winning races and championships as a team. It was still very fresh for us,' Mercedes boss Toto Wolff said.

'You know, of course, we want "the next Max". A few are already coming through our training programme, I tell you. But the only real Max Verstappen just came too soon for us.'

It is of course a convenient excuse further down the line to claim that you 'weren't interested anyway' having missed out on a generational talent, and media at the time reported that Mercedes were actively pursuing Verstappen. One Italian magazine even splashed a story that he had in fact chosen to reject Red Bull's advances and join Mercedes instead, a story that very quickly proved to be an exaggeration at best. There had been talks with Mercedes since the beginning of Max's F3 season, although about 'nothing specific'.

'They wanted to just talk with me about what we wanted to do in the future,' Max said in one of his first interviews as an F1 driver, talking to website F1i.

Had Mercedes taken on Verstappen, he would have been promoted to GP2 with Mercedes already having signed Lewis Hamilton and Nico Rosberg expected to extend his deal. With such talent readily available to them, it would have been a significant risk to take on the teenage Verstappen, and they would surely have placed him into a cooperative GP2 team. It would have been a logical and more orthodox step for a young driver impressing in his first year of single-seaters. Red Bull though, as a brand and as a racing team, had not been successful by doing the orthodox or the expected. They wanted to be bold – and they were.

The call came the day after Max's Norisring exploits. Internally, the teenager had recognised that six straight wins, across two very different circuits, might be a handy piece of evidence to present to a future team, that the results might open some doors, but he was still not thinking about F1. No more than usual, anyway. There were lots of thoughts buzzing around his head though. He and Jos drove back from Nuremberg that night discussing whether it would be worth staying in F3 for a second season, as had been the plan, if they finished second or third in the championship.

Max added to F1i: 'We already were a bit "What do we have to do?" And the other thing was we had to find a budget, which already wasn't easy in F3.'

With no obvious answer to these questions, they arrived home late, pleased but exhausted. It had been a successful but draining ten days at Spa and then in Germany. Early next morning, the phone rang. It was Dr Marko (he always rings early). They had first spoken specifically about promoting Max in May at the Monaco Grand Prix. Marko had watched every F3 event since and the second race in Nuremberg had been the final straw. He could not wait any longer.

'It was a surprise how quickly he adapted to Formula Three,' Marko said later. 'The moment I thought [he was] something really special was at the Norisring. In mixed conditions – it was more wet than dry – he was per lap over two seconds faster than anyone else.'

Franz Tost had been watching too, the team principal of Toro Rosso, and liked what he was seeing. They had already fast-tracked one teenager into the Red Bull sister team and Daniil

Kvyat had finished in the points in three of his first four F1 races. Naturally, he had more racing experience than Max but not, they thought, as much talent. They had already broken the record for the youngest ever points scorer once, so why not do it again? Marko the straight talker is unlikely to have beaten around the bush in that first phone call, but he recalls that when he said, after some internal wrangling of his own, that Red Bull wanted to take Max straight to Formula One, he was met with a lengthy silence on the other end of the phone.

'Jos? Jos? ... Jos?' Marko said. He joked later that he thought Jos might not be fully awake.

It is slightly surprising that the short-tempered Austrian did not simply hang up the phone, but less surprising that he called at an odd time of day. Another of his young drivers Daniil Kvyat recalled a less pleasant early-morning chat during a 2019 press conference.

'It was raining once at testing and I was three or four seconds off,' Kvyat said. 'He called me at 7am and said: "So, you are quite useless in the wet," and then just hung up on me. He's always tough on you but he's always right.'

Sitting next to him, Max smiles in recognition. He had the luxury of never having enraged Marko to the point of being dropped of course, allowing a little more rose tint to his glasses.

'He took the gamble of putting me in a Toro Rosso when I was still very young,' Verstappen said when asked to follow Kvyat's story. 'He's a real racer and he has a good eye of what is happening at his age, which is quite impressive to see that still. It's also no-nonsense.

'He prefers when you come up to him and tell him honestly if you made a mistake or if something went wrong, rather than make up a whole story. Then he doesn't appreciate it.

'But basically I grew up like that because my dad was the same or maybe even worse than that.'

Clearly, Jos and Helmut were cut from the same cloth, but you can imagine the turmoil that Jos must have been going through. While he had done everything in his power to prepare Max, and seen him take it all in his stride, he must have remembered those weeks when it was Huub's phone ringing in the early 1990s after a sensational performance of his own, and how much he regretted jumping into a Benetton seat so quickly, flattered by the two-year deal presented by Flavio Briatore and the chance to drive in one of the grid's best cars.

How could he in good faith advise his son to effectively do the same, at an even younger age, now that all F1's top teams were starting to call? Jos had some soul-searching to do.

He rang Max's mother and said: 'Sophie, they want Max.'

'Act normal, you're joking,' she replied. He wasn't.

In the meantime, Max had to keep racing. After back-to-back weekends, the F3 championship had a week off but the Verstappen schedule had been filled. He had agreed some time ago to head to Zandvoort and race on Dutch soil in the F3 Masters. It had previously been known as the Marlboro Masters when cigarette sponsorship was one of the big cash cows in motor sport, and in 1993 had been won by none other than Jos Verstappen. On a real driver's circuit like Zandvoort, it is still cited as a feather in the cap of anyone to have won it. More recently, Lewis Hamilton, Nico Hülkenberg, Jules Bianchi and Valtteri Bottas had all triumphed there.

With the hype around Max's name growing by the minute and high-quality motor racing in Holland a rarity, the famous dunes of Zandvoort were busy with spectators, despite the northern European weather intervening. The track was beaten and blown by fearsome conditions, with the wind more of a challenge than the rain. The grandstand was full though, under cover and sheltered partially from the wind. Even regulars at the Masters noticed there was an added excitement in the air thanks to Max's presence. A pre-race downpour, like that second race at the Norisring, left the track part wet, part dry. Treacherous, Marko had called it in Germany, and Zandvoort is a difficult track to drive on a good day. Max thought nothing of it and relished the conditions. Having dominated practice and qualifying, he led the eleven-car field from start to finish. His drive was so comprehensive that the 2015 winner, Motopark's Markus Pommer, used his data as a blueprint to take victory twelve months later.

In the aftermath, team boss Timo Rumpfkeil, who was the first person to give Max an F3 test, says what everyone is thinking.

'Max rarely makes a mistake. And if he makes a mistake, he knows how to correct it and not make it again,' Rumpfkeil says. 'His talent, skills, mastery of the car and racing art are without a doubt of an exceptional level. When I compare Max to drivers who have made it to Formula One and DTM, our internal benchmark is always Valtteri Bottas. He is one of the top drivers in F1 for me. I scale Max on the same level in terms of skills and talent. I therefore foresee a bright future for Max in Formula One.'

Timo likely knew exactly what was going on behind the scenes, but was discreet enough to stay away from specifics. After all, driver contracts are delicate things and Max had yet to solidify his future. The Zandvoort drive was handily timed though, just in case Marko or Tost were having second thoughts about signing a sixteen-year-old. He had now won seven races on the bounce.

In the background, details were being figured out between Jos Verstappen, Raymond Vermeulen, Dr Helmut Marko and Franz Tost. From the start there was no question that Red Bull would take Max on as a junior and parachute him into GP2, but that did not mean that Team Verstappen were going to sign on the line without considering everything in front of them. They had the luxury of choice and time, but Red Bull were able to offer them so much more in terms of driving opportunity by virtue of their junior team Toro Rosso.

Max headed to Russia for the latest round of the championship to race on another track new to him, the Moscow Raceway, and a circuit that looked unlikely to suit the Van Amersfoort car. Ocon had been there before in Formula Renault 2.0 and his experience showed as he broke Max's winning streak in race one, although Verstappen did log the fastest lap of the race. He was forced to retire from race two and was beaten again in race three, although not without a fight as the safety car came in with a single lap remaining. Verstappen overtook Ocon on the start-finish straight but then lost the position again in the first corner and could not claim it back, leaving him to be content with a second, a third and a retirement from the weekend. After six straight Verstappen victories, Ocon had notched three of his own and even with four race weekends to go, overhauling the lead of now 116 points seemed unlikely.

'After this difficult weekend in Moscow, I want to win again in Austria,' Max said. 'The Red Bull Ring is driven with medium downforce, which should suit us. During the test days earlier this year it also went well and I think we have a good chance.'

There was another reason to want to win in Austria. It was the home track of the team he was beginning to believe would be his new employers. Jos and Max had attended the German

Grand Prix at Hockenheim and held further talks on a rare weekend 'off'. The F3 event in Austria would coincide with the F1 summer break too, so Mateschitz, Marko and Tost and the eyes of the world would all be watching, albeit many with their minds already made up.

Unfortunately for Max his optimism had been misplaced. Desperate to get past pole-sitter Ocon at the notoriously narrow first corner of the Red Bull Ring, he collided with the Frenchman, who he claimed had not left him any space. The stewards disagreed and handed him a time penalty that demoted him from third to fifth. They would again call him up after race three too for an audacious move on Antonio Fuoco. 'Ridiculous,' he called the decision, as it sent him out of the points and left him with a meagre haul from the weekend. Away from the racing, Team Verstappen had been busy. Trying not to distract Max from the task at hand, Jos and Raymond were up at six in the morning that weekend reviewing documents with Dr Marko. Jos was waking up at half four every morning because his mind was racing.

A week later Max was back in Austria with Jos and Raymond. They had flown down to Graz the night before a typically early morning meeting with Marko. Just as he had the night before Max's first test at Pembrey, Jos sat up with a friend, Raymond taking Frits' place as confidant this time, and turned things over in his mind. 'We will see,' they had said that night, trying not to heap too much expectation on the day that lay ahead. This time, it felt more seminal.

'That moment gave us goosebumps,' Raymond said of that night as they talked about what they were about to do.

The next day, with a taxi ride at five in the morning to meet his new boss, Max began his F1 journey.

Initially, he was only announced as a member of the Red Bull junior team. He would continue racing for Van Amersfoort, albeit in a Red Bull livery, and in November he would drive the Macau Grand Prix, another F3 race. The reason for the delay was a practical one: Max was still only sixteen and could not sign a Formula One contract on his own, or even with only one parent present. He would need both Jos and Sophie to sign off on it. There were other moving parts too with Red Bull also considering promoting junior driver Carlos Sainz Jr, possibly loaning him to backmarkers Caterham for the year.

There was a hope too that by incrementally announcing Max's accession they might be able to deflate or offset the inevitable excitement, perhaps let their teenager's eyes adjust to the glare of the limelight. It was futile. If anything, it only created a crescendo that ended with his Toro Rosso contract being leaked in the Dutch media. Suddenly Pandora's box was open and the media, fans and critics came flooding out.

After the meeting with Marko, they headed to the Red Bull Ring for some publicity shots and filming. Max drove a Red Bull-branded Formula Renault 3.5, although the wet conditions, in contrast to the 30-degree heat he had endured ten days before in his F3 car, meant times were not particularly representative.

Initially, the comments about Verstappen, Red Bull's latest junior, were relatively generous. The expectation in the public sphere was that they would put him in a GP2 team and get him some mileage in an F1 car through testing and Friday practice sessions. Still, no one quite saw what was coming.

The F1 contract was being signed at Düsseldorf Airport with Sophie, Jos, Max and his sister Victoria all present, drinking coffee with Raymond Vermeulen, giddy with caffeine and excitement. Jos still has pictures of that day on his phone. It was an incredibly proud moment and the result of a lengthy thought and legal process. Was Jos allowing his son to make the same mistake he had by taking too much too soon?

'I wasn't ready for my first F1 drive but I knew Max was,' Jos said in a 2019 podcast appearance.

'The raw speed, the maturity he has and also to be honest it's the way Red Bull picked him up and trained him, put him in the simulator. They really put all their efforts into making him a success.

'Helmut offered us a seat with Toro Rosso. It's so difficult to get into Formula One so when he offered that I said: 'Okay, but we don't do it for one year, we do it for two years. First year we learn, and we do a proper job.'

On 13 August, *De Telegraaf* in Holland broke the story that Max would be driving for Toro Rosso in 2015, based on a source inside the team. He would be the youngest driver in F1 history by several years. In fact, *De Telegraaf* had jumped the gun and the final contract had not yet been signed, but it was a mere formality, and when the news was confirmed five days later, a national and international conversation had already been triggered about whether it was the right move. In some ways, it was a PR war. Anyone who had met Max or raced against him tended to believe he was in fact ready. His Toro Rosso team boss Franz Tost later described him as having the racing brain of a driver in his twenties the first time he met him. On the day of the announcement, he called the Dutchman 'one of the most skilled young drivers of the new generation and we believe he has the necessary maturity and mental strength to take on this challenge successfully'.

Tost added: 'Bearing in mind that Scuderia Toro Rosso was created with the aim of bringing young talent from the Red Bull

Junior Team into Formula One and to educate them, it will now be up to us to provide Max with a competitive car, which will enable him to have the best possible start to his Formula One career.'

The doubters came thick and fast. Particularly damning was the judgment of the FIA president Jean Todt, someone who could provide genuine impediment to Max's career. 'Personally, I do think he is too young,' he said.

Former world champion Jacques Villeneuve complained that 'he is still a boy so it is very risky, while another former winner in Damon Hill had concerns about the damage the move could do.

'For his sake I hope that he hasn't been accelerated up to that level too quickly, because that can set you back for a very long time if you're not careful,' Hill said.

Marko did not have the same fear of the hype train that Hill or Jos had, and also felt forced to defend his decision to put Verstappen, who would be seventeen years and 166 days old when he made his debut in Australia, in an F1 car. Of course, he did not hold back. He was asked to compare Max to another F1 driver, if he could.

'Most likely Ayrton Senna,' Marko said.

'He [Verstappen] is an exceptional talent that comes along only once in decades. You must not look at his age. He has been talking with people who are experts when it comes to the development of youngsters and they all say that [in terms of] his mind he is more like 22 than sixteen.

'Regarding his skills behind the steering wheel, he has been racing since he was four years old – professionally. So we expect him to be competitive from the first race.'

Jos' allies in Holland closed ranks. Giedo van der Garde, a close friend of the Verstappens and then a test driver at Sauber, seemed to sit on the fence.

'Personally, I think seventeen is very young, but some just mature earlier than others,' Van der Garde said. 'When I look at myself, I was absolutely not ready for Formula One. Of course, it helps that his father Jos was in Formula One and knows exactly how everything works.'

Another former Dutch racing driver Jan Lammers added: 'At the age of four, Max was already in a kart and the transition from Formula Three to Formula One is not illogical. Alain Prost, Kimi Raikkonen and I – we all did it. No one should forget that Max is a talent of the highest quality.'

Former McLaren and F1 PR executive Tony Jardine warned Verstappen would 'not be welcomed' in the paddock, although the initial reaction of the drivers seemed to suggest otherwise. Felipe Massa at Williams said it showed that 'teams are still interested in the talent of the driver and not the money', although he did concede that seventeen seemed a bit young. Romain Grosjean at Lotus called it 'a wonderful opportunity' and 'good to see fresh blood' but, like Massa, he added a caveat: 'He will have a lot of homework to do.' Even Jean-Eric Vergne, the largely blameless Toro Rosso incumbent Max would be replacing, found it hard to hack up much bile.

'I understand the decision,' the Frenchman said. 'I'm not pissed off. I'm a little bit sad obviously because I like the team and believe it is a good one.'

Privately, Vergne was much more frustrated. He was pissed off, although he was too sensible to say so in public.

'It's pointless to be angry – or if I do have some anger, I will put it behind the wheel and make a show!' he said, keen to earn a drive elsewhere on the grid for 2015.

The Verstappen announcement had come eleven races into Vergne's third season with the team; he had only finished six of them, but the retirements were almost exclusively down to mechanical failures on the car. When he had completed races, he had scored points three times, was narrowly out-qualifying his teammate Daniil Kvyat and had a lead over him in the Drivers' Championship too. He had beaten his previous teammate Daniel Ricciardo as often as he had lost to him. Vergne had not done a lot wrong and had every right to raise his fist to the sky and curse the cruel Formula One fates for putting him in the path of both Verstappen and Sainz, because even the installation of Verstappen did not necessarily mean the end for Vergne. Kvyat had earned a promotion to the senior team, which in theory would be filled by Verstappen, and the Dutchman was in fact keen to have Vergne at his side.

'It is important to keep Jean-Eric; I think it will be a big help,' he said, already showing a propensity to speak his own mind while the party line was likely to be 'no comment'.

'He has experience with the tyres already so he can help me a lot with that. Where I'm at with the tyres, if you have someone like Jean-Eric for sure they will help – not only for one race but I think the whole season. I think it is a win-win situation for me and the team.'

Toro Rosso were weighing up their options. Vergne had three rookies for competition: Sainz, Pierre Gasly and Alex Lynn, all of whom were impressing in the junior formulae. Vergne had watched all their progress fairly closely, but of course Verstappen had attracted the most attention.

'I heard about him you know in karting, in Formula Three. Obviously I was the first one interested to know about what he was going to do next in Formula One because it was my seat!' Vergne says from his roomy apartment in Paris, with the benefit of hindsight and now two Formula E world titles 'dans la poche' to soften the blow six years later.

'I'm okay with [him getting my seat]. He is an amazing driver and I would much rather have had him taking my place than another one that would have gone from Toro Rosso to nowhere in two years.'

Would he have had such a level-headed response in the weeks and months after being dropped?

'I was not the same driver at the time [as I am now]. I didn't have the same mentality either,' Vergne admits.

'But, when Kvyat left, I still had this seat next to me but then Helmut decided on the rise [of another rookie]. You can argue it was messed up but things happen for a reason. I'm very happy where I am.

'I was very impressed with his first season – and since then, he has been very impressive.'

The decision to pick Sainz over Vergne did not come until very late. Toro Rosso confirmed the Spaniard's elevation to the team after the end of the 2014 season, perhaps wishing to give Vergne as much time as possible to prove himself, although it is more likely that they were choosing between the three rookies: Vergne could not teach them much they did not already know in the last six months of his three-year contract.

It meant Toro Rosso would have the youngest driver line-up in F1 history with Verstappen at seventeen and Sainz yet to turn 21. The questions about Verstappen being too young to drive in F1 – or, for that matter, on public roads – would only intensify.

'If you are announced as the youngest Formula One driver ever, you can expect that criticism. I had also prepared for that,' Max says. 'I don't care about that criticism; everyone has their own opinion, fine. It really doesn't bother me. We will see how it turns out next year.'

The only way he could truly refute them was to succeed on the track.

10

TEAMMATE STRUGGLES

Even before Max made his F1 debut in Melbourne, there were some hairy moments that might have left those who had put their faith in him questioning the sanity of their decision. There is a reason that car insurance for teenage boys is so expensive, after all.

When Max's F1 promotion was announced, everyone in Holland was excited, but perhaps none more so than the organisers of VKV City Racing, the motor-sport event in Rotterdam. They had appointed Jos on the board earlier that year and in 2013 Max had taken part, speeding his go-kart up and down the streets of the Dutch city. Initially, they fear that his new employers might wrap him up in cotton wool and take immediate control of all his media appearances. Instead, they were given an even greater gift than Max's presence: he would drive his new F1 car in public for the first time in Rotterdam. Gift is perhaps the wrong word. Without the sponsorship of the car leasing company VKV, Max probably could not have driven in Formula Three at all. This was part of the Verstappens' efforts to repay some of that faith.

It would not quite be his first time in an F1 car. A few days before the late August event, he headed to Rockingham in the East Midlands, just outside Corby, to learn the Toro Rosso's set-up. There was plenty to learn too. The average F1 steering wheel has more than twenty different switches and buttons on the front which allow the driver to activate hundreds of different modes and settings. Then there is the dual clutch paddle system, the start procedure and the fact that this car is more powerful and faster than anything Max has experienced before. Max is a fast learner and always has been, but this would be a big ask.

When the day finally arrives, Max is already exhausted. He had barely been home in the last month, with flights all over Europe, racing in F3, signing contracts, seat fitting, testing, fulfilling media requirements and doing more interviews in a few short weeks than he had in his whole life. Nevertheless, he impresses. He connects with engineers and the media are baffled as to how a sixteen-year-old boy can handle the spotlight with such apparent ease, rebuffing difficult questions when they come and engaging with more positive ones. His father says that Max was always watching the way he dealt with the media and learned it that way. Many would say that Max was already far better than Jos had ever been.

On the day, the streets of Rotterdam are packed with fans trying to catch a peak of Max in an F1 car for the first time. The engine echoes off the walls of the Maritime Museum and the Allianz building as Max does doughnuts and spins up the tyres on the closed intersection of Coolsingel and Westblaak. He had driven the car sedately across the Erasmus Bridge just down the road the previous day in a PR stunt, but now got the chance to show off and was relishing it. All of his friends would be so jealous. They could not even drive themselves to the shops yet here he was producing billows of tyre smoke in the middle of Rotterdam. He tears off again at full throttle up and down the mini-street circuit they have set up before returning to the square for a few more doughnuts. Then he gets stuck. At low speeds, F1 cars are notoriously difficult to turn and he loses momentum, finding himself stationary, facing the barrier. He cannot engage reverse gear, and so he waves a few stewards on to push him back. He tries to resume his exhibition, but once again finds himself going slowly towards a barrier, so slowly that the anti-stall system kicks in and Max is caught off guard, unable to use the throttle to get himself out of trouble. He steers left to avoid it, but these cars do not turn well at 30 miles an hour and Max hits the wall. His front wing breaks and again the stewards have to push him free. The crowd giggle, jeer and then break out into applause, perhaps out of sympathy. He's only a kid, after all.

Afterwards, he admitted fault, but tried to brush the incident off with the media vultures already circling. Phrases like 'embarrassing' and 'red-faced' are used. One outlet rather cruelly suggested that Max 'Vercrashen' Jr was at least upholding the family name.

'Twice it went fantastically, one time there was a mistake,' he told *De Telegraaf*.

'It's a learning process. But after everything, this is what I've always wanted – to drive a Formula One car.'

Just a month later, Max was due to make his F1 debut in a Friday morning practice session at the Japanese Grand Prix. The Toro Rosso mechanics may have packed a couple of extra front wings, just in case.

There was better news for his father though. Jos' second wife Kelly safely gave birth to the couple's first child, a daughter they named Blue Jaye, just days after the VKV City Racing event. He had a few weeks to enjoy his third child's company before he flew with Max to Japan, much as he had when Max himself was born. Max had the chance to get to know his new half-sister a little too, despite his hectic new schedule, and still treats her with the same tenderness as he did Victoria. His new job will require him to discover a new hardiness, a boy in a man's world, but it seems he will never lose the instincts of the caring older brother he always was. He bought Blue Jaye a personalised, four-wheeled trike, in Red Bull livery of course. 'Never too early to let my little sister do some racing in-house,' he insists.

Father and son headed off to Japan and arrived on Monday. Max was due to drive the famous Suzuka circuit, in place of Jean-Eric Vergne, on Friday morning, but as yet he was not licensed to do so. Any driver needs a super licence to compete at an F1 World Championship weekend, even in a practice session, and the Verstappens were still waiting for the paperwork to come through, although there was no expectation of a problem. It was possible though that Max would simply be in the garage on a watching brief, as some believed he should have been. The complaints about him being too young were not just concerns, there were calls for review, and ultimately the opinion of Jean Todt triggered an FIA review of the qualifying conditions for a licence. They clearly felt that while they could not fail to grant Verstappen a super licence, they should not find themselves in the same situation again. Eric Boullier, then McLaren team boss but also involved for years in driver management, was one of those who supported a change in regulations – although not just because of his concerns about Verstappen's age.

'There are different problems. One is economic, in that some teams are selling Friday morning seats and are looking for some drivers who don't comply with the super licence rules,' Boullier said in October 2014.

'The other issue is that we have known for a few years that many series have appeared and there is not a clear path to F1.

'If you go to football, you have your academy and then you go to League 3, League 2 and League 1. Here we have different series and it is a bit confusing for drivers.

'So the super licence needs to be a little bit updated in the way it is given. Some series have disappeared, some series are still on, and the level of each series varies a lot.'

His words did not fall on deaf ears and the FIA acted fast. They could not, without appearing incredibly petty, change the regulations and stop Max competing in 2015, but they could make sure no one as young as him ever could again. They announced that from the beginning of 2016, super licence applicants would need to be eighteen or over and have at least two years of single-seating racing experience under their belt, along with a points system based on their success in those years, weighted to the faster series. In the meantime though, they could do nothing to stop Max Verstappen celebrating his seventeenth birthday in Japan, the day after receiving a super licence, having racked up the requisite 300 kilometres at a test in a 2012 F1 car in Italy in September. He would make his debut drive in a Formula One car at a race weekend, and at one of the most demanding tracks in the world, with a series of high-speed, high G-force corners making it a driver's favourite. It is also a gruelling track and Max's new fitness programme and neck-strengthening programme would get its first real test.

'He was still a kid arriving in a world where he wants to beat everybody, where he wants to destroy everybody and doesn't know yet how he's going to do that,' Vergne recalls of Max arriving in the paddock on that October morning.

'But of course he had something that very few drivers have.'

All the testing in the world could not have prepared Max to turn right out of the Suzuka garage and press the accelerator. His previous experiences, in Corby and Rotterdam, had been with a different generation of car from the current specification. This V6 hybrid engine was a different beast entirely.

'I almost couldn't keep up with the acceleration. I was so surprised that it was so quick,' Max said afterwards.

He tried to drive in what he called 'safe mode'. He could not win the championship or dispel any doubters in that first session, but he could certainly give them some ammunition and ruin the race weekend for Jean-Eric Vergne by crashing it. In his head, all Max was saying to himself was, 'How am I going to keep this on the road?' Fortunately for him, he did so, and some. In fact, by the end of his 22 laps of Suzuka, he had the twelfth fastest time and was only four tenths of a second off Daniil Kvyat and Sebastian Vettel, the beginning of his campaign to leave the doubters in his wake. His session was cut short by seven minutes as his Renault engine stopped him in a cloud of smoke. Despite that and the nerves of trying not to crash, Max was already looking forward to his next chance to drive the car a month later in Austin.

In the meantime, his unlikely pursuit of Esteban Ocon and a European F3 title with which to bid goodbye to his brief time with Van Amersfoort Racing had slipped into the realms of the impossible after a retirement at Imola all but handed the season's spoils to Ocon. The early-season technical problems, and a couple of rookie errors from Max himself, had left too much ground to make up on Prema's Ocon, a deserved title-winner who would battle Max in F1 in years to come. When they got to the final race of the season, he even got overhauled for second place by British driver Tom Blomqvist, but it hardly felt like it mattered. He secured ten race wins overall, a rookie season no one in Team Verstappen had dared hope for, and most importantly of all, he had a seat in F1 next year. He still had one more F3 assignment, the famous Macau Grand Prix, but his attention was predominantly focused on the start line in Melbourne next year.

As well as hours and hours on the simulator, Max was given two more practice sessions at race weekends, in Austin, Texas and at Interlagos in São Paulo. At the US Grand Prix he finished tenth fastest on Friday morning, although he is clocked at 99 kilometres an hour in the pit lane and picks up a fine of €1,000 for his troubles. The pit lane speed limit was 80.

He nearly comes a cropper in more spectacular fashion in Brazil. On the way down the hill in the last sector, he hits the accelerator a little too early and the sheer power of the engine sends the car into a spin. He starts to skid and is travelling sideways trying to regain control. Half a second later, he has caught it at the very last moment and gets it back in a straight line. On the pit wall, Jean-Eric Vergne mouths 'wow' before laughing to the engineers next to him about the close call. Team boss Franz Tost looks down in relief. Not only has Max just saved his mechanics a very busy lunch break, he must just have proved one or two things about his car control. Most drivers would have been picking bits of carbon fibre out of the tyre barrier while he was making his way up the start-finish straight for another lap.

His trip to Macau, where Max bagged the fastest lap in the main race but having started 24th due to an accident in qualifying can only finish a creditable seventh, was the beginning of a busy winter of preparation. There were award ceremonies and a couple of testing sessions, as well as the relentless physical work that Max now knew first hand was essential to cope with the G-forces of F1, but on the whole his preparation is in private. His new personal trainer Jake Aliker pushes him physically and his schedule, flying all over the world for tests, media days and glitzy dinners, where he is in high demand from those wanting to meet the new wonderkid, pushes him mentally. Still, he finds time to enjoy himself. The best drivers he can think of never abandoned go-karting and he still finds time to race a go-kart. In December, the Verstappen family have a bit of time together. Jos and Sophie have a civil enough relationship for divorced parents and are both at the Genk track to watch Max and Victoria, who has been learning the karting ropes as well, test the new Intrepid karts.

'I can learn a lot from driving behind Max. For example, how I can best take the corners and where the braking points are. Then we turned it around and Max drove after me to see if I'm doing it right,' Victoria says afterwards. Max may just have landed back in Europe from Qatar, but he still has time for his sister. Their relationship may not be as physically close as it once was, but the pair are still clearly tight-knit. At the end of the day, their parents take over for a few laps. While Max is the fastest, their times are all competitive. With Max's life about to change irreversibly, it's not clear if or when they will get the chance to do this again. The new year will bring new challenges.

The first new challenge was a driving theory test. In Belgium, the minimum age to earn a driving licence is eighteen but once Max had passed his theory, he was at least able to practise – under supervision – although he hated doing it. Even for the theory, which his mum forced him to take, he simply crammed for seven hours the night before and passed it in the morning. The media was filled with jokes that he is allowed to go over 300 kilometres an hour in his F1 car on his own, but is not even permitted to start the engine when he got home. There were physical tests too, although less formal ones. Every day would start with a two-hour gym session as his trainer tried to prepare his seventeen-year-old frame for what was to come at winter testing, consisting of two weeks of running in Barcelona. It was Max's first chance to drive long stints in the STR10, and to start to understand the Pirelli tyres. On the Friday of the first week, Max logged 139 laps and left the circuit feeling the effects. Lap times mean little on days like these – Felipe Nasr put his Sauber, a team that had not scored a single point the year before, third on the time sheets – but experience is everything, and 400 miles of running was extremely handy to have in the bank.

The Toro Rosso was not the fastest car on the grid but the chassis design was virtually identical to its parent team Red Bull, who have one of the best, designed by Adrian Newey, known as the most knowledgeable and inventive aerodynamicist in the sport. The engines the team purchase from Renault each year remained a concern, both on power and on reliability, and Max's last day of testing was hindered by a power unit change, but on tracks where downforce is a priority over power, Toro Rosso left Barcelona believing they would be able to pull off some good results, and their two youngsters were hungry to spring some surprises.

Jos' father still watched on from as close as Toro Rosso would let him. He was hardly likely to be tuning an engine any time soon, but he and Max debrief after every session and on some circuits Jos was happy to coach him about certain corners, having driven many of them in his own career. The cars have changed but on the whole the circuits have not, and Jos recalls in a *Telegraaf* column that while he had Huub Rothengatter trying to do the same for him, 'I didn't think Huub got it in terms of racing.' Jos noticed plenty of other differences in Max's experiences too, less in the car and more in the organisation of the team. For starters, the physical training was far more exhaustive than what he had undergone in the weeks before his own debut, sprung upon him after JJ Lehto broke his neck in a testing crash and upgrading him from test driver to full-time racer. Jos always felt he was not physically able to cope with his first season in F1, and was keen for his son to avoid the same pitfalls. Similarly, he always felt inferior; teammate Michael Schumacher did not even sleep in the same hotel as him, but 'at Toro Rosso, Max is central'.

He adds: 'The team will not compete for the world title, but in terms of organisation and professionalism it is really a top team.'

Unlike Marko, he was managing expectations for Melbourne. 'If he finishes, finishes before his teammate and gets a few points, I am satisfied.' Carlos Sainz Jr, although unlikely to have read the words, did not need to hear them to understand the challenge ahead of him. The first battle any F1 driver faces is against his teammate. Max had his first rival in Formula One.

Sainz was the next cab off the rank in Red Bull terms until they signed Verstappen to the junior programme, and his chance of a 2015 F1 drive looked to have evaporated a week later when he was overlooked and the Dutchman was signed by Toro Rosso. However, Sebastian Vettel's decision to leave Red Bull for Ferrari and the subsequent promotion of Daniil Kvyat gave him a second chance, and having won the Formula Renault 3.5 title, he leaped at it.

Nevertheless, as Jos says, 'Max is central' and when the F1 promoters picked six drivers for a press conference ahead of the race weekend, along with defending world champion Lewis Hamilton, Ferrari new boy Vettel and home driver Daniel Ricciardo, Verstappen was also chosen. Uncharacteristically, he was a little nervous, but he smiled his way through, giving shorter answers than usual, perhaps a little embarrassed, making the usually mature Max look more like a teenager again. He insists that the F1 paddock, sitting next to world champions, 'doesn't feel like anything new'.

True to his word, Verstappen looked entirely at home and Toro Rosso clearly had a strong package. That first challenge though, of beating Sainz, looked like a stiff one. Three years older than him and with four more years of car racing under his belt, the Spaniard flew out of the blocks and qualified eighth, beating Verstappen by about two tenths of a second on Saturday. On a track where overtaking is so difficult, it could be a decisive advantage. Verstappen though still started eleventh, and was ahead of Kvyat in the senior and theoretically much faster car. However, he was disappointed. A pain in his shoulder, he says, hampered his performance and forced a mistake that denied him a top ten spot. Points remained his target; the youngest ever driver to start a Grand Prix had not flown to Australia to make up the numbers.

Jos was, as usual, far more nervous. He did his best not to transmit the tension to his son, but just as he was in Emmen for the first kart race, grabbing on to the fence, or in the hotel in south Wales, staying up late worrying about the next day, or even when he woke up at 4am on the morning of Max's contract signing, Jos was anxious; more anxious even than when he himself raced in F1. Red Bull and Toro Rosso seemed to understand the importance of keeping him close, and also of making him feel involved. From a legal perspective, Max was not yet eighteen and Jos' presence was basically required, so it made sense for the team to keep him happy, especially given his fiery reputation. They would bounce ideas off him and talk to him about technical aspects of the car, but there was no suggestion that he was involved in the final decision-making process. F1 had evolved immeasurably since he last drove in the series, after all.

Nevertheless, he watched anxiously as Max, one of the best starters in junior racing, tried to get an F1 car off the line for the first time. He worked his way up to ninth on the harder, medium tyres while the front-runners burned through their soft rubber. By lap 33, when he finally pitted after an impressive stint conserving the tyres but still lapping quickly, he was sixth. After returning to the track in ninth, crucially ahead of his teammate who had lost time due to a wheel-gun failure, and still on course to break another record – the youngest driver ever to score points – Max panicked for the first time.

'Check the car because it's smoking I think. The engine sounds heavy,' he says to his team over the radio, his voice slightly cracking. It was an engine problem indeed and a terminal one. His race was over with no points to show for it. Jos could not contain his frustration, snatching his headphones off and storming out the back of the garage. Raymond Vermeulen stood motionless, the less hot-headed of Max's management pair. To add insult to injury, Max could not even drag his stricken car all the way into the pits. He parked up just short of the entry to the pit lane and had to walk the last few hundred yards back to the garage. His helmet hid his red face, but it also gave him time to think, to get his emotions in check. His father's first F1 race had ended in disappointment too, a huge four-car pile-up. Had it ended this way, with a mechanical failure beyond his control, he almost certainly would have been angrier. Max though always says he has some of his father and his mother in him. When he got as far as his post-race interview, he was actively smiling. A born and committed winner he may be, but he had also just fulfilled the first part of a lifelong dream and competed in a Grand Prix.

In some ways it also felt appropriate that he would now have the chance to pick up his first points instead in Malaysia, the track where he had first attended a race weekend, and where more of his friends and family could watch it together. The Australian Grand Prix had kicked off in the small hours of Sunday morning back in the Netherlands; the 9am start time for the Malaysian race was a little more palatable. His grandfather Frans was able to roll out the barrel and get the Verstappen fan club out in full voice. 'Max, Max, Max,' they chanted, just as they had his father's name. The expectations were just the same, perhaps even higher. Soon they would be shared around the world.

Malaysia was probably not a track Max was looking forward to. With its two long straights, the struggling Renault engine was unlikely to give them much grunt and the humidity, temperatures and high-speed corners always made the Sepang circuit one of the most physically challenging, certainly much worse than the autumnal street circuit in Melbourne. If Max prayed for anything, it would have been rain, to equalise some of the engine weaknesses and allow him to show off his wet-weather skills. Sure enough, it came on Saturday and he was able to produce a lap quick enough for sixth on the grid. The two senior Red Bulls were fourth and fifth ahead of him, while Sainz was back in fifteenth. It was a huge opportunity but Max also knew he would struggle to keep the likes of Felipe Massa in the Williams and the Ferrari of Kimi Raikkonen behind him. Seventh or eighth was achievable, he thought, a result that would still be historic.

Sure enough, Verstappen slipped backwards and out of the points in the early stages of Sunday's race, but eventually seemed to get his tyres up to temperature, executing textbook overtaking manoeuvres on Sergio Perez, Daniil Kvyat and brilliantly on Daniel Ricciardo, whom he gave just enough room but made it impossible for the Australian to come back at him. Eyebrows must have been raised on the Red Bull pit wall when they saw their junior drive overtake both their senior ones in the first twenty laps of the race. The only problem was that Sainz, having a fine race of his own, was running ahead of him – but he would soon take care of that. With seven laps to go, Verstappen pulled out of the slipstream to inspect the gap on the inside of Turn Three, only to move back in behind his teammate, seemingly happy to bide his time and wait until the next corner. Suddenly then, just before the braking point, he pulled out again and dived up the inside to claim seventh place. In the garage, the corner of Jos' mouth began to curl into a smile, but never cracked his face, because he knew what the team knew: Max's brakes were on their last legs on this circuit that hurts bodies and cars, and it could as easily be two retirements out of two as a first haul of points. Fortunately, Max nursed his car home to bag six points, beating his teammate and both Red Bull cars. There was one downside: he would now have to buy sister Victoria the Louis Vuitton bag he had promised her on the occasion of his first championship points. Max though was happy to do it. His team boss Franz Tost branded the 'stupid critics' well and truly 'gagged'. He was starting to cause ripples further up the team ladder too.

There was trouble at Milton Keynes before Toro Rosso started showing up their more experienced older brothers though. Vettel had walked away from the team at the end of 2014 out of frustration at the car's performance in the new era of hybrid engines.

'If things are not going well, I try to look at myself before I point fingers at others. It became clear that I wanted to do something new,' he said after joining Ferrari, subtly pointing a finger at the Renault engine suppliers. It looked to have been the right move when he won his first race of the hybrid era at Sepang, but it had also been an emotional one. Growing up in Germany, Michael Schumacher had been his hero and the events of 2014, when a skiing accident left the seven-time world champion in a coma for months, had brought things into sharp focus. Now, standing on the podium listening to the German national anthem followed by the Italian one, practically the theme tune for F1 in the 2000s, it felt right. He was another who had been criticised for being so young when he started F1, another whom Dr Helmut Marko had met as a youngster and kept an eye on to guide into the sport, and another who had the human, mature touch required to navigate the choppy waters of motor sport.

James Allison, a long-time Ferrari executive said: 'I've worked with two guys who really, really understood the value of being part of team. One was Michael and the other was Sebastian.'

In Red Bull's sister team, similar comparisons were being made about Verstappen, at first only from within the team but increasingly from without too. The doubters were a little quieter now that he had shown his mettle, especially after another impressive drive in China and a series of late-braking overtakes that earned him commentary box comparisons to Ayrton Senna, although his race ended when his Renault engine blew up two laps from the end. After the Spanish Grand Prix in Barcelona, where Max finished eleventh, he said: 'I am glad that the nagging about my age has now stopped.'

But the naggers, the doubters and the 'how old?' sceptics would not go away. They simply waited for a fall. Formula One, Jos reminds him, is a snakepit.

They got their opportunity not long afterwards when Max arrived for his first Monaco Grand Prix, a dream weekend for any driver. It had been at this venue twelve months ago that Red Bull had first started discussions about a shock promotion and now here he was with a job to do. He relishes street circuits, where it is less about downforce and there is less grip on the asphalt. It is all about feel and instinct, like karting, and there is the added excitement of trying to keep it out of the wall which is, in his words 'quite entertaining'. Monaco is the ultimate test of nerve for that very reason, even if it makes Max laugh.

Toro Rosso were optimistic, not having to worry about engine power at Monaco largely due to its lack of long straights and then watching Max finish second in the opening practice session. With that in mind, Verstappen was disappointed to qualify tenth. He was determined to make up for Saturday and, after a clean start, executed a brilliant overtake on Pastor Maldonado's Lotus at Turn One. On such a narrow circuit, passes like that don't come along too often. It was a perfect combination of timing, nerve and judgement. There was an air of opportunism about it too, something he resurrected later in the race when Valtteri Bottas moved over to allow the Ferrari of Vettel to lap him. Coming out of the hairpin, Verstappen followed him right on through and caught Bottas off guard. It was the move of a racer with 60 Grands Prix under his belt, not six. He switched on to super-soft tyres and found himself trying to overtake another Lotus, this time Grosjean, for tenth place. For five laps he could not find a way past, and then his patience ran out. He tried to repeat his move on Maldonado, something he had eyed up on the previous lap, but Grosjean moved across to cover him. Verstappen said he braked far earlier than before but Grosjean says his data did not reflect that, and the stewards agreed. Max thundered into the barriers at Sainte Devote and brought out the safety car. He was unhurt, but his reputation had taken a blow.

'Max is really, really talented, and what he has been doing is quite impressive, but he has made a mistake,' Grosjean said.

'I find it disappointing he hasn't learned from it.'

In fact he did. He learned what it feels like to crash a Formula One car at high speed.

'It was a big crash but at the end of the day then you really understand how strong an F1 car is,' he said.

'I think it even improved me. For me, it gave me more confidence. You're always a bit scared to crash or touch a wall, but now I had a big crash and it all gets a bit more relaxed.'

Verstappen did not apologise, despite getting a five-place grid penalty for the next race, and promised to keep driving the same way. Another veteran Felipe Massa had already put pressure on the FIA to act against Verstappen.

'Wasn't Massa the man who caused a rather clumsy collision there a year earlier?' he chirped back. Jos listened with a smile. That was what the grid were learning about Max. He is not afraid to overtake, and no matter who you are, he will answer back. He truly was his father's son, and never more so than two months later in Hungary. Budapest had been the site of Jos' first ever podium in F1 and his son very nearly matched him.

Both Verstappens said they enjoyed the Hungaroring because the car slides a lot there, something that drivers fresh out of junior formulae often seem to cope with better. Indeed Max's engineer Xevi Pujolar had referenced it at the beginning of the season.

'Drivers who have been driving in Formula One for years have become used to a lot of grip and a stable car,' he said.

'When their car starts to slide in a corner, those men get nervous a little earlier than the young drivers who come from a lower class where this sliding is still a daily occurrence. They just keep pushing in such a situation.'

The Hungarian Grand Prix had started on a sad note, as the grid mourned the death of Jules Bianchi, who had died after an accident at Suzuka the previous year. Several of the grid had been pallbearers at his funeral and spoke of a popular, talented member of the grid. Before the race, all the drivers placed their helmets in the middle of a circle and linked arms in a moment of silence. Once the guttural grunt of F1 car had broken the silence, an action-packed race followed, which winner Sebastian Vettel dedicated to the late Bianchi. Behind him, Kvyat picked up his first podium while Verstappen finished fourth, his best result so far, overcoming disrupted practice sessions, a poor start, front wing damage courtesy of Bottas and a penalty for speeding behind the safety car. Perhaps most satisfyingly of all, Fernando Alonso was five seconds behind him.

'Everyone is equal for me on the track, but it is nice if you can keep a world champion behind you,' Max says. He is getting used to doing so.

Several moments stand out from Max's first season in F1, on track and off it, but the one that seems to stick in many minds the most came in Belgium. Spa was Max's home race and the track where just twelve months before, he had started his remarkable run in F3 that ultimately led him to his current seat. In the summer, he had signed up with Team Redline and spent time on his simulator, playing iRacing for fun but also as a development technique. His move on Nasr at Blanchimont at closing in on 200 miles an hour was voted as 'Action of the Year' at the FIA end of season awards ceremony. He had practised the move online multiple times to understand where he could and couldn't get past another car – and when he pulled it off there were open mouths in the pit lane. Having started eighteenth, that overtake helped him secure eighth place, just a few seconds off fifth.

Blanchimont was not the only place he had a huge impact that weekend. All over the track, Verstappen was the name on ticket-holders' lips. The stand next to the Kemmel straight was not quite the 'Oranje' wall that it has since become, but it was populated with far more Dutch and Belgian fans, both claiming some ownership over Belgian-born, Dutch-licensed Verstappen, and he was happy to acknowledge them both. Race organisers had been faced with the prospect of losing the event after years of decline, but Max was starting to change that and it looked like he was here to stay too. His first ever Grand Prix in Spa saw him secure only his fourth-ever points finish, the icing on the cake. It moved him to tenth in the World Drivers' Championship with 26 points, seventeen clear of teammate Sainz. The pair were evenly matched but even with Verstappen's early-season reliability problems, he had a clear advantage with two thirds of the season gone.

So when in Singapore, one of the low-grip, wall-riding street circuits Max loves so much, Toro Rosso asked him to let his teammate through, he did not take too kindly to the request. His race had started disastrously when he stalled on the grid and had to be pushed to the pit lane to fire the car up. He rejoined a lap down, but was handed a lifeline by the emergence of the safety car just thirteen laps into the race. On lap 46, he overtook Grosjean for eighth position. On average, he had made up a position every three laps on a track where overtaking is not always an easy endeavour.

'No!' he shouted over the radio when told to swap positions with Sainz, behind him on fresh tyres, so the Spaniard could try to overtake Sergio Perez for seventh place.

'Just do it,' his engineer replied. Max would not yield.

Afterwards, dripping in sweat after a draining night in Singapore, he explained himself.

'I was one lap behind and then at the end I came back as the leading car. I was chasing the guys in front of me so for me there was no reason to let him go.'

Such a blatant disregard for team orders would usually have earned a driver some stern words in the post-race debrief. Under-pressure Daniil Kvyat had held off Max during the race, something that team officials later admitted had saved his seat, but the reaction to Verstappen's insubordination was the clearest indication yet of Red Bull's feeling towards the youngest ever Grand Prix driver. His boss Tost actually seemed to suggest that they had miscalculated things on the pit wall and that Max was entirely right to override them.

'Carlos had new tyres therefore we thought we could switch positions. But then Carlos was too slow, he was too far behind and Max was right. He saw that Carlos was not closing up and Carlos could not have caught Perez so we were right to let them go,' Tost said.

'Carlos was always a minimum of three to five tenths behind, if he wants us to swap the positions he must be closer to him or it doesn't make sense. He wouldn't have caught Perez.'

Jos' assertion that 'Max is central' continues to ring true, although he himself had told Max that if ever the team did ask him to move over, he should not do it and let them sort it out after the race. People, he said, would lose respect for him as a racing driver if he did. Red Bull might have smoothed things over publicly, and Sainz has always insisted that the pair got on fine off the track even though they were rivals on it, but it was not an incident they would want repeated. They had been through internal turmoil when youngster Sebastian Vettel ignored team orders not to race Mark Webber, and knew what strife it would cause. The team needed to find a way through, especially with what they were planning next.

11

CRITICS ARE THERE TO BE PROVEN WRONG

Red Bull had been mightily impressed with Max from the start. Every time they asked him to do something for the first time, he had mastered it almost instantaneously. When he drove an F1 car for the first time, it was wet and they were concerned that on a damp, technical track, which was not really representative of what he would encounter in F1, they would not be able to learn much. Instead, his engineer Xevi Pujolar was blown away. He was his guide for the Suzuka free practice session and watched with amazement as Max produced a faultless morning. In winter testing too, the race simulations were astoundingly fast for someone who had never driven that distance in an F1 car. Even the mechanics and engineers started to tell anyone who would listen how special this guy was. Former drivers and pundits joined the chorus, and some took plenty of stick for mentioning his name in the same breath as Ayrton Senna and Michael Schumacher. Red Bull though, with all the information available to them, always had faith in him, and with two men like Jos Verstappen and Dr Helmut

Marko pushing him to the limit, as well as his own internal drive, the doubts of the racing community were only ever likely to fuel him further. The headlines he creates with his overtaking but in fact what the team are most impressed by, even from his very first race, is his treatment of the tyres. Looking after the Pirelli rubber is difficult and something Max had no experience of, yet took to quickly. The only thing his performance coach Jake Aliker really had to work on was stopping the car on his mark during practice pit stops, which he never seemed to have a problem with during races.

From the outside though, the step from Toro Rosso to Red Bull was the biggest of his career. The Verstappens would probably argue that other moments, such as his first Formula Three race or the practice session at Suzuka were a bigger change than his previous drives, but from a public perspective, this was the big time and the expectations were higher than ever before.

Max had done an awful lot of growing up in his first year in F1 though, and not just in learning about Pirelli tyres, brake by wire, pit stops and hybrid engines. For a start, he had finally passed his driving test, the stick with which so many tabloid headlines used to beat him. He joked on Twitter that he was now 'legal to drive and born to race', passing first time on his eighteenth birthday, although not without the odd error. At one point he turned left instead of right and wasn't the most patient driver in the world.

'It would be a big, big drama if I had to do it twice or three times,' Verstappen said. 'Once, I didn't give way, but they were, like, miles behind so I didn't see it necessary to stop. So I just continued, but clearly [the examiner] thought differently.'

It was deemed a 'racing incident' by the examiner in F1 parlance and Max passed, an important step in anyone's life but particularly in his. The move into F1 had tested and changed his relationship with his father, whom Marko said Max understandably had found it difficult to exclude from his life. As soon as he could drive, he moved out and into an apartment in Monaco. He had never minded too much that his racing meant socialising always came second and was fitted in between race weekends, but by moving to the south of France, quite apart from the favourable tax conditions, he would be closer to any number of racing drivers who were now becoming his friends and rivals. You can hardly walk around a corner in Monte Carlo without bumping into a current or former racing driver. As an eighteenth birthday present, Jos and Raymond bought him a pair of jet skis, the ideal big boy's toy for Monaco's newest resident.

'Actually not much has changed, because I travel constantly,' Max insists. 'And at any time I can go back home to Belgium [to visit].'

Nevertheless, it's an important moment for any young man. There is a woman in his life as well, perhaps inevitably another racing driver, Mikaela Ahlin-Kottulinsky from Sweden, who would go on to become a Red Bull athlete as well. Her own racing schedule in the Audi TT Cup requires less international travel with most races in Germany, but their relationship is still not a simple one, even with all the private jets in the world, and when it comes to priorities, any prospective Mrs Verstappen must know she is not, for now at least, the top priority.

'My career is more important than girls,' Max said shortly before his eighteenth birthday during a joint interview with F1 head honcho and three times married Bernie Ecclestone.

'You have only one chance here – and I am going to take it.'

That uncompromising bullishness has become one of Verstappen's signatures in his first year of F1 and is part of what makes him such a fierce racer and overtaker. If he sees a gap, he is going to go for it.

So when a gap appears at Red Bull, in a seat in one of the most successful teams in recent F1 history, there is never any question in Max's mind that he is going for it.

Red Bull had already been considering dropping Kvyat towards the end of the 2015 season but drives such as his defensive one in Singapore seemed to convince Dr Marko, probably motor sport's harshest critic, to maintain his support of Kvyat. However, they were frustrated to have finished fourth behind Williams in 2015, partially down to the unreliability of the Renault engine but also because of Kvyat's inconsistency, and eventually they lost confidence in him.

In some ways, Verstappen was the worst possible man for Kvyat to have his Red Bull bosses compare him to, because he had many of the same mitigations – he was young and inexperienced, just like Max – but his weaknesses were in areas where Max was strong. He was not seen as mature enough to handle the pressure of top-level racing and he also did not have the same understanding of the tyres, something Max had developed remarkably quickly. As it became obvious that tyre management would be a huge focus of the hybrid era, Kvyat's weaknesses became intolerable, and the gap to Daniel Ricciardo, in the same car, was enormous. He was more than a second off the Australian's pace in the very first race of the 2016 season (although Sunday's electrical failure was nothing to do with him), and in Bahrain the gap was similarly large. Overtaking was becoming harder in F1 too, emphasising the importance of qualifying, where Kvyat's inability to get the tyres into the right temperature window and therefore producing a strong qualifying lap was nearly impossible. The apparent final straw was his home race at Sochi, where he started eighth, hit Sebastian Vettel in the rear twice on the opening lap, was awarded a penalty and finished fifteenth. He had also cannoned into his teammate Ricciardo who finished outside the points as a result. Furthermore in qualifying Kvyat had been just a tenth of a second faster than Verstappen, and had Max not suffered an engine failure, he would have finished sixth. According to Vettel though, and what Red Bull would probably prefer everybody to believe, the decision had been made even before what happened in Russia.

Marko and team boss Christian Horner, a long-time supporter of Kvyat's, had seen enough. Both Verstappen and Ricciardo had been consistently outperforming him, in different ways, and it was time to make the cut-throat but necessary decision. It seemed appropriate that when Dr Marko rang Kvyat to tell him of the decision, the Russian driver was watching *Game of Thrones*.

Verstappen had been pretty convinced that he would be Kvyat's seat sooner rather than later, even before the 2016 season.

'Of course there's only one seat available up there [in the senior] but I'm very confident, I know my contract and it's all looking very positive,' he said in a pre-season interview with journalist Chris Medland.

As often in Max's career, some mistook his unshakeable confidence for arrogance, especially those outside F1. It is easy to forget that the job itself requires that confidence and self-belief. F1 cars do not work when driven half-heartedly or at low speeds – as Max learned when he dinged his Toro Rosso in downtown Rotterdam. The safest way to drive them is fast and fully committed, actions that require trust in one's own hands beyond that of civilian life. Max's trainer Jake Aliker, who stopped working with him after five years in 2020, teaches his students to recognise the moment of basic instinct to pull back and to slow down, and use it as a cue to push further on. It applies as much to physical training as it does to driving. The best drivers drive on the edge, with crashes, and all the potential consequences, just one errant split-second hesitation away. What Verstappen shares with all the greats is that self-belief.

Red Bull could never be accused of failing to realise what they had either. Some characterised the early promotion – Verstappen had been almost guaranteed to move up to Red Bull Racing at the end of 2016 anyway – as an attempt to keep the Dutchman as part of the franchise as two teams who had courted him throughout his career looked to lure him away with the promise of a faster car than the Red Bull that finished fourth in 2015 and was still being outperformed by the Ferrari.

Their concern about the circling sharks was not ill-founded. Ferrari knew Kimi Raikkonen would not be around forever and Jos was interested in what they could offer, while McLaren were also trying to plan for life after Jenson Button. Red Bull could also not have predicted that Nico Rosberg would suddenly retire after winning the 2016 world title but when it looked as though his replacement Valtteri Bottas might not be up to the task, Mercedes held talks with Max and Jos Verstappen about bringing him in. Niki Lauda, the man who had lured Hamilton from McLaren to Mercedes, had hoped that the promise of a title-winning car with an utterly dominant power unit might test Verstappen's resolve but instead he signed a new, extremely lucrative contract until the end of 2020.

Back in 2016 though, he still had to prove to everyone that he was deserving of the promotion. After all, he was now driving for a team with front-running potential despite never having led a race or finished on the podium.

'Any of our young drivers must be capable of winning a Grand Prix – that's our goal,' Marko had said in explanation of his decision.

'If we see that there is no chance to achieve that, then we are reacting.'

It was a reminder to Max, as well as a simple truth, that if you live by the sword you can just as easily die by the sword. How will he cope with the pressure, one journalist asks him? 'What pressure?' he replies with a smile. The very least Max would have to do would be to match or beat Daniel Ricciardo. That would go a long way to confirming the validity of the move. He cannot have dared to dream of what actually happened, although knowing Max, he probably did.

There was one advantage to the timing of his move to the senior team. His first race would be at Barcelona, the track where he had already logged hundreds of miles in testing. There was no track he knew better in an F1 car, meaning he could concentrate on trying to make sure he knew what every button on the steering wheel does and to understand all the team's procedures. He would also have to learn his lines for what was always likely to be an uncomfortable FIA press conference. The Dutchman was seated on the front row of the six drivers, sitting next to Kvyat as he was quizzed about the whys and the wherefores of his demotion. The questioning did not shy away from it either. 'Daniil, do you think Max deserves your old seat and Max, do you think that Daniil deserved to lose his seat?'

'I think that's not up to me,' Max said, deferentially and sensibly siding with his employers. He owed Daniil nothing and certainly wasn't going to risk the wrath of Dr Marko at his first race with the senior team.

Publicly, Max took the pressure off himself by insisting that qualifying was just about trying to get a better feeling for the car and to keep producing a better lap. He certainly achieved that and finished four tenths of a second behind teammate Ricciardo, good enough for a best-ever fourth on the grid. Kvyat was only thirteenth. It was still early, but Red Bull could feel reasonably vindicated already.

The irony is that what followed, Max's first ever Grand Prix win, was by no means his best drive, and was perhaps not even the best drive of his spring. In fact, the Spanish Grand Prix in 2016 is as memorable for how it started as how it finished. The title race was quickly becoming a two-horse race once again between childhood friends turned teammate rivals Hamilton and Rosberg. The German had won all four of the opening races and Hamilton had hit engine trouble twice already. He was 43 points behind and had fewer engines available to him for the rest of the season. It was, in his words, 'an uphill battle' for him already. He was buoyed by pipping Rosberg to pole position, but that joy quickly dissipated as he was overtaken round the outside of Turn One. Pulling up the hill towards Turn Three, Rosberg realised he was in the wrong engine mode and was slower than Hamilton. He came across the track to defend his position, forcing the British driver on to the grass. He lost control of his car and crashed into his teammate, ending the race for both of them. Team boss Toto Wolff was furious and the incident echoed throughout a bitter, season-long battle between the two men. Behind them though, the race went on and all of a sudden Verstappen, who had held off a fast-starting Vettel, was in second place. With Ricciardo leading, he pitted first and Red Bull gave him the three-stop strategy while Max, who had already shown his ability to look after the tyres, was on the two-stop. The Red

Bull strategists had puffed their cheeks out when electing to put Max on to a two-stop plan. It was right on the limit of what was achievable, but they also knew that it was probably the only way to beat the Ferraris. It worked out perfectly and Max, having briefly overcome a moment of distraction with ten laps to go when he realised the win was within his grasp, drove on the limit, holding off extended pressure from Raikkonen while not overworking his tyres, winning the race by less than a second. By the end, his worn tyres felt like driving on ice, and nursing them home was the work of a much older, more experienced man. Kvyat meanwhile was comprehensively outdriven by teammate Sainz and managed a solitary point.

'I can't believe it,' Max said over the team radio.

'Max Verstappen, you are a race winner. Fantastic. What a debut. Great, great job,' said his boss Christian Horner.

He had created all kinds of history. He had become the first Dutchman even to lead a Formula One Grand Prix, and then the first to win one, as well as the youngest driver ever to finish on the podium or take victory. At eighteen years and 227 days, he had smashed the previous record held by Sebastian Vettel by nearly three years. It was an important milestone. Marko had always believed he did not want a driver in his top team who could not win a Grand Prix, and Max had proved that he could.

In the aftermath, Max was humble enough to acknowledge that they were fortunate to have the two Mercedes take each other out and that his strategy had happened to be better than his teammate and early leader Ricciardo's. And while his humility was impressive, it was also genuine. He knew enough about the sport to know that he did not have the fastest car on the grid, or perhaps even on his own team. Nevertheless, anyone wanting to question his place in the sport would have his winner's trophy from Barcelona thrust firmly in their face. He had proved something significant to the paddock, to the sport and to the world. He was now a race winner.

In the pit lane, Jos' voice had gone hoarse with shouting and celebrating.

'I knew when he was young I was working to arrive in Formula One but then that he's winning a race in his second year is something unbelievable,' he says, wiping the tears from his eyes. Max is now officially more successful than him, and he would not have it any other way. He always said that he does not miss racing because watching Max gave him all the adrenaline and excitement of driving, and perhaps even more. Now it gave him the satisfaction too.

Jos had been planning to fly back to Belgium on Sunday night after the race but Red Bull were famous for their hospitality and there was no way Jos was missing the party. 'This is so special. I want to be with Max,' he said. There was no rush away from the circuit either, with a two-day test scheduled for Tuesday and Wednesday, as well as a sponsor photo shoot on Monday. If eighteen-year-old Max had a hangover, he would just have to power through it.

In Holland, more than a million people had tuned in to watch the race, more than five per cent of the population. On Monday night, he appeared on a Dutch chat show via video link, while his grandfather Frans and one of his best friends Jorrit Pex, now karting world champion, sat in the studio, nursing hangovers of their own. Max had never forgotten his roots and was a regular visitor to the karting track in Genk or the Pex factory.

For all his popularity in Holland though, Max was not universally popular in the paddock, a consequence of being a talented disruptor in a sport where marketing modernity was often shunned in the Ecclestone era. When he had been at Toro Rosso, his bold and aggressive overtaking moves on other members of the midfield had been great highlights for the title challengers at the front to enjoy after the race. Now he was battling them for points and podiums, it was a whole lot less entertaining.

Kimi Raikkonen had spent the closing laps of the Spanish Grand Prix staring at Verstappen's gearbox and getting frustrated at his inability to pass the Dutchman. There is a skill to making one's car as wide as possible and, like most things, Max had picked it up pretty quickly and performs it uncompromisingly. As Red Bull and Ferrari's performance level converged, Raikkonen would spend more time fighting with Verstappen and not enjoying the driver who was three years old when he made his own F1 debut making his life difficult. In Hungary, Max had emerged behind Raikkonen after the first set of pit stops and could not find a way past, but in the closing stages the roles were reversed. Raikkonen tried to overtake on fresher tyres at Turn Two but complained furiously over the radio after Verstappen weaved across the road to block him. A couple of weeks later at Spa, they clashed again at the end of the Kemmel straight.

'His only interest is pushing me off the circuit completely,' Raikkonen tells his engineers and the race director.

When Verstappen defends aggressively again a few laps later, Raikkonen brands it 'fucking ridiculous'. Again, the FIA disagree with him and Raikkonen is typically blunt afterwards but unusually talkative.

'There will be a big accident if this doesn't stop. He should not do stupid things.'

Raikkonen's teammate Vettel, who would go on to clash with Verstappen later in the season, took a more diplomatic approach.

'I will try and talk to Max, not now because I think he didn't have a good day, I didn't have a good day, Kimi didn't have a good day. But I'm not a fan of penalising people; it's not the way to educate. We need to talk to each other, and we need to have respect,' Vettel said.

'I think there has been a couple of manoeuvres that the rest of the field is not happy with his behaviour. As I said the best way is to educate and the best way is just to talk rather than create a fuss in the media and try to talk via some other channels. We are men and it's best to stand in front of each other and talk to each other.

'I get along with him, I like him, he's aggressive and I think that's a strength for him, but certain movements, especially under braking which I faced when I was racing with him, I don't think are correct.'

It is a sign that Verstappen has put a number of noses out of joint, as much because of his meteoric success as his aggressive driving style, but when you have as much control of the car as he does, why not be more aggressive? He is never, the stewards tended to agree, out of control.

Max refuses to yield off the track just as he did not on it.

'I should have got a penalty if it was not correct so I think everything was also fair again today,' he says with the hint of a smile, although only a hint: he finished eleventh after suffering early floor damage and had little to smile about. In September, shortly after the Belgian Grand Prix, race director Charlie Whiting gave Verstappen 'a gentle warning' about 'getting a bad name' in racing. A month later and not for the first time, the FIA changed the regulations to deal with Verstappen and disallowed moving around in the braking zone, the tactic that many believed had become his trademark. It had little effect. Max wasn't going away and he was fighting Vettel and Raikkonen for fourth place in the championship. Vettel screamed expletives over the radio when Verstappen failed to give up a place he had illegally gained by cutting a corner in Mexico. After crossing the line, he wagged his finger out of the cockpit at the Dutchman. Max comes out swinging afterwards.

'He's shouting on the radio like a child, and then to do this after the start-finish line is even more childish,' Verstappen said, before backing up his teammate after Vettel nearly crashed into Ricciardo. 'It's ridiculous, what he did. I have never ever done something like that, not even close.'

Looking back, Verstappen would claim he was still in the right, but that perhaps he had let the impetuosity of youth get the better of him in the media pen afterwards. That was the Jos in him talking.

Aside from the copious column inches though, the weeks and month after his win in Spain had been relatively barren. His 'home' race at Monaco, driving past the apartment he had lived in for the last six months, was a huge disappointment, crashing in qualifying and then in the race to leave with no points to his name, the same as his actual home race in Belgium. There were several podiums – second in Austria and Great Britain, and third in Germany – but by the end of the European leg of the season, with fourteen of 21 races complete, he was firmly sixth in the World Drivers' Championship, although both Ferrari drivers were within striking distance.

It might have been easy to get disheartened, with the world seemingly desperate for him to fail, but Christian Horner was a constant and public defender.

'We see this always with exceptionally talented drivers. They are always criticised when they are working their way up, like

Sebastian Vettel, Lewis Hamilton, Fernando Alonso and Ayrton Senna,' Horner said after Whiting's ticking-off, and there are no concerns within the team about Verstappen's driving. In many ways, it fits in with their brand and they are happy to let the young driver learn and make the odd mistake. He has already exceeded their expectations.

He is still punctuating his season with strong results and highlight-reel moments too. In Malaysia, he took the fight to teammate Ricciardo in a battle for the race win, first asking the team to let him past under team orders and then trying to overtake him in a fair battle. The Australian held him off and led a Red Bull one-two after Hamilton's engine blew up, but Horner joked to a drained pair of drivers afterwards that they were sweating on the pit wall as the two drivers went wheel to wheel.

'Yeah, that was nice,' Max said, smiling across at his teammate, who grinned back. In a results-orientated business, nothing had gone wrong and so they could smile, but it would be a conversation they would revisit in less happy circumstances down the line.

He did go out with something of a bang in 2016 though, a year that might be considered a freebie given he started it with a different team. The Brazilian Grand Prix has so often thrown up brilliant races with rain often a possibility, and the changeable conditions of the 2016 edition made for a classic if you could cope with them. Needless to say, Max relished it.

One moment in particular stood out. Midway through the race and on the full wet tyres, Verstappen came out of the final corner and tried to get on the power, but had dipped a tyre on to the kerb on the inside. The car almost instantly went into a spin and the rear tried to overtake the front. Facing the wall, Verstappen started travelling sideways. Initially, he had tried to counter-steer, but in a split second he realised that would be futile. Instead, he steered the wheels neutral and locked up the brakes to let the car straighten out and stay out of the wall – which indeed it did.

'Well held Max, well held,' came the message in his ear.

'Yeah, heartbeat went a bit higher there,' he replied, remarkably calmly.

However, there was more work to do. An errant call to go to intermediate tyres too early cost them ten places, and with sixteen laps to go he was in fifteenth place. He had already performed the overtake of the day on Rosberg around the outside in the wettest phase of the race, but there was so much more to come. It was not long before he had sliced his way up to the sharp end of the race. His engineer Gianpiero Lambiase had been guiding him through the pack, calmly making him aware of whom he was coming up to in the low visibility and soaking conditions. When they reached Sebastian Vettel, there was a change in tone of voice.

'Okay. So. Now. Sebastian ahead ...'

It took two laps to catch him, but when he did, he dummied to the outside and then braked later on the inside of the final corner. Vettel tried to come back on the outside and Verstappen slammed the door shut. It felt like a statement as much as an overtake for fifth place.

'Atta boy!' came the cry on the radio from the pit wall. 'Go on, let's go. Let's get P3.'

Max needed no second invitation. On the penultimate lap of the race, he caught Sergio Perez in a Mercedes-powered Force India and overtook him on the same corner he had Vettel.

At the finish, he mischievously accused Lambiase of getting excited.

'Meh, you got me a little bit excited,' he retorted. Red Bull briefly thought he could threaten the two Mercedes drivers. He could not, but a place on the podium felt like a win.

'I had seen it before, in a kart. But to do it in an F1 car, in very difficult circumstances ... I was wondering why other drivers didn't try other lines. But it's a gift to know where to go, to look for the grip, having the feeling,' Jos said.

'When we were karting, if it started to rain, everyone else was packing up, but I put the rain tyres on. We would go out on the track and he learned so much.'

The clips of Max's antics in the rain were viewed millions of times around the world. The public were more interested in his overtakes than the actions of the winner Lewis Hamilton. The keenest observers of all were Liberty Media, who had just bought F1 for £3.3 billion. With dwindling viewer numbers, they would be charged with the task of bringing people back to F1. Given the choice between a dominant Mercedes and the exciting Verstappen, they knew which was the way forward. Drivers could complain about him all they wanted – Max Verstappen was the future.

12

IN PURSUIT OF HISTORY AND MORE

When Sebastian Vettel left Red Bull at the end of 2014, Red Bull were left with a four-man driver line-up across the two teams of which Daniel Ricciardo at 25 was the most senior. It was exactly what the great driver scout Dr Helmut Marko wanted and, from a marketing perspective, what the energy drink backing the team needed. They were young, high-octane and adventurous, and they didn't care what the established powers thought of them. Their motorhome in Monaco and its rooftop pool was the one everyone wanted to get a wristband for.

Max and Daniel were well matched in terms of driving style. Ricciardo was known as one of the best – if not the best – overtakers on the grid with a fearless nature and ability to 'lick the stamp and send it' from almost anywhere. Max too, while engineers had been impressed by his tyre management, was most noteworthy for his on-track passes and their audacious and tough nature. Ricciardo himself had even been the victim of a few of them. Off the track, both had a cheeky sense of humour and an ability to laugh or make a joke in the highest-pressure situations.

Ricciardo was a bit more comfortable in his own skin, but he had eight years on Max, as well as the best part of 100 Grands Prix.

So when the pair became teammates at Red Bull, it felt like a match made in heaven, and that Verstappen could learn plenty from the Australian, given their similarities. Indeed, for the first six months of his time in the team, Max largely used the same set-up as Ricciardo to give him a leg-up in a new car. It was only once they headed to Malaysia that Max and his engineers felt they could start to diverge significantly from that plan. Internally though, Ricciardo did harbour some concerns when Verstappen was promoted. The Dutchman's reputation as a fearsome overtaker was matched by a perception of self-belief that bordered on arrogance, and the presence of Jos was a concern too. Ricciardo's own strong belief that he was the best in the world looked destined to clash with Verstappen's own rigidity and unwillingness to yield. Ricciardo also regarded himself as the senior man in the team, understandable given his far greater experience, but Max had been the top dog at Toro Rosso, at Van Amersfoort, really his whole life. He would not take kindly to any suggestion that he was the number two driver.

However, Red Bull bosses Christian Horner and Helmut Marko had seen Ricciardo and Vettel blossom together, even though the latter was clearly the number one driver, and seemed unconcerned about the potential internal fireworks of two young racy drivers. They were proven right in the first year of the two racing together as they quickly became as thick as thieves, thriving on the track and enjoying Red Bull's quirky social media video ideas off it. Whether it was tasting durian fruit in Malaysia (even Max, whose favourite food is raw beef – carpaccio – couldn't stomach that one) or dancing to EDM on Eau Rouge, they seemed to embrace the opportunity to spend time together.

'If we're fighting for a world championship, and we're going hammer and tongs, then sure at some point we'll probably cross paths,' Ricciardo said after a few months of working with Max.

'It's the way you deal with it though. If you can face defeat with maturity, then I don't think there will be any type of conflict.'

The reality at Red Bull was that 2016 was another Mercedes procession and in Hamilton and Rosberg they had a great example of how world title fights can pry apart even the best friendships. Money too can start to come between friends, and while Verstappen's relationship with Ricciardo never soured too badly, it was money and status that eventually saw them go in different directions.

Max had always got on relatively well with teammates. In karting, it was hard to have enemies because the people you were racing were also generally your best friends, so intense and demanding was the racing hobby. Max spent months travelling the world with the Pex family and Stan and Jorrit became like brothers too him. When he moved up to Formula Three, they would watch and cheer from wherever they were karting that weekend, just as they did when he stepped up again. During his whirlwind year at Van Amersfoort, he hardly had time to get to know Gustavo Menezes or Jules Szymkowiak. He and Sainz raced hard on track, but both always insisted they got on reasonably well and objected to the media portrayal of them as enemies. Even his best friends ended up asking him whether they were fighting within the team.

'Everyone thinks Max and I hate each other, and that's absolutely not the case,' Sainz said, eighteen months after Verstappen had been promoted.

'We were having fun that year, I promise. We had a lot of fun out of the track. In the track, we were extremely competitive.

We knew we were battling for our careers, for our Formula One pedigree in our first year, rookie season, and I got on with him a lot better than what people think.'

More recently, Sainz is clearly sick of the question. He got on with all his teammates, he says, and the Max stuff is just hot air. He is privately bitter though that Verstappen was first promoted to Toro Rosso ahead of him (although Vettel's departure meant he ended up getting a seat too) and then to Red Bull ahead of him. He always felt the 'Max Verstappen phenomenon' was destined for the top and got the fast-track treatment from the team. He could not hate Max for that, but it was a feeling that he would not be the first to experience.

The first time Ricciardo and Verstappen's 'bromance' really hit trouble was in the searing heat of Budapest in 2017. Max had endured a frustrating start to the year with five retirements in ten races and a series of mechanical problems on the car, which was clearly third-fastest behind Mercedes and Ferrari. It added to Max's frustration, despite his friendship with Ricciardo, that Daniel had fared much better with five consecutive podiums including a win in Azerbaijan, a surprise given the Renault power unit was so much weaker than its competitors.

Red Bull were keen for things to go well at the last race before the summer break, not least because Dietrich Mateschitz was in attendance, so could hardly have been more frustrated when Ricciardo did not even make the fourth corner of the race. Verstappen had locked a front wheel at Turn Two and smashed into the side of his teammate, breaking the radiator and forcing the Australian to retire. He was furious.

'Is that who I think it was?' he asked over the radio.

After confirmation that it was Max, he spat out: 'Fucking sore loser.'

He had not calmed down much by the time he got in front of a TV camera either: 'That was amateur, to say the least. I don't think he likes when a teammate gets in front of him. You've got the whole race to try to repair a mistake but the pass was never on. It wasn't even an attempt to pass, it was just a very poor mistake.'

In fairness, Max recognised his error. Team boss Horner insisted the nineteen-year-old would be 'man enough' to hold his hand up and as soon as he finished the race, he went to apologise to his teammate and the whole team.

'I was trying to avoid Daniel of course, but unfortunately that was not possible,' he said to the media afterwards. 'It is of course never my intention to hit anyone but especially not your teammate and especially not with the relationship I have with Daniel; it's always very good. We always can have a laugh so this is not nice.'

It also earned him a penalty that probably cost him a chance at a second race win, adding insult to injury on a difficult day in the hot Hungarian sun, a rare track where Red Bull seemed to have the fastest car on the grid. Everything seemed to have been resolved by the time the pair got to Japan in October though. The pair disrupted the post-race press conference, after finishing second and third, by throwing towels and water at each other and over race winner Lewis Hamilton, with smiles all round.

However, the tumult of 2017 was mounting and while Verstappen and Ricciardo's relationship was intact, Max was not having an easy time of it. In April, Jos had been involved in a brawl at a lakeside bar in Roermond, emerging with cuts to his face and a black eye. He got divorced from his second wife Kelly van der Waal a few months later.

The Verstappen family were concerned that Jos' difficult year would start to impact on Max's career and his grandfather Frans rang up Dr Marko in an attempt to smooth things over. The Austrian did not seem overly concerned.

'I made it clear that Red Bull has a contract only with Max, and everything else that happens in the family is not our business,' he said, seemingly washing his hands of the incident.

However, the call seemed to have some sort of impact. Just a month after the fight, Jos was recruited as a scout for the Red Bull driver academy programme.

'This is a good cooperation and expansion of the Red Bull junior team,' Dr Marko said.

'It is a question of time, as there are clashes with junior races so that I cannot see them. So we asked if he has the time and the inclination to visit certain races for us.'

Presumably, those clashes would be with the Grands Prix that Dr Marko and other members of the team cannot miss – but that Jos can. It seems as though Red Bull are drawing Jos in closer with one hand and pushing him further away from his son with the other.

'Jos was always closely involved in karting,' Dr Marko added. 'He can not only coach the drivers with his experience but also look at the teams. The success in the development phase that he managed with Max is also obvious.'

Dr Marko was also becoming increasingly concerned about Max's long-term future at the team. The rumours of Lewis Hamilton moving to Ferrari were gaining momentum and Red Bull executives, despite back-channel denials to the hilt, remained confused about how to read the situation. As such, they swooped and did a deal. Dr Marko said he was not interested in playing poker, instead offering Max just a one-year extension until the end of 2020, when a sweeping regulation change was expected, but a huge uplift in salary to keep him in place. The deal was worth an estimated $30 million plus bonuses over the three seasons. It was a show of faith from both sides; Verstappen had little reason to suspect Red Bull would have a title-winning car any time soon given the Renault engine's struggles, while he was technically being outdriven by his teammate. Nevertheless, Red Bull never wavered from their belief in Verstappen and vice versa.

It had helped that Max produced two timely wins at the back end of the season. A day after his 20th birthday, he overtook Lewis Hamilton in Malaysia in textbook fashion and controlled the race from the front to bag his second win in F1. In the Red Bull garage, his sister Victoria, due to turn eighteen a month later, burst into tears as he crossed the line. The siblings had remained close throughout Max's manic early racing career and in September he had started wearing a lion of her design – she had been working with Red Bull in the Netherlands and was launching a fashion label – on the top of his helmet. The stress of his year, the family turmoil and not having the escapism of racing and travel that Max had was understandably too much to handle. Behind her, Jos hugged his new girlfriend Amanda Sodre. He said at the time that he was 'on the way to happiness again', although the pair split just a few months later. Max too was more settled and had started dating Dilara Sanlik, whom the German gossip pages report was introduced to him by long-time family friend Dr Marko, although the Austrian denied ever getting involved.

Max added his second win of the season before the year was out, overtaking Vettel in robust fashion to win the Mexican Grand Prix from second on the grid, showing the best of his abilities while Hamilton sealed the world title further down the pack. The luck at Red Bull had seemed to flip as Ricciardo recorded three retirements in the last four races, but it was not enough to allow Verstappen to overhaul him in the drivers' standings. Of any driver completing a full season, no one had logged fewer laps than Verstappen, and it did not feel a lot like his fault: of his seven retirements, four were mechanical and three were first-lap crashes, none of which earned him a penalty or a reprimand. In races where both drivers had finished, he had been the better Red Bull on five of seven occasions and on average was three tenths faster than Ricciardo in qualifying. While he only finished sixth in the title race – last place effectively on a grid where three teams were far and away better than the rest – 2017 felt like a victory, all things considered. At the FIA Prize-Giving Ceremony, notoriously the booziest affair on the F1 calendar, Verstappen won Personality of the Year for the third time running, but failed to bag a fourth straight Action of the Year gong. Accepting the award, he called it an 'educational year about remaining positive in difficult moments'. It was another thinly veiled dig at Renault, but also an acknowledgement of his resilience in the face of his own fallibility, a quality that would be tested in the next twelve months.

The relationship between Red Bull and Renault was becoming increasingly frayed. At the end of 2017, Toro Rosso terminated their agreement with the French team to supply engines and switched to Honda, while McLaren's disastrous relationship with the Japanese team ended and they took Renault engines instead. The move was a piece of political posturing that would potentially pave the way for Red Bull to follow suit – if Honda could prove at Toro Rosso that they were up to the task. The gradient, starting from an extremely low point admittedly, had been a positive one at McLaren and they seemed to be trending in the right direction. A Red Bull switch to Honda was starting to seem inevitable, but there was uncertainty across the garage from Max too. Ricciardo only had one year left on his contract and was starting to get concerned about his role in the team. The Australian wanted to win a world title and genuinely believed he could ('Why else would I be doing this?' he told one interviewer), and with the growing momentum and resource towards Max within the team, it felt as though he would not necessarily be given the chance to do so, even if and when Red Bull developed a car capable. The uncertainty and inconsistency of the Renault engine was not helping either, nor was the impending departure of his race engineer Simon Rennie. Increasingly, it felt to Ricciardo that Red Bull was not the right place to be, while Max had never felt so at home.

Equally, he had never been so pessimistic about his chances of winning. Ahead of the season-opening 2018 Australian Grand Prix, traditionally a week where talking up the team and the car is acceptable no matter how far from reality your claims might be, Max undercut the power of the Renault engine.

'The straights will still be a bit painful for us. I am certainly positive, but also realistic,' he said. He prayed for more reliability, but performance improvements were what they were. This was not his usual effort to underplay his hand, the kidology that some drivers like to deploy to hoodwink their rivals. This was the truth.

Nevertheless, 2018 would prove to be a big year for Max in terms of personal development. He would turn 21 in September, but before even that his father would step further back from his career, Ricciardo would confirm his move away to leave Max as the senior driver and Red Bull would join up with Honda to move them forward on the grid.

It started in conflict though, as all great stories do. Ricciardo was desperate for a fast start to the season to bolster his negotiating position with his preferred teams Mercedes and Ferrari, as well as to convince Red Bull he might be worth forking out Max Verstappen kind of money to keep him. There was still a chance, and many of the paddock still believed, that Ricciardo would end up staying, but privately he seemed to prefer the idea of leaving.

Red Bull were keen to reinforce that the rivalry that had developed between Ricciardo and Verstappen, from their perspective, was not a problem – until it was. In Azerbaijan, one of the fast, bumpy, low-grip street circuits that Max so loves, he was defending hard from his teammate Ricciardo. After the longest straight in F1, they collided, the Australian slamming right into the back of Verstappen, taking both cars out of the race.

'That's about 30 points we've just spunked away there,' Horner said to Marko in the garage, head held in hands in disbelief.

It was not the first time Horner had seen his two drivers crash into each other. Mark Webber and Sebastian Vettel had collided when leading the race in Turkey in 2010, and Red Bull had insisted on letting them continue to race each other going forward. Racing after all is central to the Red Bull brand, which is the whole point of the team; they did not want to turn into the kind of team Ferrari were in the early 2000s, forcing Rubens Barrichello to pull over and allow Michael Schumacher to win races he had not dominated on the day, but equally, they had seen what Hamilton and Rosberg did to each other in 2016. When Verstappen hit Ricciardo though, Horner came close to changing his tune. Both drivers knew they had done wrong – most apportioned blame 50:50 between the two – and in the briefing room afterwards, the usually calm Horner let rip at them. They stared back at him like naughty schoolchildren being chastised by a head teacher. Afterwards, they both left with their heads bowed and promised not to do it again.

Red Bull arrived in Monaco a month later then and both drivers had points to prove. Max had never finished on the podium here and on his first two visits failed to finish at all. Media pressure was mounting and the name 'Vercrashen' was being whispered once again. Around the streets of Monte Carlo though, the strong Red Bull chassis and low reliance on straight-line speed meant this would be an opportune track for the team to grab a race win. Once again though, Max was walking back rather than driving, angry and frustrated. At least this time, it was on Saturday morning during practice when he hit the wall. Nevertheless, his team now faced a speedy repair job ahead of qualifying at a Grand Prix where it is more important than ever because overtaking is such a challenge. In the end, he did not even complete a lap in qualifying, despite a remarkable repair job. As if to add salt in the wound, Daniel took pole position.

From Red Bull's perspective, it summed up why they were so keen to keep the Australian. Ricciardo's consistency was what enabled him to beat Max in 2017 and it was his consistency that made him a safety net if Max pushed over the limit, as a young driver is occasionally bound to do. When he converted Monaco pole into victory, it only strengthened their resolve. Max's critics were back out in their numbers after he was only able to finish ninth on Sunday in the wake of Saturday's disaster.

He sits in the back of the garage, hurting, wishing he could just ghost through the principality's now-packed streets and disappear up to his apartment for some carpaccio and a long sleep.

'It will come,' Horner reassures him, and he believes it too. Having just invested an eye-watering sum in the youngster, it has to, for all their sakes. 'Be happy for your teammate today, celebrate with him. You know how this business is, it's up and down.'

Max says: 'I should have won that race.'

He picked himself up and swapped his fireproof race suit for a team-branded polo before heading to the coolest party in town, Daniel's celebration. He smiled and chatted with an elated Ricciardo. Inside, he just wanted to go and help pack up the garage, especially after how much his mechanics had sweated on Saturday. It was the same feeling as that day in Italy, when his dad made him clean the kart and load it himself after a mistake had cost him the win.

That anger, shame, frustration and embarrassment boiled over two weeks later in Canada, when he was asked a series of questions about his crashes and mistakes in the early part of the season. They were starting to stack up against him: along with the incidents in Monaco and Baku, he had spun out in Australia, Bahrain and China, all while attempting ambitious overtakes, and in Spain he had damaged his car trying to get past a backmarker. Max grew tired of the questions.

'If I get a few more, I might headbutt someone,' he said, staring back at the offending journalist. The opportunity did not arise, but clearly the pressure was mounting on him.

With his son clearly struggling, Max's father took a conscious step back. He had told assembled reporters in 2016, when his constant and influential presence had fuelled rumours of a rift within Toro Rosso, that he would take a less active role in his son's career now he had stepped up to Red Bull Racing, but he was no less often seen in the garage on race day. As so often, what Jos says and what Jos does seemed to differ in that respect, although the experienced hand of Christian Horner on the tiller and his quickly formed closeness with Max may have helped ease him aside. This time though, it was Dr Marko who later in the season suggested that Jos had moved away again, making it ring rather truer.

Lewis Hamilton had endured a rather more public split from his own father Anthony, although the pair are now reconciled and have a more traditional, less business-focused relationship now that he is not managed by his dad. Speaking in 2019, Jos insisted he remained a confidant throughout his son's career.

'I don't think we will come to the point that he thinks that way because I really leave him, I let him do his own things, but I always have my ears open,' he said.

'I'm not there to only complain but also to tell him what's good and we also have Raymond so he speaks to him too.'

Vermeulen was an increasingly crucial figure. Anyone who wanted a piece of Max's time or image, and there were plenty of them, had to go through Raymond, who had become part of the Verstappen furniture, and was an important layer of protection from the circling sharks inside the paddock and outside.

Meanwhile, in the aftermath of Monaco and with the summer break approaching, the chips started to fall on the plans for 2019. Red Bull pulled the plug on their deal with Renault after twelve years of partnership and, impressed by the operation's progress at Toro Rosso, signed up with Honda.

For Renault, it was a significant blow to their pride and their revenue streams, at a time when their participation in the sport had been under review. The French team bit back. With Red Bull still under the assumption that Ricciardo, as other top teams closed their doors to him, would eventually sign a new deal, they were informed that he had agreed to join Renault. Horner was stunned, and surprised. He said he would have understood a move to Mercedes or Ferrari, but Renault were midfield runners at best. However, they were midfield runners backed by one of the world's biggest car companies and had offered Ricciardo 40 million reasons, and some big ambitions, to sign a two-year contract. Red Bull responded by promoting Pierre Gasly from Toro Rosso to be Max's new teammate. Horner had been heard telling Ricciardo's father Joe that 'there are no number one drivers here' when trying to convince him that Daniel should stay. It seems unlikely that he could have told Gasly's people the same thing with a straight face.

The season ended, from Verstappen's point of view, in typically two-faced fashion. It was a year when he had landed the odd punch on the imperious Mercedes of Lewis Hamilton, but for the most part had been scrapping for podium places with the Ferraris of Vettel and Raikkonen. With three races to go, he still trailed Raikkonen by 30 points in the battle for third in the championship. Returning to the Mexican Grand Prix he had won the year before, he beat Ricciardo off the start to Turn One and despite being told midway through the race by his engineer that 'this race was not going to be straightforward to the end', he made it look easy. He had Vettel, desperately trying to stop Hamilton winning the title, bearing down on him, his tyres were losing rubber rapidly, his teammate's engine had blown up so they had to turn his down – and yet he calmly controlled the race to the end and picked up his fifth race win. Two weeks later in Brazil might have been his sixth, but he got out of the car at the end anything but calm.

Leading the Brazilian Grand Prix courtesy of brilliant early overtakes on Vettel and Bottas, Verstappen looked certain to drive away from Hamilton and win. The lapped Esteban Ocon, Max's former F3 rival who was now driving for Racing Point, emerged from the pits behind him but on far fresher tyres, and looked to unlap himself by overtaking the leader, who happened to be slower. The two collided and Verstappen, having stuck his middle finger up at Ocon, would end up finishing second, while Ocon was handed a ten-second penalty by the stewards.

'I hope I can't find him in the paddock,' Max said over the radio. Unfortunately for Ocon, he did. As the drivers queued to weigh in after the race, Verstappen confronted the Frenchman. According to Max, Ocon laughed when he asked him what happened and Verstappen flew into a rage, pushing and shoving his rival in scenes caught on camera and quickly beamed around the world. He called him 'a pussy' in the post-race press conference. Later asked if Ocon had apologised, Max said: 'No, he gave a really stupid response ... we're all passionate so those things happen.'

Many people would have recognised his father's son in the moment, and a year later, once Max had finally calmed down, he joked that the incident was karma for when Jos had done something very similar to race leader Juan Pablo Montoya.

'We should not make it bigger than it is,' Jos wrote of his son's reaction at the time. 'Football players do that to each other every weekend and Max is professional enough not to beat up anyone.'

Jos seemed to think that if it had been him, punches would have been thrown, but he praised his son for not going further than a few pushes and shoves. It was an odd take.

The incident cost Verstappen a race win and left him needing to finish second at least in the final race of the season to catch Raikkonen for third in the title race, not that he cared. Max does not spend his off-season sweating in a gym to fight for second or third. He is in F1 to win.

The angry scenes in Brazil though, even Max eventually recognised, were not desirable, like his headbutt threat in Canada. They might have done wonders for his rock-and-roll image and F1's overall visibility (the official F1 account posted the Ocon spat with the caption 'In the blue corner ... Max Verstappen'), even playing to the Red Bull crowd quite well, but he knew what lay further down that path of anger; his father was the perfect cautionary tale. In 2019, he made a conscious effort to chill out.

'This year I was a lot calmer in front of the cameras. More Zen,' Verstappen said in a TV interview with Ziggo Sport.

'Generally, that works better. I never throw things anyway as my father has never allowed it' – some irony there, you feel – 'but sometimes you cannot help being angry.

'That's just being human but, if I am angry, I have learned to wait before I go in front of the cameras. When I was very angry, sometimes I skipped the media altogether. That was a problem, but I don't do that any more.'

It may be a chicken-and-egg situation, but his Zen year coincided with his best-ever season in F1. He produced three race wins in a season for the first time, finished third in the World Drivers' Championship and compiled a career-high 278 points. Max must take much of the credit, but it was also in no small part down to the switch to Honda power units, for whom Max bagged the engine supplier their first win in any form since 2006 when he, fittingly enough, won Red Bull's home race in Austria, in front of an entire stand wearing orange. Despite being a ten-hour drive from Max's home town, the Austrian Grand Prix had become a home from home for Verstappen. Nevertheless, when Max got on the podium, it was the Japanese Honda mechanics whom he was thinking of.

For Jos, it was a poignant moment too. He had been signed up by the Japanese company in 1998 as the test driver for the project that was supposed to see the company, and Jos, return to F1 as a works team. They had been testing in Spain and been confident of convincing Honda HQ that they had the pace to produce a winning car, when the technical director and Jos' former ally at Tyrrell, Harvey Postlethwaite, a universally popular team boss, suffered a fatal heart attack in his office at the track at the age of just 55. The project died with him. When Red Bull eventually earned their first victory with Honda, Max innately knew how big a moment it was for the engine manufacturers.

'They went through such a difficult time with McLaren and it was so good [to win again],' Jos said. 'And then when Max stepped on to the podium and pointed to the Honda logo on the podium, which was never talked about before, it was because he had the same feeling. Then seeing the Japanese in the garage they had tears in their eyes and you could see how much heart and effort they put into the whole thing.'

It had been an atypical Verstappen start and he was eighth by the third corner. He lost more positions on the first lap than he had in his fourteen previous races. After that though, it was a classic Max attack, a masterclass in overtaking, passing three different world champions in Vettel, Hamilton and Raikkonen before closing in on Leclerc, his former karting rival, with five laps to go. The Monegasque driver defended desperately but on the 69th lap of the 71-lap race, Verstappen sent it up the inside of Turn One. The pair banged wheels but Max emerged ahead and Leclerc had nothing left to give. 'What the hell,' he cried over the radio. 'He turned in on me,' Max said in reply to his own engineer. Seven years ago, Leclerc had overtaken Verstappen for the lead in the Euro Series karting and pushed him off the track, leaving the Dutchman seething. Now Verstappen had returned the favour, albeit with a rather bigger prize at stake this time.

The result was massive for everyone involved, for even bigger reasons than anyone knew at the time. When Max had signed his new contract in 2017, there was a clause inserted that would allow him to leave the team as a free agent a year early if certain conditions were not met. One of those was that he would be in the top three in the Drivers' Championship, a position at that point he had still never achieved at the end of the season. The date for reaching this target was the 2019 summer break, and before the Austrian Grand Prix, Max was eleven points behind third place occupied by Sebastian Vettel. Not only were Red Bull looking at another year in no man's land between the midfield and the front-runners, they were staring down the barrel of losing the best driver of his generation while their second driver Pierre Gasly floundered in a distant sixth. Everybody wanted Verstappen to stay, as did he, but he wanted to win, first and foremost. Were it not for that victory in Austria, Red Bull might have lost him for good. A chaotic race in Germany at a wet Nürburgring, a disastrous weekend for Mercedes and a masterful drive by Verstappen in changeable conditions confirmed things.

Max's forthright decision-making, of which that contract clause is a good example, meshed well with the team's own style. With Gasly unable to match their expectations, Red Bull got to the summer break, when they knew Verstappen would be staying, and dumped the Frenchman back to Toro Rosso, replacing him with Alex Albon, who clung on to his new teammate's coat-tails sufficiently to earn another year with the team in 2020, but was still nowhere near as fast. At last, Verstappen had a car fast enough and an engine reliable enough to take the fight to Ferrari, but sometimes in F1 that still is not enough, and two cars are certainly better than one. On the track, Verstappen could beat both Vettel and often Leclerc, who was fast becoming the Italian team's preferred driver, but up against a team who could split their strategies and play both sides, Red Bull would more often come off second best.

As such, 2019 became a season of highs and lows, when strategic gambles were high-risk, high-reward, but with no real title challenge even thinkable in the face of another year of Mercedes dominance; it suited Max well. His driving style was developing too: his overtakes remained feisty and uncompromising, as Leclerc found out in Austria, but his ability to remain calm when things weren't going his way or when a quiet, tyre-managing stint was required, was growing. He had always understood the tyres well, but now he was beginning to understand himself with, as so often, a maturity to belie his years. In an interview with GQ, he is asked to compare himself to the teenager who had made his F1 debut in 2015.

'I feel a lot wiser. If you ask anyone that question when they look back from when they were seventeen to when they were in their twenties, it's just very standard and normal that you have that same feeling,' he replied.

'It's the same in racing as well. When you do a lot more races, you have a lot more things you come across during a race or during a weekend, which gives you more experience in life in general, and more experience on track as well.'

He would secure one more win in the 2019 season at a track that was fast becoming his favourite, Interlagos in São Paulo. A popular track and often the site of the year's most exciting races, there were serious concerns, not least from Verstappen, when it seemed as though the race would not continue there beyond

2021 because of a political dispute, but its future was preserved until 2025 late in 2020.

Given that the race was one of those cancelled by the coronavirus pandemic in 2020, it was not impossible that Max Verstappen could have gone down in history as the last winner of the Brazilian Grand Prix at Interlagos. He started on pole for just the second time ever and led the race comfortably until he was blocked by the Williams of Robert Kubica in the pit lane and was forced to slam on the brakes, allowing Lewis Hamilton to undercut him and effectively take the lead. Max did not panic. He knew he would be fast on fresh tyres and it took him just two laps to get back ahead of Hamilton, executing a perfect overtake on the inside of the first corner and defending hard to stay in front. A safety car with sixteen laps to go saw him dive in for fresh tyres while Hamilton stayed out, setting up another grandstand finish as the already-crowned world champion (for a sixth time) tried to hang on to the lead. His defence lasted just a few hundred metres as Verstappen this time went round the outside of Turn One. Hamilton tried to come back at him into the corner known as Subida do Lago but Max hung him out to dry on the outside. The race had one final twist in the tail though. The two Ferraris tangled and the safety car was once again deployed, returning to the pits with just two laps to go. Red Bull were denied a one-two when Hamilton crashed into Albon in a last-gasp overtaking attempt, but Max was well clear of the trouble.

'If you can battle against the world champion for the lead, it's better than battling for P10. We gave each other enough room and it was cool,' Max said afterwards.

While Pierre Gasly answered questions next to them in the post-race press conference, Hamilton and Verstappen joked off-microphone about the race. The six-time world champion was hardly bitter about the defeat, having already sealed the overall win. A year before, they had chatted about his clash with Ocon when their positions were reversed, and Hamilton had been the voice of reason.

'He is allowed to unlap himself, you know,' Hamilton said to him, leaving Max briefly speechless. As someone who had grown up surrounded by F1, Verstappen's respect for Hamilton is obvious, and now it seems that respect is mutual.

Somehow Brazil had ended up being a place of growth for Max. In 2016, he had stunned the world there in the wet, two years later he had shown his teeth with Ocon, and this was probably his most mature victory yet, winning from pole for the first time since his F3 days. His racing education was nearing its completion. Not so long ago, these drivers were calling him dangerous and the FIA were changing the rules because of him. Now he was an equal among the likes of Hamilton and Vettel, and will one day surpass them.

When Covid struck in 2020 and cut off most international sport in the world at its knees, no one was immune to its effects, but the likes of Verstappen were among the lucky ones. With his racing simulator in Monaco and more money than he could have dreamt of as a teenager, he was able to keep life relatively normal, although it was his longest spell in one country for a decade. While he is not as prolific a streamer or social media user as the likes of Lando Norris or Charles Leclerc – Max's maturity broadens the minimal age gap between himself and other members of the 'next generation' in F1 – his profile certainly benefited from the chance to show a different side of himself.

It was not the same though. Max is a very skilled sim racer and much of the time uses his simulator for fun or spending time with his friends. Like Norris, he does not see it as like his job and perhaps being so young and enthusiastic, the lack of distance between his hobby and his occupation does not feel like a problem. He doesn't mind his own company either and his apartment in Monaco is decked out with equipment to keep him busy; not only is there a racing simulator in his living room, but his balcony is like a mini-gym complete with a Watt bike, a skiing machine, a rowing machine and weights. He's a keen road cyclist too – as many of the racing drivers who live in Monaco are – and eventually he had his personal trainer for company. Nevertheless, racing was what he wanted to be doing, something F1 finally made possible in July 2020 in a strict system of bubbles and testing. Crucially, drivers were allowed to get back on the black stuff and race. It was all any of them wanted and the world was welcome of the distraction from grim reality.

When the season had been expected to start as normal, Red Bull were extremely optimistic. In the second half of the season in particular, they had shown excellent pace. Verstappen had finished the year with three straight podiums to beat Charles Leclerc into third place and they were less than 100 points behind Ferrari. They were also buoyed by the fact that an FIA investigation into Ferrari's engine had ruled that they had been operating illegally at times in 2019, or at least through a loophole, and their power advantage over Red Bull all but vanished. In February's winter testing, Red Bull were the second team on the grid and optimistic of challenging even Mercedes. The confidence had convinced Verstappen to sign a new contract in January that would keep him at the team until 2023, well into the new set of regulations that were due at the end of 2020, only to be pushed back by a year due to the Covid-19 shutdown. It was a bold move, particularly with Ferrari and Mercedes seats opening up within that period. Once again, it was a tremendous show of confidence.

They were hurt though by the shutdown of factories that essentially froze development between testing and the start of the season, even though that gap had been extended from two weeks to more than three months. Traditionally, Red Bull are a team that comes on stronger at the end of the campaign because they seem to be better at in-season development. In what was to be a seventeen-race season over six months (rather than 21 or 22 over nine or ten), there was less opportunity for that, and Red Bull felt the pinch.

Tracks like Mexico, Brazil, Monaco and Singapore were all crossed off the list and replaced by more achievable events in places like Turkey and Portugal. The Dutch Grand Prix was a victim too, denying Max the chance to race on the Zandvoort dunes in an F1 car for the first time. Instead, there were double-headers in Austria, Great Britain and Bahrain.

'I think it certainly hurt us at the beginning,' Max said, looking back on the year.

'We had to get things in order, and if the races follow each other so quickly it's a bit unfortunate.'

If he thought the beginning of the season went poorly, it is a sign of the relentlessly high expectations of himself. The very first race ended in early disappointment because of an engine problem and two weeks later he would wish he hadn't crashed embarrassingly on the way to the grid in Hungary – although his team did a remarkably speedy rebuild and he ended up finishing second. In fact, for the first thirteen races of the season, he finished on the podium every single time he did not retire, which he did four times, all because of mechanical problems. The frustration though was that in those thirteen races, even though he had accumulated just one win and was still trailing world champion Hamilton by 120 points, yet again he did not have a teammate capable of racing fast enough to support his efforts against Mercedes. If the Red Bull team wanted his attitude to the season summed up in one comment, it was the one he made during the 70th Anniversary Grand Prix at Silverstone.

He had just been told by his engineer to back off because the turbulent air from the back of Hamilton's car, and the extremely high air temperatures of a British heatwave, were starting to hurt his tyres.

'Mate, this is the only chance we have to challenge the Mercedes instead of just sitting behind like a grandma,' he replied. If he backed off, he would give Hamilton enough of a gap to compensate for the fact that he would have to pit earlier on softer rubber. If he stayed on his tail, he could force the British driver to push harder, wear out his tyres quicker and perhaps even make a mistake. Starting on a harder tyre, Red Bull were aiming for a one-stop that would be faster than Hamilton's two-stop, and so it proved. They beat the Mercedes by eleven seconds. Had Verstappen not pushed his engineers to let him stay in touch early on though, he might never have made it work.

'We were just quicker today, mate,' they told him over the team radio after the chequered flag, but the truth was that if he hadn't been insistent, and they had not trusted him, it would never have worked. It is the kind of override function that few modern drivers are allowed by their teams: Hamilton, Vettel, Raikkonen and Verstappen. Max is the only one of those without a world title, which speaks volumes.

One thing that 2020 will be remembered for apart from the Covid pandemic is the rise of the global anti-racism movement that started as a series of demonstrations in the US and steadily grew into worldwide conversation about racial inequality in society. It hit sport too, with stars across a wide range of events 'taking a knee' in solidarity. It got so big that it generated significant blowback, with many claiming that Black Lives Matter, the organisation that led the protests, had more nefarious and destructive aims against law and order than merely equality.

As such, when it came to 'taking a knee' at Grands Prix, the paddock was divided. F1's own response was muddled, cutting away from the drivers' demonstration at a key moment on the world TV feed at one race and then botching the organisation of it at another. A number of drivers, Max included, chose not to do so while thirteen did at each race. It had been fourteen initially, before Kevin Magnussen chose to stop during the season.

'I am very committed to equality and the fight against racism,' Verstappen posted on social media, explaining his decision not to kneel.

'But I believe everyone has the right to express themself [sic] at a time and in a way that suits them. I will not take the knee today but respect and support the personal choices every driver makes. #WeRaceAsOne #EndRacism'

As it did in almost every country, especially in Europe where the culture war of right vs left, of 'freedom of speech' vs 'wokery' was raging on with as much vim and vigour as it ever had in a tumultuous decade. Back home in Holland, Max's decision not to kneel became a national conversation. Even the national football team manager Ronald Koeman was asked about it.

'I do not understand that not everyone does that,' he responded, with the same confusion that many felt at such a disunited show of unity.

'It surprises me. This is something you discuss with each other? In England you see football teams kneeling. Then it would be very strange if three or four players just stand there?'

It wasn't so much a criticism of Max, but of the sport's response as a whole. Eventually, with the most successful driver of all time and the grid's only black driver Lewis Hamilton driving it, F1 coordinated its own show of solidarity with the fight against racial inequality.

For Max, it dragged him into a political sphere he had always been keen to avoid. When BLM came to F1, he was instantly cautious.

'It's good to do something, but you also have to be very careful in these situations, and be careful what you write or post,' he said.

'I can't decide for others, and I don't want to do that. I can only speak for myself. But I can't imagine anyone favouring racism. Everyone is equal in this world to me.'

Max's reaction could be read in any number of ways. No one doubted his own personal moral view, one of anti-racism and equality, but clearly some drivers were doing more than others. It could be said that Max did not feel, still a relative youngster, senior enough on the grid to be a leader; Hamilton had already achieved a great deal in his career when he knelt in front of his colleagues wearing a 'Black Lives Matter' T-shirt. Max though was already a senior figure on the grid. He may only have turned 23 in 2020, but it was his sixth season in Formula One. Indeed when at the end of the season the drivers presented a signed helmet to outgoing F1 CEO Chase Carey, it was Hamilton and Verstappen who did the presentation.

Perhaps though a lack of security in his achievements on track also informed Max's apparent lack of conviction in social activism. He was still not a world champion, nor had he even finished in the top two. In his mind, he was yet to conquer F1, even though everyone regarded him as one of the best drivers in the world, perhaps the best beside Hamilton.

On the track, Verstappen ended the season on a high, although celebrations were arrested by his signature high expectations. With Hamilton still recovering from contracting Covid, driving after a negative test but still lethargic, Verstappen took pole position on Saturday before driving away from the field on a short run to the first corner. Just as he had at Silverstone for his only other victory of the season, he managed his tyres to perfection, although this time he was running in clean, cool air at the front rather than the turbulent stuff behind the two Mercedes cars. At no point did Max really look threatened during his one-stop strategy, even though he had told his engineer with twenty laps to go that he had little confidence in the tyres lasting.

'That was the best most static race we've enjoyed for a long, long time,' Christian Horner said afterwards, referring to it as a marker for the 2021 title challenge.

Verstappen resisted the urge to perform a few celebratory doughnuts on the track. He let Drivers' champion Hamilton and his teammate Bottas, who had helped secure the Constructors' title, create an enormous smokescreen on the start-finish straight. He was already thinking about getting home for Christmas, celebrating with his family and then beginning pre-season training again. It would be a short winter with less than three months between the last race and the first day of testing, before rushing into the 2021 season again – and he had a title challenge to prepare for. He had come within nine points of pipping Valtteri Bottas, in a vastly faster and more reliable car, to second place in the championship, a feat that would actually have been a feather in his cap.

'For me, that's not very interesting,' he said without a hint of a smile on his face when asked two races from the end of 2020 whether he was thinking about reeling in Bottas for second place. It was win or bust. He had no time to drive around like a grandma behind the two Mercedes. Lewis Hamilton had just drawn level with Michael Schumacher on a record seven world titles. It was time to start chasing them down.

13

A TRUE RIVAL TO LEWIS

There is a saying in Formula One so prevalent that it has become a cliché: it is one thing to catch the car in front of you, but another to pass it.

For Max, overtaking was the thing that had won him such a tremendous reputation. The move on Felipe Nasr in Belgium had drawn praise from just about everyone who had driven an F1 car before. His tiptoeing round the outside of Turn One to overtake Hamilton in Brazil in 2019 was as aggressive as it was brave. But he didn't want to be known for moments of brilliance. He wanted to be known for winning titles.

He was probably ready to do so even before his seventh season, but his car wasn't. Red Bull, the team that had shown the faith in him required to capture his signature when he was still a teenager, had taken some time to reach parity in the hybrid era, but the second half of 2020 was a step forward. Significantly, the Honda engine was no longer being outmuscled by the Mercedes powertrain that had been virtually unstoppable since 2014 and the dawn of hybrid technology in the sport.

Nevertheless, Christian Horner's talk of mounting a title challenge in 2021 at the end of the previous season was very much just that: talk. His team would need to walk the walk that they had practised but not executed since 2013. But self-doubt was not something Red Bull ever dealt in, and Verstappen was no different. His only real doubts were whether the car was good enough to challenge, and even early on in 2021 it became clear that it was. In that sense, Red Bull had caught Mercedes. Now what they needed Max to do was pass them.

It is probably a coincidence that shifts in Max's personal life happened at the same time as what might be termed a 'levelling up' in his professional one. Late in 2020, he began a relationship with Kelly Piquet. Kelly, nine years Max's senior, had been a familiar face in the paddock for some years. Her father Nelson Piquet had been a three-time F1 world champion and she had worked in motor sport in her own right. Through those connections, she met Daniil Kvyat, the former Red Bull driver with whom she had a child, Penelope, in 2019. Sadly, she and Daniil broke up later that year. In October 2020, she and Max got together and she was soon being spotted in the Red Bull garage on race weekends alongside Raymond Vermeulen. Racing drivers' relationships are often like their professional lives – exciting, fast, furious but ultimately fleeting – even though you never hope that they are. At least in Kelly's case, Max has someone who has seen much of what goes with life in the paddock before. You would think that little about the insane circus of F1 can shock her at this point.

One person seen a little less in the Red Bull garage in 2021 though was Max's father. He had always insisted, although not very convincingly, that he would not get in the way of his son's career. Certainly the team at Red Bull have at times been keen to keep him at arm's length where possible, his fiery reputation and track record a potential risk to the branding that makes the team possible. He had already started staying away from some races – when Max crashed on the warm-up lap to the grid half an hour before the race at the 2020 Hungarian Grand Prix, Jos was frantically texting the team from afar trying to find out whether they would be able to fix the car in time. For context, that 30 minutes of engineering was one of the more remarkable turnarounds of the modern F1 era, as frantic radio messages that were later published will testify. They did manage to get the car in one piece and functioning before the lights went out, something for which Max gave a lengthy and heartfelt apology. But you can only imagine how it went down with the team at the time when the driver's father, who had spent decades building go-karts and managing his career, kept asking for updates. The team manager was the one responsible for rebuffing him and assured Verstappen Sr that everything would be fine, and could we just get on with it please? Any schoolteacher whose students have so-called pushy parents can sympathise.

In 2021, Jos spent a little more time on the sofa trying not to get nervous, although he would still reappear at key moments. As the title race ramped up, he was nearly ever-present. Clearly, he was never going to miss the Dutch Grand Prix at Zandvoort, and he still turned up to places like Silverstone, Barcelona and Budapest – lesson learned from 2020 on that last one perhaps. But he was certainly more hands off. After all, he had an ever-growing family to devote time to as well; Jason Jaxx and Mila Faye were still in nappies, as was his daughter's first child Luka, who was soon to be joined by Lio. Now a grandfather as well as a father, Jos had less and less time to flit around the world for Grands Prix.

'I have a private life, so I can't be everywhere,' said Jos after someone quizzed him about his absenteeism.

'I now have a beautiful family, so I don't want that [travel] anymore. I'll go there if I have to be there, it's an important year and it's looking good.'

He even admitted the racing was often more exciting at home – or perhaps just more nerve-wracking – because he didn't know everything that was going on. And he had a new protégé to work with in the shape of Thierry Vermeulen, Raymond's son, whom he was mentoring through the early stages of his motor sport career.

Meanwhile, his old mentee Max suffered an early setback when Mercedes out-strategised him in Bahrain. Seven-time world champion Lewis Hamilton took the chequered flag and thanked his team in Bahrain and back at the Brackley factory. But it was not the same. This was certainly different.

'We know we're not quick enough,' Hamilton said to his engineer despite having held off Verstappen in the final five laps, painfully aware of the fact after the Dutchman had overtaken him, although he had done so with all four wheels off the track and was told by his Red Bull engineer to give the place back.

'Why didn't you just let me go?' Max complained on the radio afterwards. He knew his move would incur a five-second penalty but trusted that he could pull out a larger gap than that over Hamilton and retain the victory. It was an impetuous, frustrated moment of someone so very sick of finishing second, and even sicker of having to literally give the race away. It would not be the first that season he had to do it – but it would probably be the least controversial.

Bahrain is a hot, sticky place, and afterwards, with the benefit of a cold towel, a frank debrief with the ever-calm Horner and despite Max's frustrations, there was real optimism from him in the paddock. He told the team that a race weekend like that, which included pole position only for Hamilton to undercut him when Red Bull were slow to respond during the pit stop phase, would have delighted them in 2020, and it was a measure of the progress and expectations of the team in 2021 that they were annoyed to have only taken second. His reaction was a measure of his own growing maturity too.

What he could not necessarily know, although he might have guessed, was that his maturity and character would be tested and indeed questioned in the course of a campaign that would be dominated by the battle between himself and Hamilton: the pretender and the champion pitted against one another in a showdown that even the producers of Formula One's own fly-on-the-wall documentary series *Drive to Survive* could not have dreamed up.

The list of drivers who can truly claim to have outdriven Hamilton is vanishingly small. Teammate Jenson Button at McLaren and Nico Rosberg at Mercedes, who pipped him to the world title in 2016, can perhaps be the only ones to claim they have done so. Fernando Alonso came close, finishing on the same points as him when they were both at McLaren in 2007, but he did finish third in the standings to Hamilton's second. You can ask all three what they think of Lewis and all believe him to be a brilliant racer, possibly the greatest of all time, but they all also know one thing: you can get under his skin. It may be less true every year as he gets older and, somehow, better, but all three of them gained some mental edge over Hamilton that made him easier to beat. In Rosberg's case, it was playing on an insecurity over internal Mercedes politics. In Alonso's, it was underhandedness like delaying in his pit box in Hungary to stymie Hamilton's qualifying run. The ever-affable Button says he always found a way to be quicker on a Sunday – and he made sure Hamilton knew it, even subtly.

Verstappen, just as he had upset drivers when he first arrived in F1, started to get under Hamilton's skin in the second race of the season. Having yielded to allow Hamilton past in Bahrain, he was determined to be hard but fair – but primarily hard – for the rest of the season. Nice guys rarely finish first, particularly in motor racing, and Verstappen was done with being a nice guy, if indeed he ever was such on the track. That first race would stick out as an anomaly rather than the norm. Battle was joined on both sides.

In damp conditions at Imola that could hardly be further from the ones in the desert in Bahrain, again it was Verstappen first into Turn One, although Hamilton was alongside him. Just as Lewis had afforded him no space in the closing stages of the first race, so Verstappen left him none this time. Hamilton bounced over the sausage curbs and could only watch as his rival drove off into the distance. A safety car bunched the field back again, and on the restart, Hamilton positioned his car on the outside of the same corner. The gap was there again but his lesson had been learned. It felt like a poignant moment. You can't exactly make eye contact with each other in a Grand Prix but if you could, Max might have detected a flicker in Hamilton's gaze.

A mistake by Hamilton later, one that he himself called impatient and human – words we don't usually associate with him – meant Verstappen was largely unchallenged on his way to victory. The British driver fought his way back to second though, meaning two things had quickly become clear: that Hamilton and Mercedes were a little rattled, and that this title would be a case of who made the fewest mistakes, who could stay the coolest. For now, though, Hamilton and Verstappen – and Mercedes and

Red Bull – were still in the realms of civility. Perhaps with so many races still to go and no clashes that had cost either man more than a few points, it was hard to get too upset. That would come, but not yet. Even when Verstappen elbowed pole-sitter Hamilton aside at Turn One of the Spanish Grand Prix, the Mercedes' dominance of that track meant he reeled him in later.

'They had all the options,' Horner reassured Max afterwards, noting that Mercedes were so far clear of the rest of the field behind them that they could hedge their bets between Hamilton and Bottas.

Red Bull had been painfully aware of how much easier Mercedes found it to bat off their new rivals in 2020 by having two cars at the front rather than one. They had hoped in 2021 that they had solved that problem by dropping Albon, whose performances had yielded just two podiums in the 2020 season and a seventh-place finish in the championship, and bringing in Sergio Perez. It is difficult to explain quite how radical a move this was from Red Bull, but at their very heart they are a team built on driver development and daring. After all, promoting young drivers was what Helmut Marko had wanted to do right from the beginning, and how he had tempted Dietrich Mateschitz to get involved in motor racing in the first place. So when they handed a 2021 contract to Sergio Perez, a 31-year-old Mexican driver with a hefty sponsorship package and nearly 200 F1 races behind him, it was a significant departure from the team's DNA and sent everyone two clear messages: Max is our number one and we will do anything to get him on the top step of the podium. The only problem? It wasn't working. Hamilton had won three of the first four races, had arguably only lost at Imola through his own mistake, and even there he still finished second. Perez meanwhile was yet to force his way onto the podium and could not effectively rear-gun for Verstappen. By his own admission, Perez was still struggling to get to grips with the car, designed so specifically with Verstappen in mind with its high rake concept and notoriously slippery, unstable rear end. Mercedes had their own problems between drivers as Bottas ignored an order not to hold Hamilton up, but at least the Finn was quick enough to do so. Perez did not even have the pace to get ahead of Verstappen, never mind hold him up. Red Bull were also in a quandary from a technical standpoint. Max did not think the Barcelona defeat had been down to strategy.

'It helps a lot when you're clearly just faster,' he said in typically blunt fashion, mirroring the messages of Hamilton to his own team after the first race suggesting that they 'did not have the pace'. When two teams in F1 are saying the other is quicker, they probably both believe they are lying.

Red Bull though did not think they were significantly quicker, and pressed ahead with an aggressive development strategy. With regulation change on the horizon at the end of 2021, teams started to devote resource towards the 2022 car at some point during the season. Back-markers Haas even said they would not be developing the 2021 car at all, merely focusing on the sea change due to take effect from the start of 2022. Red Bull had no such thoughts, and believed that their relentless factory work would eventually pay off.

In the meantime, they had to capitalise on Mercedes' mistakes, and opportunity beckoned shortly after the disappointing Spanish Grand Prix in Monaco. The race in Monte Carlo is something of a homecoming, with so many present and past drivers calling the principality home. Max of course remains one of them: his apartment overlooks the quay that hosts millions of dollars' worth of yachts. However, the actual Grand Prix there had invariably been an occasion of frustration for him. In 2018, he had ended the day slumped in the corner of an anonymous room in Red Bull's mobile HQ, angry at himself for the qualifying crash that had ruined the weekend. He had dragged himself into the shower and then across town to teammate Daniel Ricciardo's celebration after he had delivered victory, but even though he smiled for the cameras and for Daniel, whom he genuinely liked, Max's heart was not in it. He had not proven the point he was so desperate to prove, and three years later, he still hadn't; Red Bull had given him a car that was, on some days, quick enough to compete with Hamilton and he had yet to beat him mano-a-mano.

Monaco is not always the greatest race on the calendar. F1 cars have only got wider and the streets of Monte Carlo have not. It is so narrow and the track so short that overtaking is virtually impossible. Max learned as much the hard way in 2015 when he smashed into the barriers at Turn One after trying to overtake Romain Grosjean, and when, with a vastly faster car, he was only able to advance from last to ninth over the course of the 2018 race.

So it was a point of some frustration that he was not able to take pole position on Saturday, beaten by two tenths of a second by the grid's only Monégasque driver Charles Leclerc. That frustration was doubled by the fact that Leclerc crashed late in the session, causing a red flag and terminating all other runners – including Verstappen, who was halfway through a lap that probably would have earned him pole. A string of expletives followed down the radio back to the pit wall when the red flag came out as he bombed it through the tunnel.

'This is pissing me off,' he said, already feeling like the dice were loaded against him.

His anger turned to relief 24 hours later when Ferrari found a crack in Leclerc's bodywork that meant they could not start the race and Verstappen, albeit from the second-placed grid box, would effectively drive off from pole. Hamilton meanwhile, after a difficult day trying to heat up the tyres, was down in seventh. His teammate Bottas did not complete the race after a wheel nut got stuck on during a pit stop and had to be removed with a blowtorch much later. In other books about other drivers, this will go down as a nightmare weekend. For Max, it felt like a bit of redemption. After years of undeserved bad luck on the riviera, things had finally turned his way. The only jeopardy on race day would be the start, which he nailed by driving across the track and covering off Bottas. The rest was almost a procession, as much as driving a 1000-horsepower car round a narrow seaside city with race-ending consequences for every smallest mistake can be. In the cockpit, he just laughed. It had not been a particularly draining or adrenalin-fuelled afternoon. It was as routine as he thought it should be.

He could not conceal his smile afterwards. He was fully aware he had never even finished on the podium in Monaco. He knew there was a long way to go in the season and said he was already thinking about the next race in Azerbaijan; he barely even noticed Serena Williams standing next to him in the post-race ceremony.

From the outside though, there was a feeling that this title race between Hamilton and Verstappen was still waiting to ignite. In reality, they had not raced on track against each other an awful lot, and when they had it had been in circumstances where the two cars had quite different amounts of pace. The wider sports media were obsessing about the chances of two heavyweights Anthony Joshua and Tyson Fury meeting in anger;

if these two racing heavyweights could get together too, it would be the kind of antidote to eighteen months of Covid hell that the sporting public needed. Once again in Azerbaijan they were kept apart by fate – Verstappen halted by a tyre failure and Hamilton by an inadvertent bashing of a switch in the cockpit that rendered his brakes useless during a late restart – but those baying for a gladiatorial showdown would not have to wait too much longer.

The narrative thus far had often been that the pressure of Verstappen and his rock-and-roll approach to racing had forced Hamilton, these days an ultimately calm driver, into mistakes, but in France those roles were reversed. Max, by his own admission, made a mistake at the first corner and let Hamilton through. Red Bull reacted eighteen laps later by trying an undercut that Ricciardo at McLaren had already deployed with great effect further down the order. That grabbed him track position, and Red Bull pulled the trigger again to pit Verstappen when they realised that the two-stop strategy would allow them to be quicker at the end of the race, on fresher and softer rubber. It was a typically bold move from a team who have made such bravery their calling card. With just a lap and a half to go, Max caught Hamilton and passed him with ease. He extended his lead at the top of the standings to twelve points. It was a starter pistol on the title race in earnest.

Verstappen said: 'The whole race we've been fighting each other. It will be like this for the rest of the season.' His prediction would of course prove to be right.

And anyone who had been doubting whether Verstappen could really challenge Hamilton for the title, or would just tail off like so many had before once the meat of the season was reached, could not doubt him anymore.

'If we can beat them here, we can beat them anywhere,' said Horner triumphantly.

Mercedes knew it too. 'We've got to find some pace,' Hamilton said on a radio message that would have rung in the ears of almost all of Mercedes' 891 employees. He knew they were in a fight.

And if anyone was still unsure, Verstappen cemented his place at the top of the standings with a double victory at the Austrian double-header, his team's home track, the place where he had impressed the bosses for the first time and where he had first driven a Red Bull car in any format. It was also a race where an entire stand would be decked out in orange. The reinstatement of the Dutch Grand Prix to the calendar means Max has many home races now – Netherlands, Belgium, Monaco – but Austria's relative proximity and placement in the heart of the summer means there is always a strong travelling Dutch contingent to make the Red Bull Ring feel like a home from home.

Max added to that feeling with two imperious drives in the space of eight days. In both he took pole position, got away cleanly and won the race at a canter. Mercedes even conceded defeat before the chequered flag in the first one, and in the second, Hamilton, Bottas, Perez, Leclerc and Norris produced one of the races of the season scrapping for the podium places, but Max was long gone, finishing more than 45 seconds ahead of Hamilton, who was wide-eyed in his amazement at the pace differential afterwards. He knew Red Bull had brought a significant aerodynamic upgrade to Austria, but cannot have predicted how much extra pace it would add.

'Keep turning the screw,' was Christian Horner's advice to Verstappen, incendiary words he might have regretted a few weeks later.

What followed was the most memorable moment of the season to date, and in any other year would have been the iconic moment. In fact, you could argue it was actually more impactful than 2021's dramatic finale, because it so changed the timbre of Verstappen and Hamilton's relationship for ever. Over their years racing against each other on occasion and so far in 2021, when the majority of their clashes had been no more than sparring, they had built up a level of respect. In 2019 in Brazil they had even enjoyed giving each other enough room to jostle safely. 'That was cool!' Max said at the time. Not so much, two years later.

The context of the British Grand Prix is important. The race at Silverstone holds special status within motor sport and is historically one of the best attended. So too it would be in 2021 as it obtained permission from the UK government to welcome hundreds of thousands of spectators back to the event, despite ongoing pandemic restrictions. Best of all, the sun shone, and the Woodstock of F1 went ahead in a tidal wave of overpriced cider, sunburn and worn-out grass.

That transmitted to the drivers too, particularly Hamilton, whose relationship with the British public was not always so rosy. By this point, he had graduated close to national treasure level, and anyway the petrolheads who come to Silverstone had never doubted him. Either way, the scenes after he went fastest in qualifying on Friday night, part of F1's experimental format that included a sprint race on the Saturday that would determine the starting order for the race in full, will live long in the memory. It was an emotionally charged celebration in front of an adoring Friday night crowd that had felt a world away when Hamilton was sitting in a Middle Eastern hotel room suffering badly from Covid just a few months before. Even for the non-Hamilton fans, the occasion was a tonic.

The sun came out again on Saturday and so did the crowds. They were disappointed when Verstappen got ahead off the line in sprint qualifying but thrilled when Hamilton stayed within touching distance. At Copse Corner, a fast right-hander surrounded by some of the biggest grandstands on the course, Hamilton slid up the outside. Modern cars take the corner only just lifting off the throttle, at around 175 miles an hour. Guts barely even covers it, but also tremendous trust in the driver on your inside. Hamilton got halfway through the move but then thought better of it. Were he to spin or crash, it would send him down the order and leave him fighting from the back on Sunday. In such a close title race, the risk was not worth the reward. He might get another chance, he thought, but Red Bull closed the door. Verstappen never got more than two seconds away, but Hamilton never got within one. Max held him at arm's length in the dirty air as Lewis found himself butting up against that invisible barrier. Starting from behind on Sunday, he would need to do something special to get past.

The first lap was virtually identical, albeit with Verstappen starting eight metres ahead of Hamilton on pole instead of behind. He got the better start once again, held off Hamilton (just) through the first part of the lap and hung him round the outside of the Brooklands hairpin. They drove up the old pit straight and once again, Hamilton pulled alongside Verstappen into Copse. Only this time, Max had weaved to the outside to cover off the racing line while his rival had dipped to the inside and started to come alongside him. This time, he did not withdraw, and they collided. Verstappen was nudged sideways and careered into the tyre barriers. He had lost one wheel before he even hit them. The gravel did little to slow him down and he hit the wall at a terrific speed. It was the type of accident that would have been fatal in years gone by, maybe even killing spectators too. The advances in safety mechanism saved many lives. Had they not existed, the fallout would have been considerably greater.

As it was, there was still plenty of contention. Once it had been established that Verstappen was broadly fine (he walked out of the car under his own steam but was helped into an ambulance and taken to hospital for checks), Red Bull and Mercedes frantically started radioing to Michael Masi the race director, stating their man's case. Mercedes boss Toto Wolff sent Masi an email with telemetry that they said proved it was Verstappen's fault, while Red Bull said they had data that proved the opposite. Masi told them he didn't check his emails during racing and it would be handled in time by the stewards. They eventually decided it was 'predominantly' Hamilton's fault and gave him a three-place grid penalty for the next race.

The toss of that coin was argued for months. Was Hamilton given 'racing room'? Was Verstappen too aggressive? Was Lewis too impatient? Should the two have their heads banged together in an effort to make them see sense? Everyone had an opinion on the incident and the penalty doled out. Even Piers Morgan.

Predictably, no one on the Red Bull pit wall thought the penalty was anywhere near enough, including Max. Before he even left hospital he had tweeted about it, watching on TV with Jos as Hamilton sprayed champagne and drank in the atmosphere after eventually sealing victory and closing the gap in the world title race to just eight points.

'Glad I'm ok,' Max wrote. 'Very disappointed with being taken out like this. The penalty given does not help us and doesn't do justice to the dangerous move Lewis made on track. Watching the celebrations while still in hospital is disrespectful and unsportsmanlike behaviour but we move on.'

That sentiment remained too. Even the morning after the last race of the season, when Jos and Max sat down for a hungover interview with David Coulthard, they talked about it and how appalled they were by the celebrations.

Additionally, the crash had cost Red Bull more than a few points. The repairs to Max's car would run to more than £1 million in the first year where F1 was subject to a spending cap. They felt it had become open season for firing shots at Max too, with the accusations of aggression and arrogance that had dogged his early career returning to the fore, even from members of the Mercedes team. Red Bull fought fire with fire. Days later, Horner clapped back at Max's critics and promptly submitted an appeal, suggesting to the FIA that Mercedes and Hamilton had not been punished enough. They wondered aloud in interviews whether Mercedes should be forced to foot the bill. The noise was deafening.

Max, apart from the social media outburst, tried his best to stay out of it. He was not seriously hurt, other than the kind of stiffness you might expect from a smash involving forces of up to 51G. He spent the best part of six hours in hospital that night, waiting until the CT and MRI scans of his brain had come back clear, but he was released back to his team hotel early enough to get to bed before 11pm. At 10.30am the next morning, he flew back to Monaco for a week of rest before the Hungarian Grand Prix, traditionally a race where Red Bull have dominated. But if Max was hoping that Red Bull's past successes and the swinging pendulum of the season would ensure he had a peaceful and unchallenged race, he was duly disappointed. Rain greeted drivers on race day and the track was not quite completely wet or dry for the start, conditions that in fact the likes of Hamilton and Verstappen might have relished, but both their races were compromised before they had even really begun.

For the second race in a row, Verstappen was taken out by a Mercedes – although not quite so directly or so violently. At the very first corner, Bottas missed his breaking point and shunted into the back of Norris, who in turn collided with Verstappen. The Red Bull was badly damaged, although not irrevocably, and he was at least able to drive it back up to what was eventually (after late penalties elsewhere) upgraded to ninth. He was also fortunate that Hamilton was the only car not to pit behind the safety car when the track dried out, meaning he lost out to the entire field still wearing his intermediate tyres. However, with a fully functioning car rather than Verstappen's damaged one, Hamilton was able to recover to third place and salvage enough points to retake the lead in the World Drivers' Championship, while Mercedes also overtook Red Bull in the Constructors'. To do it at a track where Red Bull had traditionally been so strong, especially having been knocked off their perch at old strongholds like Paul Ricard in France, must have felt particularly sweet. Verstappen and Red Bull now had the four-week summer break in which to ponder how they could swing the advantage back their way.

The truth was that the team did not think there was much to swing back. But for some poor luck in Azerbaijan, Britain and then Hungary, they would be leading. That was no reason to sit on their laurels though. Mercedes were vulnerable. Hamilton had almost passed out on the podium in Hungary and admitted he believed he was suffering from Long Covid, the effects of which no one fully understood at the time but which were certainly not conducive to peak physical performance. The usually serene Mercedes PR machine was starting to look ragged and disjointed.

They had finally decided to drop Bottas, who had gone from willing No. 2 to petulant wannabe superstar, for the rising star George Russell – but in the meantime would have to see Bottas out until the end of the year. There were cracks in the armour – all Red Bull had to do was find them.

There was also the small matter of Max's reputation to defend. He was not happy at being painted as the bad guy, and nor were the team. It was going to get worse before it got better though – and for many, it may never get better. It took Hamilton years of ruthless success to win over the world, and it may yet take years for Verstappen to do the same. At least at Silverstone the stewards were on his side, albeit not as comprehensively as Red Bull would have liked. The same could not be said a few weeks later in Monza.

Talk of the growing rivalry between Hamilton and Verstappen had taken a backseat in the build-up to the Italian Grand Prix by virtue of the worst kept secret in F1 – Russell's accession to Mercedes – finally being confirmed. The hype was around what challenge Russell would mount against Hamilton, rather than Verstappen's own efforts to dethrone the great champion. It was a welcome smokescreen for the Dutchman, for whom the heat of the fallout from Silverstone had been distinctly unpleasant. Max is hot-headed and confrontational, but those things tend to fade quickly. Lingering animosity is not his style.

So it can hardly be fair to characterise what happened at Monza as malicious, although many would like to paint it that way. Hamilton had erred in the sprint event on Saturday and would start fourth, with Verstappen (by virtue of an engine penalty for Bottas) on pole. 'It should be an easy win for Max,' Hamilton predicted in one of the more obvious attempts to get in the younger man's head.

Hamilton was also disconsolate though. 'They bring upgrades every week. There's only one week they haven't brought an upgrade.' And it was true. Red Bull had been constantly adding pace to their package and Verstappen was benefiting. The joker in the pack on race day though was his old teammate Daniel Ricciardo. McLaren's development had also been rapid and Ricciardo, in his Mercedes-powered car, launched brilliantly from second on Sunday at Monza and got past Verstappen. Hamilton moved up to third and was, all of a sudden, in Verstappen's gearbox. He was alongside a corner later and tried to go around the outside of one of the notoriously narrow chicanes at Monza. Max left him precious little space, held position and they bumped wheels. No serious damage but advantage Verstappen, for now.

That advantage faded when Red Bull, the kings of the sub-two-second stop, fell foul of the new pit procedures and left him sitting still for eleven seconds. Less than a minute later, Hamilton re-passed Norris for effective third place, and if he could find the pace before his own pit stop, maybe second ahead of Max. A perfect stop would have put him ahead of the Red Bull. As it was, a split-second hesitation forced him to wait for an extra second, meaning he emerged side-by-side with... guess who? The pair whom the fates had largely kept apart in the early weeks were now inextricable.

Hamilton arrived at the first corner, a tight right and then left-handed chicane, half a car length ahead and on the inside. It would mean Max would have the inside line for the second corner, but probably too far back to make it count. In the cockpit, Verstappen braked marginally later than he normally would, planning to go deep into the corner and swing around the outside of Hamilton to compete for the second apex. As they reached the second part of the corner, he ran out of room.

Hamilton forced him into the orange kerb, placed to make cutting the corner impossible. In the blink of an eye, Verstappen was propelled up into the air and was powerless to stop his car careering into Hamilton's. Albeit at relatively slow speed, the sight of his car crushing the top of Hamilton's and his rear tyre rubbing against the British driver's helmet was a terrifying one. Had the halo structure, introduced in 2018, not been in place, Hamilton might have been killed or at the very least badly injured. As it was, he was merely left with a sore neck and a totalled car.

'That's what you get when you don't leave the space. Fuck!' Verstappen complained, conveniently forgetting his own failure to leave Hamilton space merely minutes earlier. Such is the short and selective memory of a racing driver, especially one who knows the stewards are listening to his every word.

It wasn't enough. The stewards decided that, as Hamilton was at pains to point out after the race, Verstappen was behind going into the first corner and therefore had not earned the right to racing space in the second part of the corner. That was a point of some contention, naturally, and Max did not even feel Lewis had given him the space he deserved in the first part. Red Bull called it a racing incident, which rather suggested they knew what was coming from the stewards – namely a three-place grid penalty for Max, matching the penalty they had given his rival a few weeks earlier. Fair's fair, perhaps.

Nevertheless, the knives came out for Max once again. Hamilton criticised the move, naturally, but also Verstappen's failure to check on him after getting out of the car. Certainly, having been so critical of Lewis' celebrations after the British Grand Prix, there was an opportunity to take the moral high ground there. Instead, Max walked straight off to the pit lane. In all likelihood, it was the right decision. Anyone who knows him knows his emotions would have been running too high at that moment for civility. Plenty joined in on the Max-bashing, given licence by the stewards' decision. Former driver Jackie Stewart accused him of taking a long time to mature, a familiar script for Max's detractors.

And the great tragedy was that nothing could be further from the truth. He had proved as much just a week before, when he had overcome the pressure of a race on home soil, one that had been organised specifically because of his own popularity, to take victory in the Dutch Grand Prix.

After one cancellation and one delay, both due to Covid, from May to September, the Netherlands would finally host a Grand Prix for the first time since 1985. The race had been wiped off the calendar by Bernie Ecclestone for not making enough money, and organisers were determined to prove that despite the limits of fading Covid restrictions and having refunded more than £8 million worth of tickets, that would not be a problem this time. With Max flying in the world championship, they were never surer that they were on to a winner. By the time it got to lights out on Sunday, the race appropriately sponsored by Heineken felt more like a football match than a Grand Prix race. F1 fans have become accustomed to seeing one stand decked out in orange on race weekends in northern Europe; the site of 15 or 20 of them lining the banked corners of the sand dune circuit was something to behold.

It was not exactly a low-key weekend either. Max had never had such a frantic media schedule but tried to enjoy every moment of it. He even did a track walk, something he claimed not to have done for four years.

The great and the good of Dutch society turned out. On Sunday, King Willem-Alexander, Queen Máxima and their daughters Princess Catharina-Amalia and Princess Ariane were given a tour of the garage and enthusiastically bumped fists with Max before he showed the King around his cockpit. Dutch DJ Tiësto had the honour of waving the chequered flag. And hundreds of thousands more turned out too – with millions more watching from home. Ziggo, the satellite TV channel with the Dutch rights to F1, threw their doors open to the whole country, a record 3.5 million of whom tuned in to watch the race. There are only 17 million people in Holland, meaning one in five of every man, woman and child was watching one way or another. Many millions more worldwide would have watched it too, but doubtless it was that bit more special for those watching one of their own.

As had become customary in 2021, Max shared the front row with Lewis. When he beat him to the first corner, the crowd roared its approval. You would have forgiven them for losing their voices by the end after another flawless drive by Verstappen. Only when Bottas' long stint at the front held him up and allowed Hamilton to close up behind him did victory look in question, but once he passed the Finn he drove off into the late summer sun once again.

'It's nice pushing for 72 laps here!' Max told his team with a giggle. Zandvoort may not be a great place to watch wheel-to-wheel racing, but it certainly is visually spectacular and feels fast all the way round. After a stressful summer and the enormous pressure and circus of driving your home race, Max had clearly enjoyed getting back to what he loves: driving fast. Winning a home Grand Prix is something few drivers get the chance to do. Doing it for the first time will never leave Max. It was a special day.

For that weekend, the world title seemed almost irrelevant, or at least secondary. When Max jumped onto the top step of the podium with the Dutch flag draped around his shoulders, it was a moment of such freedom from all the trappings and pressure of F1. Max rarely looks bothered by them, but he wouldn't be human if he weren't.

Zandvoort felt like a pause, a moment of pulling his head above the tumultuous waters of the title race to breathe the fresh North Sea air and fill his lungs with the adoration of a home crowd, before diving back below the surface for one final, epic tussle with Hamilton. Just five points separated the pair after they crashed into each other at Monza, and as the F1 circus flew away from its European heartland at the end of the summer, it became clear that the race was unlikely to be decided much before the final Grand Prix. No one could have predicted quite how close it would be.

14

KING OF THE WORLD

You could have forgiven Max Verstappen for sacking off his 24th birthday party. He got back home from Russia a few days before, a race where he had to serve a grid penalty due to the Monza crash, took an engine penalty that forced him to start from the back, and took no meaningful part in qualifying. While he fought his way back up to second place, victory for Lewis Hamilton in the changeable conditions (Lando Norris' failure to put wet tyres on cost him a maiden victory) meant that he took back the lead in the title race.

But Max was grateful to have been able to limit the damage to just a seven-point swing and have taken the engine penalty that was inevitable at some point under the new regulations. Mercedes would have to take one too – but the analysts also knew that the last three tracks of the season in the Middle East were likely to favour Hamilton's car. The next four would have to count for Red Bull in Turkey, Texas, Mexico and São Paulo.

Maybe that is why Max got up on the morning of his 24th birthday, lifted some weights on his balcony, worked on his core and went for a run along the Monte Carlo seafront before spending the evening on a yacht with his family. His birthday cake included a custom-made helmet on top (complete with sponsors), a 1:1 replica of a Red Bull can made entirely of fondant and an edible picture of his nearest and dearest: Max, Kelly and little Penelope. (Not pictured: the two newest additions, cats Jimmy and Sassy, perhaps in the doghouse after interrupting one of Max's online streaming sessions by curling up under the pedals.)

Two weeks later, he was rolling out of the garage in Turkey. The race was supposed to have been the Japanese Grand Prix at Suzuka, but for yet another pandemic rearrangement. In celebration of Honda's last year in F1, Red Bull had designed a special livery for the occasion of the engine manufacturer's home race. It would have been particularly poignant for the Verstappens: Jos was at the very heart of Honda's F1 works team for the 2000 season, testing their all-white prototype over hundreds of laps at the Jerez circuit before Harvey Postlethwaite dropped dead in the team office and the project was terminated; Max had sat in the same white Honda car as a toddler and then more than ten years later driven an F1 car in anger for the first time at the Suzuka circuit. What should have been a special moment was yet another, albeit comparatively minor, victim of the pandemic.

The special livery was still a big hit, but Red Bull could not reward their engine suppliers with a race win, as Valtteri Bottas navigated his way through the treacherous conditions in Istanbul to take victory. There were more signs though that Hamilton, who finished fifth after taking a grid penalty, was feeling the pressure. Verstappen's second place behind Bottas was good enough to edge him back ahead of Hamilton, who had been running just behind him in third. His team called him in with sixteen laps to go but he refused to box, only to finally be worn down nine laps later.

'Why the fuck did we give up that space,' he complained to the team over the radio, who told him they thought they would have lost third place no matter what.

'We shouldn't have come in, man. I TOLD you.'

Such heated exchanges of opinion are not uncommon during a race; in the driver's case, they are trying to make their point while also driving at the limit of their abilities and holding down a radio button with a thumb they cannot really spare. But Hamilton was fuming. After taking the grid penalty, Turkey was always going to be a damage limitation exercise, but Lewis could not hide his frustration. Verstappen's teammate Sergio Perez had held him up on the track, then overtaken him thanks to the pit stop. At least his own rear gunner Bottas had held up his side of the bargain and prevented Max taking an even bigger lead. In the grand scheme of things, the gap was just six points, less than the gap between first and second on a race weekend. The road to Abu Dhabi and an eventual champion had rarely looked more tense or tortuous for either party.

One other emerging theme of the season was the role of race director Michael Masi. The Australian took over from Charlie Whiting, the much-loved official who died suddenly of a heart attack just days before the start of the 2019 season. It was never going to be easy to fill the boots of Charlie, to whom Masi had served as a deputy; Whiting was affable, laidback, relaxed and approachable. When F1 started letting cameras into the drivers' briefing, a meeting where all twenty athletes gather in one room before the race weekend to discuss the previous week's events and any safety concerns going forward, the general public got to see him deal with something that resembled a difficult class of teenagers. Charlie appeared to handle the nest of vipers with ease and always appeared even-handed and unflustered. He and Max had spent a day together in Geneva just a few weeks before he died. They talked about everything and anything, for Charlie was that sort of man. The last thing Max said to him was how excited he was to see him in Australia for another season of racing. That reunion never took place. Charlie Whiting died on March 14th, 2019. He was just 66.

Quite apart from the huge hole left in the heart of Charlie's friends and family, his sudden passing meant Masi was thrust into arguably the most difficult role in sport: refereeing twenty cars at 200 miles an hour over miles and miles of track. Whiting had been working for the FIA since 1988; Masi was only ten years old at the time and despite having spent years in motor sport, he could not dream of having the same kind of experience and gravitas as the man he replaced in Melbourne.

For the most part, he had managed to navigate his way through the first two years of his reign without controversy. The best referees go unnoticed, so perhaps he had been doing a decent enough job. Most of the disputes seemed to take place off the track rather than on it, his dominion. The 2021 season though was different. With two racers battling for the title more closely than any since Nico Rosberg pipped Hamilton to top honours in 2016, the rules were being repeatedly tested.

Masi had tended to operate a soft-touch approach, partially because of the desire of F1's new owners Liberty Media to 'let them race' rather than taking an overly officious approach to the sport, but the incidents between Hamilton and Verstappen at Silverstone and Monza in particular had forced him to intervene and remind both men of their responsibilities to each other's safety and to the integrity of the sport. It would be the latter that came into tight focus just a few months after he did so.

Masi's warnings seemed to have taken some effect on the duelling pair, although his efforts to keep the peace were aided by circumstance: in Austin, Verstappen pushed Hamilton to the edge of the track but the British driver still got past before Max got the lead back thanks to a strategy move rather than an on-track overtake; in Mexico, Verstappen did the same back to Hamilton into Turn One and they never really got near each other again. Two races, two wins, advantage Red Bull and Masi was fading back into the background. The title race, the Australian must have hoped, would have little to do with him.

However, the Hamilton–Verstappen battle needed refereeing again in Brazil. Probably in a pre-social media era, Max's quiet inspection of the Mercedes rear wing would have gone unnoticed. But the scrutiny of endless Twitter accounts with access to hundreds of cameras all filming just about every move ended with a campaign to, frankly, get Max in some trouble. Had it been Lewis, doubtless his own supporters would have mounted something similar. The upshot was that both men got in trouble: Mercedes and Hamilton were disqualified from qualifying and sent to the back of the grid for an irregularity in the rear wing that broke technical regulations; Verstappen was fined €50,000 for touching the piece in question while the cars were in *parc fermé*, when not even the driver's own team are allowed to touch the car.

'We had our suspicions that something was going on there in the beginning of the year. We all had to change our rear wings ... so I think there is still something going on with the main plane that is opening up and giving them more top speed,' Max explained.

'There's clearly something going on.'

Teams in F1 always think there is something going on in other garages, because it is a sport with a long history of subterfuge when it comes to the technical regulations. The line between clever solutions, loopholing and straight-up cheating is extremely thin and often vague. Red Bull and Mercedes did not invent such sniping and they will not be the last to engage in it. Max's investigation, in many ways, was rather heavy-handed compared to some of F1's more high-profile spying scandals. More controversy was to come too, and in far more high-octane fashion. When Hamilton challenged Verstappen for the lead round the outside of Turn Four of the famous circuit in Interlagos, he found himself blocked off the track by Max. His team said afterwards he had a slip of understeer mid-corner, forcing him to correct the skid wider to where the Mercedes was trying to overtake him.

'Michael, that is all about let them race,' Red Bull told Masi over the radio, pre-empting his scrutiny. They need not have worried though. Hamilton's engineer called it 'running you off the track' when he radioed his man to inform him the stewards had deemed there was 'no investigation'.

'Of course,' Hamilton answered wryly. Both Max and Lewis have a shared belief in the same thing: that the world is out to get them, and that in order to win, they regularly have to go over and above what others might require.

Fearing the stewards were against him, Hamilton ensured they would have no excuse to penalise him. The second time he challenged Verstappen, Max made the same move to the inside and went deep into the corner, but Hamilton pulled out and kept his powder dry. The third time, he was so much faster that he raced past before they even reached the braking zone.

In doing so, and driving away from Verstappen for the rest of the race, he ensured that Mercedes would head to the three-race finale in the desert only having to make up fourteen points on Max. They were confident they could, even if they thought the FIA didn't want them to.

In theory, neither man had much time to contemplate the race. They were due back on track 7,000 miles away in Qatar just five days later – but both recognised the importance of mental freshness before what would be an intense run-in. Hamilton stayed in Brazil for a day and spent some time on the water, enjoying the southern hemisphere temperatures. Meanwhile, Verstappen flew back to Monaco that night to reflect on a difficult weekend and have at least one night in his own bed. It is somewhat typical of the life of an F1 driver that he was in his eighth-floor flat for less than 24 hours before he was back on his black-and-orange private plane and bound for Doha.

In Qatar, it was Max who caught the attention of the stewards, earning a five-place grid penalty for failing to slow down enough for yellow flags in qualifying, a penalty that virtually guaranteed he could not catch pole-sitter Hamilton. But he did fight back to second in what he called, for the second time in a week, a decent damage limitation effort. The gap had narrowed again and after a ten-day break, F1 returned to the Middle East. Controversially, Saudi Arabia would welcome its first race before Abu Dhabi played host to the finale, a venue that has now become traditional for the final Grand Prix of the season. Any sports-washing-related controversy paled into insignificance, though, compared to what went on between the white lines – and beyond.

The organisers of the race in Saudi were probably pleased as punch that the title race, one of the greats, was still alive and that millions of eyeballs would be trained on it. They would remember this, Hamilton and Verstappen battling it out on the streets of Jeddah. They did remember the race, but few would be able to identify it as iconically Saudi Arabia. That is because perhaps the two most startling moments occurred when both cars were doing very low speeds or, in one case, not moving at all.

The pair had swapped positions already several times when the race was red-flagged for the first time because of a crash. At the standing restart, Hamilton out-dragged Verstappen to the first corner but Max braked much later and had to cut across the second corner, re-joining the racetrack ahead of his rival. Max impeded him so much that Esteban Ocon's Alpine moved into second, meaning that while Max wanted to give the place back to Hamilton after taking it illegally, he could not do so without losing two places. Seconds later, another major crash stopped the race again, and Mercedes jumped on the radio to complain.

By the letter of the law, Verstappen had performed an illegal overtake and would have to be penalised. Masi, presumably not wanting to interfere in the title race by penalising Max in the penultimate race, made Red Bull 'an offer'. He told them he would drop them down to third on the grid to start one place behind Hamilton with Ocon on the front of the grid for the second restart. It was a highly unusual piece of improvisation. Race directors are not in the habit of making offers to teams, more often handing out judgments and penalties. Red Bull politely accepted the offer, before Max rather less politely barged his way to the front of the pack from the subsequent restart. Hamilton though had good race pace and once he got past Ocon, he set about chasing Verstappen down. At the end of Lap 36, he pulled alongside and got most of the way past him by the time they got to the first corner, but Max does not like to yield. He braked late again and had Hamilton continued to turn, he would have crashed into him. Verstappen once again went straight on and largely skipped Turn Two, cruising back into the lead.

'That was fucking crazy,' Hamilton complained.

Red Bull agreed and told Max to give the position back, just as they had under the red flag. This should have been more straightforward, given that Ocon was some 25 seconds behind. Max slowed on the back straight and tried to let Hamilton by.

'I was just down-shifting, braking and waiting for him to go by and then he runs into the back of me,' Max said afterwards, still unable to comprehend what had happened.

It seemed as though Hamilton had not noticed Verstappen slowing down. F1 cars do not have brake lights or indicators and drivers cannot really communicate with each other beyond the odd, usually angry, hand signal. So Hamilton bumped into Verstappen for what must have been the most watched low-speed fender-bender in history. It could have been title-deciding. Hamilton lost some bodywork but not a critical amount and Max avoided a puncture that could easily have happened. An epic title race decided by an incident that might not have made the local newspaper if it had happened on a high street.

As it was, both men emerged unscathed. Max successfully gave the position back five laps later – only to overtake Hamilton again a few hundred metres later. It was not enough to keep Hamilton at bay, as he retook the lead a lap later, running Verstappen wide at exactly the corner where he had lost the lead two minutes earlier.

Max was racing as hard as he ever had. He had the luxury in Saudi Arabia of knowing that a DNF for Hamilton would be virtually fatal for his chances given Max was in the lead on points. He could race with that abandon that some called recklessness, while Hamilton had to make discretion the better part of valour. He fumed with injustice afterwards, despite having claimed victory. While sitting next to Max in the post-race press conference, he cited an incident in 2008 when he had pulled the same 'give the position back then overtake' move that Verstappen had pulled on him. Race director Whiting had told the team it was initially permitted but later slapped him with a penalty. Max, he felt, was not playing by the same rules as everyone else. If he felt hard done by after Jeddah, far worse was to come.

In what had quickly become as much of a war of words as a motor race, Hamilton had set his stall out clearly. He talked about racing between the white lines.

'I know that I can't overtake someone off track and keep the position,' he said in Saudi Arabia. It could have been setting himself up for a fall. Max was less committal, saying he had to move forward, that he didn't spend too much time thinking about it.

'Lately we are talking more about white lines and penalties than proper Formula One racing.'

Both attitudes would be borne out in the finale.

It's difficult to overstate the furore that preceded that final race. Looking back, it could so easily have been a damp squib. The Yas Marina Circuit in Abu Dhabi has rarely provided classic racing, although it had been remodelled in an effort to do so. In both Max and Lewis' home countries, the satellite broadcasters who owned the rights to the action did a deal to make it available for free; Ziggo and Sky both realised that the day would be a spectacle worth throwing open to a massive audience. More than 5,000 Dutch fans defied the difficulties of travelling in the pandemic and the expense of the journey to travel to the Middle East, noticeable by their bright orange outfits and ability to seek out anywhere in the dry city for a late drink. Lewis was not short of fans either; there are few places in the world where he is.

Much was made in the build-up, predictably, of whether we would see a repeat of the infamous incidents between Ayrton Senna and Alain Prost in 1989 and 1990, where crashes ended the race between the two fierce rivals. Michael Masi reminded the drivers of their responsibilities, not for the first time, and also pointed out that post-race sanctions could be taken if either driver was judged to have deliberately caused a race-ending collision – although realistically it would be Max because he was ahead on countback. The discourse was febrile. The newspapers talked of little else. It was almost as if Max had *already* crashed into Lewis and the post-mortem was now being conducted.

Perhaps if the pair had collided, it would have been easier for the FIA. There would have been clear blame and culpability on the track, and their role as judge, jury and executioner would have been far easier. Instead, Masi ended up in the spotlight he appeared so keen to avoid within half a lap.

Verstappen was overtaken off the line for the second weekend in a row, but fought back at the hairpin Turn Six to retake the lead he had earned in qualifying on Saturday. Hamilton had to cut the next corner to avoid a crash, much as Max had in Saudi Arabia, and just as Max had, he emerged ahead. Hamilton had gained the place, off the track, outside the white lines he said were his limits.

'He has to give that back,' said Max on the radio. The stewards disagreed. Masi told Red Bull that Hamilton had slowed on the straight and given back the advantage he gained. The team pointed out he was still in the lead. They heard nothing back. In many eyes, Max had been given a taste of his own medicine.

Perhaps Lewis was playing on the squeaky-clean image he had been trying to portray in the phoney war.

What Red Bull had to their advantage was a second ace to play. Verstappen soon pitted for fresh tyres and Mercedes covered him off a lap later, but Red Bull left out Sergio 'Checo' Perez, who inherited the lead of the race. It was for this very situation that Max's previous teammates had been sacked but Perez had been hired. If Red Bull wanted to end Hamilton's supremacy, they would need to gang up on him. As the defending world champion approached the back of Perez, the Mexican was told to 'think about how best' to hold up Hamilton, who had an eight-second lead over Verstappen. Perez made his car as wide as he could. He saved battery when he was able to and challenged Hamilton every time he tried to overtake. Twice Hamilton got past him and twice Perez got him back straight away. A lap later, he could not fight back, but the damage had been done. Verstappen had closed up the road behind him and Perez obligingly got out of the way.

'Checo is a legend,' Max told the team.

'An absolute animal,' his engineer agreed.

It wasn't enough though. Max caught up but could not pass Hamilton and he started to stretch the gap again. With five laps to go, the gap was twelve seconds. It was Hamilton's title. In the live betting exchanges, Max was being offered at 25/1 to win it from here, equivalent to a probability of under 4 per cent. Even his father Jos had left the Red Bull garage and gone upstairs to sit away from the prying eyes of the world's cameras. Raymond came to join him with twenty laps to go. They sat quietly and watched the title slip away. Jos had some custom-made hoodies in his bag that said 'Max Verstappen, World Champion' that he was probably thinking of ways to destroy.

Then the miracle that opens this book, and that will probably define Max's life for ever. The moment that was so incredibly timed that it seemed like a Hollywood ending. Nicholas Latifi crashed and set in motion a chain of events that would end with Max sitting behind Lewis with one lap to go, points level in the title race and fresh rubber on compared to his rival's far older tyres.

Entire libraries will be written about what happened in the seconds, minutes and hours – and indeed days, weeks and months – that were all triggered by Latifi, who finished 17th in the championship and will probably never have as big an impact on any title race as he did on that day, running wide at Turn Nine, getting his tyres dirty and lacking the grip to recover from his mistake at Turn Fourteen, colliding with the barriers and forcing Masi to bring out a safety car.

Michael Masi will never forget a moment of that afternoon. His name trended on Twitter for days afterwards, as fans of Hamilton raged at his decision-making. In the storm of rage and blame that erupted after the race, Masi was the lightning rod.

The use of the safety car in F1 is a judegment call, but ultimately the decision to deploy it comes down to safety. If there is a car to be removed or debris to be cleared off the track, it's a no-brainer, because the marshals have to emerge from behind the relative safety of the Armco barriers and chain-link fences into the firing line of cars that would otherwise be travelling at 200 miles an hour. In this case, there was little controversy about its introduction, but its removal before the end of the race caused all hell to break loose.

The safety car looked like a miracle, until the pack finally bunched together. Verstappen did not, as he had hoped and expected, find himself staring at Lewis Hamilton's gearbox. Instead, he had to peer over the vehicles of Lando Norris,

Fernando Alonso, Esteban Ocon, Charles Leclerc and Sebastian Vettel. Even if the safety car did come in before the end of the race, and all five cars were as obliging as possible in allowing Verstappen through, he would have no chance of catching Hamilton. In the Mercedes garage, there was a silent sigh of relief. The gods had thrown them one more curveball, but with the other hand taken it back. Hamilton's record-breaking title was surely safe.

Then Masi made his decision. Instead of telling all the cars that had been lapped to overtake the safety car, something that would take longer than the race had left, essentially a call to 'get out of the way', he only stipulated that those five between the front two cars would have to do so. Then the race would recommence, with just one lap left. Mercedes' sighs of relief turned to panicked fury. They knew that Verstappen, having pitted, had every advantage he needed. Mercedes had stayed out – 'gone long' – on old tyres to save the time spent in the pits. Max had pitted behind the safety car and saved time by doing so. Red Bull had acted with the freedom of being second, with nothing to lose and everything to gain.

Mercedes boss Toto Wolff hammered Masi over the radio.

'No, Michael, no, no Michael! That was so not right!' Wolff said in a clip that has been replayed millions of times since.

'This race has been manipulated,' Hamilton told his team over the radio afterwards. He said little else for weeks afterwards.

Masi, who was sick of being the subject of intense media speculation (although it was only to get much worse), was curt in his response: 'Toto, it's called a motor race. We went car racing.'

What was most surprising was the apparent ease with which Max made the final overtake. (In fact, he had a massive cramp in his right leg that made it painful to push the accelerator to full throttle, although he did manage to fight through the pain for just one lap.) Clearly, he had a huge mechanical advantage, achieved by strategy as much as skill, and had a lot more in his tyres than Hamilton, but it was surprising that the defending champion did not, frankly, defend harder. When Max lined up the lunge into Turn Five, one of only two realistic overtaking spots with Turn Six being the other one, Lewis did not revert to the inside line, the obvious way to defend that corner. Once Max had got past, Lewis had one chance to get back at him, the hairpin at Turn Six. With everything on the line and nothing to lose, you would have thought if the positions were reversed, Verstappen would have thrown everything at that corner. But Hamilton was strangely subdued. He followed Verstappen on the straight to try to get the slipstream, but when it came to the corner, he was just outdone. Perhaps he had so little left in his tyres that there was just nothing left to give, but the whole incident felt like a neat summing up of their two styles. Max had been bold and it had paid off; Lewis had tried to hang on at the front, managing his tyres, and it had not.

Few fans will remember the celebrations: some because they were at the heart of them, one of the 5,000 Oranje in the Middle East enjoying themselves as much as possible without incurring the wrath of the police in a country where being drunk in public is a criminal offence; others will not remember because the newspapers and websites were covered in pictures and words of or about Michael Masi. He was in danger of overshadowing Max altogether – albeit not in the Netherlands.

'It's a really tough job he has,' Verstappen said the next day. 'People say maybe he needs help. Yeah, fair point. Everyone needs help. I need help as well. Michael is a nice guy and he tries his very best and it's very unfair to now start hating on him because it is a very tough job.'

But on the night, there was no thought of what role Masi had played, only of celebrating. Within seconds of victory, Jos and Raymond had their customised hoodies on and were hugging anyone they could see. If anyone was carrying Covid that night, everyone was going to get it. Social distancing was impossible, and implausible frankly. When Max got out of the car, still wearing his helmet, he ran straight for his girlfriend Kelly before being engulfed by Raymond, Jos and everyone who had been part of the Red Bull journey. Christian Horner could not stop crying.

A few minutes later, once Max had weighted in and done his first of many post-race interviews, he found himself alone for a second. He sat down on a piece of staging and tried to compute what had happened. His father knelt down next to him and they shared a moment. It was this they had always worked for, always believed they could do, and even until perhaps 30 minutes before that moment, thought they might never achieve. Awaiting them were many things: a Red Bull private yacht that would finally be vacated at 7am the next morning, a private jet back to Holland where millions had watched in ecstasy as he became the first ever Dutch world champion; questions about Masi, about Lewis, about everything; awards, audiences with great dignitaries, phone calls with the royal family; and then a pre-season and the rematch with Hamilton that was only a few months away.

But that could all wait. It was not the most intense of debriefs. There would be no discussion of whether they could have won more easily or why, as Jos believed, Max had not waited until Turn Six to make his move instead of risking being overtaken again on the straight after Turn Five. There was a temporary moment of stillness. Just father and son, sitting in a garage, smelling of fuel, burnt rubber and sweat, knowing the hard work had paid off.

And they were just getting started.

MAX VERSTAPPEN
PROFESSIONAL RACING RECORD

2014

FLORIDA RACING SERIES, HOMOLOGOUS SERIES: 12 races, 2 wins, 5 podiums, 3 fastest laps, 3rd overall

EUROPEAN FORMULA THREE, VAN AMERSFOORT RACING: 33 races, 10 wins, 16 podiums, 7 fastest laps, 441 points, 3rd overall

ZANDVOORT MASTERS, MOTOPARK: One-off race, winner

2015

FORMULA ONE, TORO ROSSO: 19 races, 0 wins, 0 podiums, 0 fastest laps, 49 points, 12th overall

2016

FORMULA ONE, TORO ROSSO: 4 races, 0 wins, 0 podiums, 0 fastest laps, 13 points, 10th overall at point of promotion

FORMULA ONE, RED BULL RACING: 17 races, 1 win, 7 podiums, 1 fastest lap, 191 points, 5th overall (including Toro Rosso points)

2017

FORMULA ONE, RED BULL RACING: 20 races, 2 wins, 4 podiums, 1 fastest lap, 168 points, 6th overall

2018

FORMULA ONE, RED BULL RACING: 21 races, 2 wins, 11 podiums, 2 fastest laps, 249 points, 4th overall

2019

FORMULA ONE, RED BULL RACING: 21 races, 3 wins, 9 podiums, 3 fastest laps, 278 points, 3rd overall

2020

FORMULA ONE, RED BULL RACING: 17 races, 2 wins, 11 podiums, 3 fastest laps, 214 points, 3rd overall

2021

FORMULA ONE, RED BULL RACING: 22 races, 10 wins, 18 podiums, 6 fastest laps, 395.5 points, Champion

RECORDS HELD BY MAX VERSTAPPEN

Youngest driver to drive at a Grand Prix weekend (17 years, 3 days)

Youngest driver to start a Grand Prix (17 years, 166 days)

Youngest driver to score points at a Grand Prix (17 years, 180 days)

Youngest driver to finish on the podium at a Grand Prix (18 years, 228 days)

Youngest driver to lead a Grand Prix for at least one lap (18 years, 228 days)

Youngest driver to win a Grand Prix (18 years, 228 days)

Youngest driver to set a Grand Prix fastest lap (19 years, 44 days)

Most podium finishes in a season (18 podiums, 2021)

CAREER F1 STATISTICS
(AS OF BEGINNING OF 2022 SEASON)

141 Grands Prix

20 wins

60 podiums

1,557.5 points (Eighth in all-time rankings)

13 pole positions

16 fastest laps

ACKNOWLEDGEMENTS

First and foremost, to Hannah, who has put up with my endless whingeing throughout writing it and longer. She clearly has the patience of a saint.

To Alice, who bought the first copy before I had even finished writing it. To Manus, for keeping me sane. To my family in advance, for smiling politely when they unwrap a copy every Christmas. To Julie and Charlie, for lending me their flat in which to write, and to Linda and Nick, for their spare room in which to do the same.

To all those who chronicled Max's life. Verstappen.NL was a website dedicated first to Jos and then to Max, which recorded Verstappen Jr's life from the very first day. I am indebted to their dedication to Dutch motor racing, as I am to every writer, sub-editor and editor whose newspapers, magazines and websites detailed the growth of their most successful driver from long before it was clear he would become that.

And finally, to my editor Michael and agent Melanie, both of whom believed in me from the start. I would not be writing these words had they not.